THE SOCIETAL SUBJECT

THE SOCIETAL SUBJECT

Edited by Niels Engelsted, Mariane Hedegaard, Benny Karpatschof, and Aksel Mortensen

AARHUS UNIVERSITY PRESS

Published with the financial support of the
Faculty of Humanities, University of Copenhagen
and the Aarhus University Research Foundation.

AARHUS UNIVERSITY PRESS
Building 170, Aarhus University
DK-8000 Aarhus C, Denmark

Acknowledgments
The editors wish to thank R.G. Tharp and R. Gallimore for the permission to
redraw a figure from their book *Rousing Minds to Life*.
We also wish to thank Lisbeth Nielsen, Chris Sinha, and Thomas Teasdale, who
have checked and revised the English of the manuscripts, and Ole E. Rasmussen
for assistance in drawing figures.

CONTENTS

AT A CROSSROADS – AN INTRODUCTION

Niels Engelsted
University of Copenhagen

Every book has its own story, immersed in other stories. To provide context and background for this book, I want to sketch some of these stories. Primarily this is the story of what motivated the present collection, but, further, it is the story of how a particular psychological understanding intertwines with the development of Danish psychology; and in the last instance it is the story of psychology itself.

1.

The 14 articles presented are enlarged and revised versions of papers and commentaries delivered at the *2nd Danish Conference of Activity Theory* held at Roesnaes, Denmark, 1991.

Activity Theory, a theoretical position initiated in the late 1920's by Lev Vygotsky, and developed by his coworker Alexei N. Leontiev, was discovered in earnest by Western psychologists in the early 1970's, when the most important Russian works were translated into major languages. As the interest spread, international communication and cooperation on the subject of Activity Theory grew; and soon – in large part due to the tireless efforts of professor Michael Cole, San Diego, professor George Rückriem, Berlin, and professor Charles Tolman, Victoria – an international association had formed, complete with standing committee, journal, and international congresses.

The adoption of Activity Theory in Denmark very closely parallels this development. Vygotsky's seminal work *Thought and Language* was translated into Danish in 1971, and the general psychology of Leontiev was introduced soon after (Dreier, 1974). Leontiev's major works, *Problems in the Development of Mind* and *Activity, Consciousness, Personality,* appeared in Danish translations in 1977 and 1983 respectively. In 1986 Michael Cole, educational psychologist and American authority on Vygotsky, was invited to give the first *Alfred Lehman Lectures* at the University of Copenhagen, which served to broaden the scope and foster transatlantic cooperation.[1]

This progression reflects the interest with which the Activity Theory approach was received in Denmark. The theory formed the basis of much subsequent work, and this again led to organizational initiatives of which the Danish conferences – held between the international congresses – are an example.

The establishment of Activity Theory as an international collaborative approach has been of great value. Yet, it would be a mistake to consider Activity Theory a unitary approach. The work left by Vygotsky at his premature death from tuberculosis in 1934 is for the most part an assembly of visionary outlines; while Leontiev's work can best be characterized as a conceptual framework for a general psychology. The Activity Theory handed down by the founding fathers is thus more a frame than a finished body of theory. Not denying the importance of ongoing research in studying and interpreting, and even recovering, the past work of Vygotsky and Leontiev – especially since their approach suffered considerable adversity in the form of repression and coercion from authorities – the major attraction of Activity Theory has been its open–ended quality and future prospects. It is precisely as a frame to be filled out and a set of insights to be utilized according to the agenda and priorities of the adopting parties that Activity Theory has been embraced internationally. The Activity Theory approach subsequently was inscribed onto the different psychological traditions of various countries, and today encompasses a wide variety of diverse issues and problems. Depending on whether it is looked upon through North American, Russian, Japanese, German or Finnish eyes, the theory shows itself in different perspectives.

Danish eyes are no exception to this rule. The contributions from the Danish conference, accordingly, reflect an adoption of Activity Theory that is distinctive for Denmark and should be understood in light of the history of the Danish psychological tradition.

Merely to introduce the present articles as a local conception of Activity Theory would be misleading, however. The conference had its own very special agenda. People knowledgeable in Activity Theory will notice right away that many of the contributions considerably overstep the recognized bounds of this theory. The present collection is consequently more like a fair of different theoretical visions than it is a unified theoretical approach. It was intended to be. This, however, does not mean that Activity Theory serves merely as a pretext. The aim of the conference and the project of Activity Theory as adopted in Denmark spring from the same venture. A venture that reflects fundamental and – so it seems – timeless problems in

---

[1] Thanks to Cole and the new electronic mail medium this cooperation today takes the form of daily worldwide communication between researchers in the field.

the science of psychology to the same extent as it reflects the particular history of Danish psychology.

2.

Geographically Denmark is placed at a crossroads, bridging the Scandinavian countries to the North with Continental Europe to the South, and the British Isles to the West with Eastern Europe and the Baltic to the East. This placement shaped the Danish intellectual landscape, with traffic of ideas following the traffic of commerce, and parochialism being counterbalanced by the opportunism of a small trader. (A small country cannot afford provinciality, it is said). Over the years, the main trends of Western thought were quickly adopted in Denmark, which – befitting its geography – came under the sway of both Anglo–Saxon and Continental philosophy.

This being so, it is not remarkable that the innovation of experimental psychology – being an Anglo–Saxon notion bred on Continental ground – was quickly adopted in Denmark, where we pride ourselves of having the world's second oldest university–established psychological laboratory, dating from 1886.

The founder of the laboratory, Alfred Lehman, an engineer, was, as would be expected, a student of Wundt in Leipzig; the route taken, however, was decided by his successor, Edgar Rubin, philosopher and cousin of Niels Bohr. Rubin was a student of G.E. Müller in Göttingen, and this apprenticeship – plus Rubin's strongwilled temperament – was the crucial factor in the creation of what became known as *the Copenhagen School of Phenomenology*.[2]

G.E. Müller entertained the belief that psychological problems were those that could be investigated by experiment in a laboratory. The method was description of phenomenological experience. Theorizing was to be avoided as – at best – premature. Lectures and seminars, accordingly, were superfluous. If they must, students could attend the lectures of faculty-member Edmund Husserl. Entirely irrelevant was also, of course, the writing of a 'Grundriss' or 'Grundzüge', otherwise obligatory for German psychologists. The only thing that really mattered was methodological stringency.[3]

Müller's puristic conception came to dominate Danish university psychology during Rubin's directorship, thus ending the prior tradition for theoretical synthesis laid down by Rubin's old teacher, philosopher Harald Høffding.[4] A body of beautiful experimental work was produced, unsur-

---

2   For a review see Moustgaard & Petersen (1986) and Moustgaard (1987).

3   For an analysis of the impact of experimental psychology on the development of psychology in Scandinavia see Nilsson (1978).

4   See Høffding (1882).

passed in descriptive acuity – Rubin's own work on the perception of figure and ground being a prime example[5]; but it was a slim body.   Having inherited very little of the go–getter quality of the Continental phenomenological tradition founded by Husserl, and further developed by thinkers like Heidegger and Merleau–Ponty, The Copenhagen School of Phenomenology was more related to the Anglo–Saxon neo–positivist tradition[6], and with its narrow conceptual scope hardly able to adress the rich array of issues confronting theoretical and applied psychology.

The reign of the Copenhagen School of Phenomenology came to an end in the late sixties and early seventies.   Its demise coincided with a period of massive student unrest and rebellion sparked by substantial social transformations in the system of higher education and parallelled by similar student activism in France, Germany, and the United States.   According to legend, the school was actually – in a very Kuhn–like manner – unseated in 1968 by rebellious students of psychology revolting against professorial authority.   Looked upon in retrospect, it was not a clear break at all; but at the time it seemed to be.

In place of the repudiated tradition, other traditions were soon brought in, spurred by a great appetite for new understandings. From the United States, Germany, France, and England were imported behaviorism, ethology, cognitivism, psychoanalysis, humanistic psychology, Rogerian and other traditions in personality psychology, and various brands of social psychology.   It was like a great natural experiment, where the vacuum created by the sudden extinction of the native species was rapidly filled up by migration of all major species of psychology.

In such an experiment, sharp inter–species competition will be the immediate outcome, gradually giving way to coadaptation.   This happened to be the case in Danish psychology where years of strife – reminiscent of the war between psychological schools of the early part of the century – eventually subsided into a state of reasonably peaceful (and indifferent) coexistence among different psychological understandings.

Comprising all major psychological understandings, Danish psychology became a small scale model of psychology *in toto*.   The basic problems of psychology, not least of which was the problem of coherency, consequently were very acutely felt in Danish psychology, now unprotected by   the shield of one ruling viewpoint.

3.

The lesson learned from the years of strife was that unification cannot be gained by conquest.   As it reflects this lesson, the principle 'live and let live'

---

5   See Rubin (1921). See also Moustgaard (1990) for a recent example of the keen descriptive ability of the Copenhagen tradition.

6   See Erik Schultz this volume p. 109–130.

is hard–won and to be treasured. Yet one must wonder how such a principle of pluralism can apply to a science? Intuition tells us that the diversity of psychological theorizing does reflect the many–sided nature of mind, and that insights will be lost if perspectives are closed and diversity attenuated. At the same time, the very talk of perspectives and many–sidedness presupposes that something has these many sides which different perspectives can reveal. The recognition of diversity presupposes some unifying order.

The lack of agreement as to the nature, not to say existence, of such an order or subject matter has been a hallmark of psychology from its first inception. This, of course, threatens psychology's claim to be a science, since it is the existence of a particular domain of lawful order in the universe that sanctions a particular science and gives it the mandate to investigate and uncover this domain.

This lamentable state has – as was perhaps forecast in the ancient Graeco–Roman myth of *Psyche* and her sisters – made psychology *the Cinderella* in the sisterhood of science. It was the judgment of Sigmund Koch, the sage of psychological theory, that psychology could never become a coherent science; that it could be a science at all has been denied from Kant to Rorty. From every side another science has stood ready to eliminate – cannibalize in the word of Edward O. Wilson[7] – psychology in a great reductive sweep.

Since psychology has not yet been felled by these harsh verdicts, but, on the contrary, has flourished as both a profession and a scientific institution, and continuously grows in practical application and theoretical scope, however diverse, one could perhaps dismiss such denunciations as mere bickering. As long as our science works in practice and can solve the particular problems it set out to solve, why should we make a fuss; let each man follow his own drummer.

Much can be said for such a pragmatic stance. Nevertheless, the critical judgments of the sisters should not be taken lightly. They reflect the fundamental conceptual problems that form the core of the psychology's scientific domain; if psychology is not to be reduced to a collection of ingenious visions and a bag of sagacious tricks, these problems must be addressed. Moreover, psychology cannot simply renounce its claim for scientific status; among the sciences a very special responsibility befalls psychology.

4.

Every science has its measure of theoretical differences and confusions, what sets psychology apart and threatens it with incoherence, is the special place it occupies in scientific geography.

---

7   Wilson (1975:6).

The scientific world has three great continents: the natural sciences, the social sciences, and the humanities. Set apart by subject matter, and consequently, methodology and philosophy, these continents are not easily bridged. Rather, they have come to constitute worlds of their own, and traditionally have eyed each other in ways that are very much reminiscent of the ways of enemy tribes.

To which of these worlds does psychology belong?

As Ebbinghaus observed, psychology has a short history, but a long past. Until Wundt – inspired by the psycho–physiological work of Fechner and Helmholtz – at the end of the last century launched psychology as a science adopting natural science's outlook and methodology, psychology had throughout millennia been an integrated part of philosophy, investigating the possibility, forms, and conditions of knowledge, experience, desire, and the will. Wundt's project was, therefore, a coupling of two markedly different worlds. As such, it immediately invoked vigorous protest. There is, asserted Wilhelm Dilthey, *Naturwissenschaft* (natural science), which explains; and there is *Geisteswissenschaft* (humanities), which understands. Psychology belongs to the latter, since humans are agents with consciousness and must be understood in terms of meaning. Wundt did not really disagree, as his subsequent work on the *Völkerpsy-chologie* proves. He only thought that, for some purposes psychology, should adopt a natural science position, for others a hermeneutical science position.

Irrespective of the validity of the distinction between explanation and understanding, a solution based on division hardly seems tenable, however. After psychology's appropriation of Darwinism, it became very clear that mind is a phenomenon belonging *simultaneously* to the world of natural science and to the world of hermeneutics. Only by spanning the great divide can psychology bring into focus the essence of mind, as attested by the achievements of William James and Freud.

No one has, however, to this day, shown how the divide can be spanned in a principled way. Here is the *Catch–22* of psychology: If it is true to its subject matter, it becomes unprincipled. If it tries to remedy this, it becomes untrue to its subject matter. Humanistic psychology and behaviorism can be seen as prototypical examples.

If, to this problem, further is added the necessity of tying psychological understanding into the historical understanding of the social sciences, we have the real reason why incoherence rules psychology.

It is not because psychologists are less intelligent than other scientists, even though they may be. It is not because psychology is a young science, and it can be debated whether it is. It is not because psychology is still an immature science; even though it is, this is a symptom and not the cause of the problem. It is not because psychological problems are complex; they are, but every science is confronted with complex problems. Unless, of course, this complexity refers specifically to the problem of bridging simultaneously the understandings of hermeneutical science, social science, and natural science. Because this is the real problem: that psychology in order to capture the essence of mind, must span all three scientific continents, and therefore must suffer their mutual incompatibility as her own incoherence. Hence also the special responsibility of psychology; on her territory open up the fissures of science, so it is from here that the possibility of redemption is to be sought. Only psychology fits the shoe.

5.

In psychological history, periods where the coherency problem – also called the crisis of psychology – is in focus alternate with periods in which the problem is largely ignored. In America, for example, a period of strenuous search for theoretical rapprochement, brought about by the exodus of European scholars in the thirties, ended in the late forties, at which time there seemed to be "no question of tongues blending into a single narrative" (Koch, 1959:1). Then again, two decades later, the theoretical quest was vigorously resumed, this time spurred on by the new *Cognitive Science*; and not surprisingly so, since Cognitive Science in its very conception is an attempt at a synthesis across the continents of science and consequently faces formidable conceptual enigmas.

In other words, it is the meeting of incongruous understandings that makes the incoherence problem stand out and calls for theoretical work to provide a larger and more synthesizing view.

This was exactly the situation confronting Danish psychology in the seventies, and explains the upsurge of theoretical interest in this period. The adoption of Activity Theory was one attempt at meeting the challenge of incoherence, and a befitting one, since the Vygotsky–Leontiev approach was developed originally as an answer to the crisis of psychology. Further more it contained certain insights, which from the Danish point of view are considered *sine qua non*.

Vygotsky – young art critic and teacher – entered psychology as an ardent believer in objective psychology, but soon came to have second thoughts. Without wishing to renounce Pavlov or behaviorism, he nonetheless found psychology without psyche or mind rather senseless. His 1924 paper *Consciousness as a problem in the psychology of behavior*[8], which calls for an effort at synthesis, propelled him unto the scene of Soviet psychology where, in 10 short years, he – as composer and conductor – produced such brilliant work that he has been considered the Mozart of psychology by Stephen Toulmin.[9]

---

8   See Vygotsky (1934,1979).

9   See Toulmin (1978).

In keeping with his time and place, Vygotsky saw the key to the necessary synthesis of objective and subjective psychology in Marxist philosophy. This choice could hardly have been more appropriate since the philosophy of Marx is essentially an attempt to synthesize the classical, continental, idealist understanding of the human as subject and producer with the classical, Anglo–Saxon, materialist understanding of the human as object and product.

The renaissance of Marxism in Europe in the 1970's greatly facilitated the discovery of Vygotsky and his school.[10] There was, however, another important reason for the adoption of this understanding in Denmark.

After the long reign of subjective idealism that governed The Copenhagen School of Phenomenology, objective psychology came to hold great attraction. Brains were dissected, and rats run in mazes. Yet, the lesson of the Freudian father–murder was not to be escaped. You are yourself the father. Less poetically, a psychology, it was realized, which does not accredit subject and subjectivity a decisive place is not tenable. Why? Because the mental phenomena undisputable tells us so, and – another legacy of the Copenhagen School of Phenomenology – the phenomena are not to be talked away, but are to be taken serious.

The Copenhagen School of Phenomenology did not see things wrongly, it only saw them too narrowly. The subjective as well as the objective are crucial for the psychological understanding. Psychology must encompass both worlds.

Both worlds were seemingly what Vygotsky offered. Believing himself to be dying, he writes in 1927 his major methodological work, *The Historical Sense of the Psychological Crisis,* in which the very cause of the incoherence of psychology is identified as the existence of two psychologies – "the natural science, materialist, and the spiritualist". "Everything else is differences in view points, schools, hypotheses...", often in a confusing and intractable manner[11]. Only a general psychology that addresses the basic rift can sort out this confusion.

6.

The answer to Vygotsky's call was Activity Theory. Outlined originally by Vygotsky and developed by Leontiev in the following decades, it attempts to mediate the cleft between objective determination and subjective agency through the concept of the subject's activity. Immersed in a world of objective determinations, the organism or person is capable of actively

---

10 Scholarship can have a hard time crossing ideological boundaries, as is well known. Despite the long overdue arrival in the West the basic ideas of Vygotsky luckily have not diminished in actuality.

11 See Vygotsky (1985:192).

confronting this objective world, and this process calls forth the phenomena of mind.

Rejecting Watson[12] the theory draws an important dividing line between animals and human beings. Animals are not by this division denied mind. On the contrary, it is of singular importance to show how at a certain stage of phylogenesis mind occurs as a natural development. Leontiev's dissertation is dedicated to this problem, and in his subsequent work the prehuman stages of mind are thoroughly dealt with.[13] Nevertheless, the theory is naturally primarily devoted to the particularly human stages of mind, consciousness and personality.

The investigation of the ontogenetic development of human consciousness occupies the larger part of Vygotsky's work. His basic idea was that cultural signs – words and tools – constituted a particular class of stimuli, which the child could use to control itself. Vygotsky here found a common ground for objective determination and subjective agency. Further – in the words of Cole and Scribner[14] – Vygotsky became the "first modern psychologist to suggest the mechanism by which culture becomes part of each person's nature." This work – not least the part of which was the conception of *the Zone of Proximal Development*[15] – made Vygotsky famous as a developmental and educational psychologist.

In references to this work, and in the supplementary work done by Alexander Luria in Ushbekistan[16], the term the *Cultural–Historical School* is often used, while the term *Activity Theory* is reserved for the subsequent work of Leontiev and his coworkers and students. Whether or not this distinction is theoretically important, it does reflect different focuses of interest in the adoption of the Vygotsky–Leontiev approach. One reflects the interests of general psychology, as mentioned; another reflects the interests of developmental and educational psychology. The Danish adoption followed both courses, as can be clearly seen from the present contributions.

7.

The issues motivating the two courses are not identical, but they can never–

---

12 Watson (1914:1) "recognizes no dividing line between man and brute".

13 See Leontiev (1981).

14 See Cole and Scribner (1978:6).

15 See A. Mortensen: Notes on Activity Theory, Communication and Zone of Proximal Development, this volume p. 229-240, and K. Baltzer: Where does personality go, when the child goes to school?, this volume p. 250.

16 Alexander Luria, later to be known as a brilliant neuropsychologist, was a coworker of Vygotsky. In the thirties he was commissioned by Vygotsky to investigate the effect of radical social change on the modes of thinking among peasants in Ushbekistan. The study, however, was afflicted by not easily overcome cultural bias. See Luria (1976).

theless be traced back to the same social changes, namely the moderniza-
tion of Danish society incited by the economic boom of the 1960's. Not
only was higher education for the few changed into higher education for the
many, resulting in problems of adjustment and student unrest, but women
were also brought into the labor market *en masse*, creating no fewer
adjustment problems. The need for day care institutions grew rapidly, for
instance, when temporary relief had to be found for working mothers.
This, in turn, created a great demand for qualified personnel, which only a
special education and educational facilities, schools and teachers, could
meet. *Teaching* the art of taking care of and instructing children, however,
requires some kind of conceptual understanding of children's development.
Hence a great need arose for theoretical contributions from educational and
developmental psychology. Vygotsky and his school obliged, and Activity
Theory subsequently formed the basis of much empirical and theoretical
work in this field, which came to constitute the decisive forum for the dis-
semination of Activity Theory in Denmark. The scope and originality of
this work are well represented in the paper of Sven Mørch and Søren Frost
(p. 273).

8.

There are many ways in which a theoretical framework can support inquiry.
It can provide guidelines for empirical research, which leads to the organic
growth of a body of empirical results with supplementary theoretical
observations. The article of Hedegaard and Chaiklin (p. 259) provides a
good example of the artful combination of practice and theory.

It can also be the starting point for conceptual rethinking, leading to
extensions of the framework, perhaps even transgressions of its boundaries.
The open state of Activity Theory makes such work particularly relevant.
After all, Activity Theory has not provided a definite solution to the crisis
of psychology. A. A. Leontiev (1992:44), son of A. N. Leontiev, even goes
so far as to say: "Vygotsky and Leontiev each intended to develop a new
conceptual system, and each failed to do it. That is, it would appear, the
next problem that will motivate the development of psychology in the
decades to come." Actually, the concern of Danish general psychology has
been to search for the missing elements in Activity Theory, while still
remaining within its framework.[17]   In this collection, Jens Mammen's
forceful article on the elements of psychology (p. 29) and Henrik Poulsen's
astute discussion of conations (p. 17) are good examples of this approach.

A theoretical framework can also serve as the springboard to a different
framework. The work of A. N. Leontiev serves this function in the *Berlin
School* of Klaus Holzkamp, also called *Critical Psychology*, which can be

---

[17]   See for example Engelsted (1989) and (1992); Mammen (1989); and Poulsen (1989) and
    (1991).

considered a cousin of Activity Theory. Born of, and keeping alive, the social critique of the student rebellion years, Critical Psychology is a general psychology which places special emphasis on human emancipation.[18] The critical acumen of Critical Psychology – here with Leontiev himself as the target – is exemplified in the contribution of Erik Axel and Morten Nissen (p. 67).

Yet, a theoretical framework should do more than this. It should also, like a good parent, provide confidence, make you trust your own judgment, and furnish you with a secure base from which you can move out and boldly explore the world. This is not, admittedly, the way theoretical frameworks usually function. More likely, they will hold you captive behind the self–erected borders of your own understanding, viewing different understandings with great suspicion and disdain. Evidently, such all too common bent and bias, when added to the truly great conceptual problems, makes the incoherence problem of psychology absolutely insoluble.

9.

An explicit objective of The Second Danish Conference of Activity Theory was, for this reason, to address the necessity and problem of going beyond the single understanding. This choice was hardly accidental. The biases of theories are merely special cases of the biases of ordinary life, and, like them, socially constituted. When social change upsets the latter, the former follow like Hegel's owl.

The breaking–up and opening of borders, which in more ways than one characterizes the social changes of recent years, does not leave psychology untouched. On the contrary, it not only forces the examination of new questions, it also urges the reexamination of old issues. A.A. Leontiev's reappraisal of Activity Theory quoted above, is a case in point.

Temporarily adopting Feyerabend's principles of theoretical proliferation and methodological pluralism[19], the Danish conference set out to investigate this new window of opportunity. In addition to papers securely within Activity Theory, contributions from outside the tradition were invited, and authors were asked, if possible, to search for possibilities for alignment between views.

The call was heeded, as the contributions show. In his paper on the psychodynamics of activities and life projects, Preben Berthelsen hands us a possible synthesis of Activity Theory and Freudian psychodynamics (p. 83). Benny Karpatschof, in his analysis of social anomia based on Activity Theory, returns to the discarded and forgotten social psychology of Le Bon, and proves that old issues can provide insight into contemporary under-

---

18   For an English introduction and appraisal see Tolman & Maiers (1991).

19   See Feyerabend (1988:34 note).

standings (p. 201). Arne Poulsen, in his thoroughly worked out analysis of the disembedding of human capacities in modernity, relates this phenomenon rather relevantly to Activity Theory (p. 141). Kinship is also evident in Erik Schultz', at the same time phenomenologically – and realistically – based, exposition of methods, content, and theory in humanistic research (p. 109), as it is in Ole Elstrup Rasmussen's deeply thought–provoking merging of issues from organizational psychology with general principles of social intercourse (p. 165).

Heterogeneity abounds, of course. But even with a scope spanning from Mogens Hansen's paper on the development f the conscious body, (p. 67), to Mads Hermansen's platform for modern didactics in postmodern society, (p. 131), the common ground is never out of sight.

Norms of orderly presentation made us choose a tripartite division of the contributions into those dealing with general psychological foundations, those dealing with the deep interrelationship between human social living and mind, and those dealing with more specific issues from educational psychology. This convenient partition should not, however, obscure the profound parity of the contributions. Across the different perspectives there is a common manifestation of the genuine intent of general psychology, namely the pursuit of proper units of analysis to be used in unravelling the intricacies of mind. Across the diverse comprehensions, there is a deep commitment that renders the human individual a true subject. Across the various views, there is a mutual assertion that it is imperative to recognize the societal nature of human life and, hence of human psychology.

The close affinity with the quest of Vygotsky and Activity Theory is obvious. Choosing *The Societal Subject* as title for the book is a recognition of this.

10.

Looking for the other person's insights rather than his mistakes turned the exercise into a constructive one. Suspension of criticism and unprincipled compromise, however, is not hereby advocated as a solution to the crisis of psychology; neither is eclecticism, pluralism, not to mention relativism, which Jerry Fodor (1984) rightfully teaches us to hate. Quite on the contrary, to approach the problem of incoherence, one must be committed to psychology's claim for scientific status. That is, one must be convinced that some underlying order of mind really exists, that a genuine prince lurks out there in the mist for Cinderella to find.

Or, if not a prince, then at least the elephant encountered by the wise, but blind, men of the old Indian fable. Being blind, each of them got very different images of the elephant, as they touched it from different angles. Being wise, they understood, however, that their incoherence problem could be overcome if, and only if, the existence of a real, if still undefined, beast was maintained. Further, they understood that the image of the next person, however lopsided, rather than threatening their image, provided potential clues for its refinement, bringing it closer to the reality of the beast. That disparity of vision, once the equations are solved, is the source of vision in depth. Kirsten Baltzer's paper (p. 241), critically taking on one perspective after another in an attempt to capture the vicissitudes of the child in school, could be seen as an exemplary manifestation of this approach. If the coherency problem is to be tackled, the wisdom of this approach should not be ignored.

Adopting this approach, the Danish conference – paying tribute to the spirit if not the letter of Activity Theory – adopted general psychology's quest for synthesis. This was not without precedent. In 1882 Harald Høffding observed – quoted in part in Vygotsky's treatise on the crisis of psychology[20] – that, considering psychology's many sources from across all the sciences, it could be pursued in many ways and by many avenues. Consequently there would be not one, but many psychologies. However, with a psychology of subjectivity as pivot, a drawing together should naturally be pursued.[21]

And so – with history taking a full turn – the chickens have come home to roost.

References

Cole, M. & S. Scribner (1978): Introduction. In Cole, M. & al. (eds.): L.S.Vygotsky: *Mind in Society*, Cambridge, Mass.

Dreier, O. (1974): En præsentation og vurdering af Leontjevs almene psykologi. (A presentation and evaluation of the general psychology of Leontiev), *Udkast, 2,* pp. 247–351.

Engelsted, N. (1989): What is the psyche and how did it get into the world? In N. Engelsted, L. Hem & J. Mammen (eds.): *Essays in General Psychology. Seven Danish Contributions.* Aarhus, pp. 13–48.

Engelsted, N. (1992): A Missing Link in Activity Theory?, *Activity Theory, 11/12,* pp. 49–54.

Feyerabend, P. (1988): *Against Method,* rev. ed., London, New York.

Fodor, J. (1984): Precis of the Modularity of Mind, *Behavioral and Brain Sciences, 8,* pp. 1–5.

Høffding, H. (1882): *Psykologi i omrids på grundlag af erfaring,* Copenhagen. German edition: Psychologie in Umrissen auf Grundlage der Erfahrung, Leipzig, 1887. English edition: Outlines of Psychology, London, 1891.

---

20   See Vygotsky (1985:65).

21   See Høffding (1882:32).

Koch, S. (1959): General Introduction, In S. Koch: *Psychology. A Study of a Science*, Vol. 1, New York.

Leontiev, A.N. (1981): *Problems in the Development of Mind*, Moscow.

Leontiev, A.A. (1992): Ecce Homo. Methodological Problems of the Activity–Theoretical Approach, *Activity Theory*, 11/12, pp. 41–45.

Luria, A.R. (1976): *Cognitive Development: Its Cultural and Social Foundations*, Cambridge, Mass.

Mammen, J. (1989): The relationship between subject and object from the perspective of Activity Theory, In N. Engelsted, L. Hem & J. Mammen (eds.): *Essays in General Psychology. Seven Danish Contributions*, Aarhus, pp. 71–94.

Moustgaard, I.K. & A.F. Petersen (eds.) (1986): *Udviklingslinier i dansk psykologi fra Alfred Lehman til idag* (Developments in Danish Psychology from Alfred Lehman to the present), Copenhagen.

Moustgaard, I.K. (1987): Dansk eksperimentalpsykologi og dens pionerer (Danish experimental psychology and its pioneers), In I.K. Moustgaard, J.M. Pedersen & K.H. Teigen (eds.): *Seculum primum – glimt fra 100 års psykologi i Norden*, (Seculum primum – glimpses from a 100 years of psychology in Scandinavia), Copenhagen, pp. 9–18.

Moustgaard, I.K. (1990): *Psychological Observation and Description*, Søreidgrend.

Nilsson, I. (1978): *Själen i laboratoriet* (The Soul in the Laboratory), Lund (English summary included).

Poulsen, H. (1989): The concept of motive and need in Leontiev's distinction between activity and action, In N. Engelsted, L. Hem & J. Mammen (eds.): *Essays in General Psychology. Seven Danish Contributions*, Aarhus, pp. 7–12.

Poulsen, H. (1991): *Conations*, Aarhus.

Rubin, E. (1921): *Visuell wahrgenommene Figuren* (Visually perceived figures), Copenhagen.

Tolman, C. & W.Maiers (eds.)(1991): *Critical Psychology. Contributions to an Historical Science of the Subject*, Cambridge.

Toulmin, S. (1978): The Mozart of Psychology, *The New York Review of Books*, September 28.

Vygotsky, L.S. (1985): *Ausgewählte Schriften* (Selected Works), I, Köln.

Vygotsky, L.S. (1934,1979): Consciousness as a Problem in the Psychology of Behavior (1934), *Soviet Psychology*, 1979, *XVII,4*, pp. 3–35.

Watson, J.B. (1914): *An Introduction to Comparative Psychology*, New York.

Wilson, E.O. (1975): *Sociobiology. The New Synthesis*, Cambridge, Mass.

ON FOUNDATIONS OF MIND

CONATION, COGNITION, AND CONSCIOUSNESS

Henrik Poulsen
University of Aarhus

Since Kant the mind has traditionally been divided into three mental functions: Cognition, conation, and emotion. In modern textbooks one finds a similar tripartition of the field of psychology into cognition, motivation, and emotion. Motivation has here replaced conation, because conation has erroneously been identified with motivation.

The British empiricist philosophers of the 17th and the 18th century conceived of the mind as consisting of beliefs and desires. They were thus correctly pointing to cognition and conation as the two conceptually basic categories of the mind. Emotions, on the other hand, are complex mental phenomena with cognitive as well as conative aspects.

In early German and Danish philosophy and psychology, conation was referred to as volition. I, however, prefer the concept of conation, because I believe we need a concept covering more than volitionary phenomena. The concept should, for instance, encompass striving or purposive behaviour in animals as well as in human beings. It should moreover cover phenomena like human wishes, passionate cravings, and interests.

The concept of conation is often referred to as purposive or goal-directed behaviour, but I want the concept to cover more than conations embedded in motor behaviour. It should, for instance, also comprise consciously experienced wishes, desires, and appraisals (cf. Poulsen, 1991, pp. 41–45).

Instinctive activities

In trying to develop a concept of conations and a conception of the relations between conation, cognition, emotion and motivation, I shall first attempt to characterize conative activities of animals. I shall do this by showing how these conative activities contrast with phylogenetically older and more primitive instinctive activities, the so-called fixed action patterns.

Lorenz (1977, p. 55) has illustrated the nature of fixed action patterns through an account of a kestrel being "fooled" by reflections from a polished marble surface into going through its bathing pattern, and subsequently cleaning its feathers. The kestrel was not in the least distracted by the fact that the "bathing" did not take place in water. The kestrel's drive to carry out its bathing behaviour seemed to be reduced quite as effectively by its "bathing" on the dry marble "pond", as it would have been had it taken place in water.

This bathing and cleaning of feathers belongs to the category of consummatory, instinctive behaviour characterized by the following properties:

– it is a species–specific, rigid, motor pattern which is triggered by a releasing stimulus when the animal's inner drive has reached a certain magnitude,

– and it is the execution of the motor pattern itself which reduces the drive, and thereby, for a period of time reduces, the probability of this motor pattern being triggered by another releasing stimulus.

The biologically relevant *effects* of a consummatory activity like, for instance, cleaning feathers, or food consumption will, of course, have a fairly high probability of being attained when the fixed action pattern is being released within the stable ecological niche to which the animal is adapted. If this were not the case, the fixed action patterns would be dysfunctional to survival of the species. But, as illustrated by the bathing pattern of the kestrel, one might say that these effects are not sought by the subject. They are only side effects of what the animal is really trying to do, i.e. carrying out a certain rigid pattern of movements.[1]

The kestrel's bathing on a marble surface illustrates another interesting property of the instinct–mechanism: Sensing the releasing stimuli does not function as cognition. It does not inform, or misinform, the animal about objects in the world.

A releasing stimulus triggers a consummatory activity, but the releasing stimulus from an object does not function as a signal informing the subject about other object–properties. The releasing stimulus does not make the animal anticipate anything. It does not prepare the animal for future events. Another way of expressing this fact would be to say that the animal does not react to feed–back from the object with which it has been brought into contact by its motor pattern. The kestrel's bathing behaviour was triggered by reflections from the polished marble surface, but there were no signs in the behaviour of the kestrel of its being "surprised" by not being splashed with water. It would, therefore, be unwarranted to say that the kestrel saw the slab of marble *as* water. It would be unwarranted to mean literally that

---

1   Mechanisms of instinct may be considered rigid and primitive, but they are, in terms of species survival, highly efficient means of existence within stable environments. And let me remind you that human beings form equally rigid behaviour programs, called habits, within stable parts of their environment such as, for instance, their bathrooms.

the reflections "fooled" the kestrel into believing that the marble surface was water.

At the evolutionary stage of instinctive mind, sensation does not function as cognition (perception). It functions only as registering of releasing stimuli which trigger motor patterns. Ascribing cognition to animals requires the existence of observable aspects of behaviour, which may be interpreted as signs that the animal is able to realize that *it has made a mistake*.

Sensing of stimuli has the character of cognition only when it functions as providing information or misinformation about objects in the world. Cognition requires more than sensitivity to releasing stimuli. Cognition does not, however, come into existence in phylogenesis until animals are capable of carrying out conative activities.

Conative activities

In mammals, conative activity seems to be the dominant form of activity. I do not, however, want to express any opinion on the question of differences between the species in this respect. And I must particularly stress that in taking an activity in birds to exemplify fixed action patterns, I did not intend to imply that conative activity is not characteristic of this species. I am concerned with distinctions between forms of activity, and not with distinctions between the different species.

An activity being conative, means that it consists in a striving – with behaviour which adjusts itself to the conditions of the activity – towards establishing a certain relation between the subject and an object.

This relation between subject and object, which the subject is striving to establish, is what I will call the *goal of the activity*. Instances of activity–goals are, for example the animal's comsumption of food, its finding of a resting–place, its passing of an obstacle, and its feeding of its young.

An activity with a certain goal can be carried our via various *modes of activity*: The animal will use the ways and means of activity which under the existing conditions will lead to the goal. A certain activity–goal may be obtained through different modes of activity, depending on the conditions with which the animal is confronted.[2]

A mode of activity may consist in the striving towards a certain goal by the use of other activities, as for example jumping over or by–passing obstacles, when the animal is progressing towards its hunting territory. Modes of activity may also consist in different motor features concerning, for instance, motor pattern, direction of movement, speed of movement, or quantity of muscular power.

---

2 Modes of activity have been called operations by Leontyev (1981).

A conative activity has a constant and a variable component. The constant component is the *goal* of activity. The variable component is the *mode* of activity. The conative or striving character of an activity is signalled by a perceptible distinction between the activity's goal and mode. In contrast, a distinction of this kind cannot be made where instinctive, consummatory activities are concerned. With conative, striving, goal–directed activity the animal is trying to establish some relation or other between the subject and an object, and it varies its mode of activity until the relation has been established. An instictive, consummatory activity, on the other hand, has been carried out when a certain rigid pattern of movements has been executed, quite irrespective of whatever relation between subject and object has been attained thereby.[3]

The conations we may ascribe to animals, capable of conative activities, are not conceived of as inner, mental phenomena (desires) lying behind outer bodily behaviour. The conations of animals exist only in the striving, goal–directed, purposive character of their motor activities. Conations are aspects of their motor activities. These motor activities are "inhabited" (Taylor, 1983) by conations.

In human beings, conations may also occur as embedded in conative, motor activities.[4] Human conations occur, however, additionally in the form of consciouly relating to objects in the world in wishes or desires, without the conations being embedded in motor activity. Although this is a possibility for human beings, one might still say that conations are, to use a phrase of Taylor (1983), "fundamentally articulated" in the striving, goal–directed character of motor activities.

Conative activities and cognition

With its conative activities the animal not only establishes goals, i.e. relations between the subject and objects of the world. It also perceives these objects as suitable *goal–objects*, i.e. as objects to which certain relations may, or must be, established by the activities in question. In addition, with its mode of activity the animal perceives the object as lending itself to this particular activity–mode.

The animal's repertoire of conative activities constitutes its store of *concepts* with which it can perceive, describe, or categorize objects. The animal has, as a matter of fact, no other kind of concepts, neither verbal nor

---

3   My attempt to determine the nature of conative activity (here as well as in Poulsen, 1991) is directed at the same problem which Engelsted (1989) has tried to solve in his discussion of "teleological" activity. I believe, however, that I have, by introduction of my concepts of activity–goal, modes of activity, and goal–object (see below), come closer than Engelsted to our common goal.

4   Human conative activities are usually called actions, and human conations, when imbedded in actions, are then called intentions.

pictorial. By striving to establish a certain relation between the subject and an object, the animal is perceiving and describing this object as suitable for the activity in question with respect to its goal and mode. It shows, by directing its activity towards this particular object, and by using a particular activity–mode, that it has taken the object to be suitable as goal–object of this activity, and as lending itself to this particular mode of activity:

-      X is perceived and described as something which may be eaten,
-      Y as something to escape from by flight,
-      Z as something to be explored,
-      Q as something to be neglected,
       etc., etc.

The conative activities of an animal constitute its conceptual media of cognition.

Let me explain why I consider the describing of objects in terms of conative activities to be cognition. To this end, let me first remind you of the kestrel's bathing behaviour. We saw, in this case, that reflections from the marble surface acted as releasing stimuli, triggering the fixed motor pattern. The kestrel's landing on the slab of marble, and thus coming into close physical contact with it, had, however, no influence on the kestrel's behaviour. Functionally speaking, the kestrel was, within the context of its instinct, sensitive only to those stimuli from the slab of marble which by an inborn mechanism served as releasers. All other properties of the object were functionally of no importance. It would, therefore, not be warranted to say that the kestrel had been informed about the nature of the object by the reflections of light from the marble surface. If it had been so informed (or, if you will, misinformed) this would have shown up in its behaviour following its landing on the object.

When animals use conative activities, the situation changes quite drastically. The animal does not merely react to releasing stimuli. Stimuli from an object make the animal engage in an activity which also functions as a preliminary description of the object as being suitable for a certain activity with respect to a given goal and mode. This desciption is thereafter tested when the animal, through its activity, comes into contact with other properties of the object. It is as if, with their activities, the animals are posing questions: Was it in fact possible to slip under this obstacle or to by–pass it? Was it in fact possible to catch the prey? to hold it? to eat it? Etc. The test may turn out negatively, in which case the activity must be broken off, or its mode changed. Alternatively the test may turn out positively, and the activity may then be continued or brought to its end.

With their conative activities animals describe and ask questions about objects. This is a necessary precondition for their being informed about objects in the world. Thus the conative character of their activities is a precondition of cognition in animals. Conation must therefore be considered the primary mental function, and cognition the secondary. This fact may easily be overlooked by psychologists, taking the human mind as their point of departure. Recognition of the phylogenesis of the mind is important for an adequate understanding of the human mind.

Cognition is tightly interwoven with conation. The mind of subhuman mammals is a *conative–cognitive mind*, and this mind exists only as embedded in motor activities. But the connection between conation and cognition is even closer, the animal's cognition being unavoidably *cognition of the conative relevance of objects*. Translating and slightly rephrasing a passage from Mammen (1983, p. 227), I will express this idea in the following way: Subhuman mammals peceive objects only as objects of their conative activities. Objects are not perceived as objects with objective properties beyond those which are involved in the ongoing conative activity. I have referred to this property of mammalian cognition, when saying about these animals that they know the objects as something to be eaten, as something to take flight from, to copulate with, to give parental care, or as something to be used by the particular individual as a tool in a specific activity, etc.

The conative character of cognition in the subhuman mammals entitles us to assume, in the words of Prinz (1992), that cognition and conation, or perception and action, are coded "in the same format of representation" in the brain of these animals.

Prinz (ibid.) argues that "since the basic biological function of perceptual systems is to supply the organism with information for planning and guiding its actions, it is likely that these systems have developed such that they satisfy the needs of action control". This point of view is highly relevant to the account I have given of the conative–cognitive mind in subhuman mammals. But the paper by Prinz brings experimental evidence, concerning temporal and spatial coincidence of perception and action, in favour of his assumption of a common afferent and efferent code in human brains as well. To this line of evidence, I should like to add some observations by Lewin (1926).

The observations by Lewin concern perception of the *aufforderungscharacter* (or valency) of an object: Objects may, so to speak, call out to us to be eaten, to be fondled, to be slapped, to be crawled upon, to be kicked, etc., etc. The object's *aufforderungscharacter* is sometimes its most salient mode of appearance. Perception of *aufforderungscharacter* is a human form of cognition of the conative relevance of objects, and this human form of cognition is not necessarily embedded in motor action. Lewin considers this kind of perception to be especially characteristic of children. He thereby indicates kinship between human perception of *aufforderungscharacter* and the form of cognition characteristic of subhuman mammals.

In my discussion of instincts and conative activities, I have up till now sketched sensation and cognition as having evolved

- – from pre–cognitive sensation of releasing stimuli,
- – to conative cognition, embedded in motor activities,
- – and to human conative cognition, not necessarily embedded in motor action.

The next step to be mentioned in this sketch of cognitive evolution, is connected with the concept of consciousness.

Before I turn to this subject, I would like to make a few comments on the relation of conation to emotion and to motivation.

The relation of conation to emotion and motivation

The roots of human emotionality are found in the mammalian mechanism for maintaining a stable body temperature. The sympathetic part of the autonomic nervous system, which controls the visceral reactions, originally evolved as a mechanism for managing the organism's reactions to the dangers constituted by environmental temperature fluctuations. This system gradually developed further to support the animal's reactions to other external dangers as, for example, predators which must be fought or avoided by flight (Pick, 1954). To serve this end, it became a mechanism for mobilizing energy needed in situations of external danger. Conative-cognitive activities in fight and flight, accompanied by sympathetically aroused visceral reactions, are the emotions of the subhuman mammals. In cases where, in connexion with the unity of conation and cognition, there occurs a relatively powerful activation of visceral reactions with ensuing consequences for behaviour, we have emotional syndromes resembling to some extent the emotions of anger and fear we are familiar with from human life.

Psychological theories of emotions have searched for the essential characteristics of human emotions. The theories differ as to what feature or features they consider to be essential: Visceral or cortical arousal; intuitive evaluations or appraisals embedded in cognition; certain conative activities or different kinds of conation (including a variety of forms of evaluation); cognition of those features of the situation or event which specify the the category of emotion. The theories have often been unreasonably one-sided in their stressing of what features characterize the human emotions. On the basis of an analysis of many different theories of emotion (Poulsen, 1991), I have suggested that we understand human emotions as syndromes of conation, cognition and affect. By affect I mean a considerable visceral and cortical arousal and the different behavioural effects thereof. The variety of kinds of conation and cognition possible in human emotions is extremely large.

We have a human emotion when conation occurs together with cognition, and when this combination is accompanied by considerable affect. In contrast to the subhuman mammals, human beings may have cognitions without conations. Human cognition and conation is probably, more often than in subhuman mammals, "cold" cognition and conation, i.e. unaccompanied by affect.

One may easily feel confused when confronted with the many different motivational concepts and phenomena: Drives, instincts, needs, incentives, purposes, wishes, conations or intentions, etc. It may be tempting to try to escape from this confusion by searching for *internal* characteristics common to the different motivational phenomena. Such an attempt would, however, be in vain. The different motivational phenomena have, as a matter of fact, no internal characteristics in common. The only feature they do have in common is a certain type of *external relation* to a certain kind of phenomena. What they have in common is their explanatory function concerning intentions of action, or, in the case of animals, conative activities.

An explanation by motivation, or by motive, explains the intention of an action (or the conation of an activity) by specifying how and why a certain intention (or conation) has attained a positive value for the individual. Such positive value may be indicated by, for instance, the force and energy used in trying to realize an intentional action. Or it may be indicated by the inconveniences or disadvantages which the individual accepts in order to realize the action in question.

There are no limits to what kind of phenomena may have motivational function. Motivational phenomena may be organic needs, perceptual incentives, purposes, beliefs, or conations. Even though it is the function of motivation to explain conations of actions or activities, nothing precludes a conation from being a motive for another conation. Conations may function as motives, although it would be unwarranted to identify conation with motivation, because a conation is not necessarily used as a motivational explanation of another conation.

The word "motive" is preferable to the word "motivation", when the motivational explanation refers to reasons which are or might be given in consciousness. It is my feeling that "motives" should not be used when we speak of animals or young children. In such cases "motivation" is to be preferred.

Psychological theories differ as to what kind of motivation they are concerned with. They differ also as to what kind of motivation they consider fundamental, inborn or acquired. But they do not – or they ought not – differ as to their understanding of the explanatory function of motivation.

Before leaving the subject of motivation, I should like to remind you that the concept of motivation is not always used as an *explanatory concept* in the way I have spoken about it until now. In ordinary conversation motivation is sometimes employed *descriptively* to characterize the nature of a person's conations. When speaking about a person being strongly motivated, we do not refer to the causes or reasons for his activity. We mean, instead, that the person takes pleasure in what he is doing, that he is highly interested in his task, or that he is firmly committed to it. In Anglo–Saxon psychology, motivation is primarily employed as an explanatory concept, whereas in Continental–European psychology there has been a tradition for using it decriptively to characterize the nature of conations.

Animals without consciousness and consciousness of human beings

From amongst the different concepts of consciousness, I choose to mention two.

"Consciousness" may refer to an ability to express one's cognitions and conations in another medium than motor activities. Animals do not have consciousness in this sense.[5] They do not have at their disposal any medium for perceiving, describing or categorizing objects of the world other than their conative, motor activities. Nor do they have any other medium available for articulating their conations.

Their only medium of desciption being motor activities, and it being impossible to make their own motor activities the objects of other motor activities, animals cannot be conscious of themselves.

Human beings have other media of description at their disposal than their motor actions, verbal concepts being the primary other media. As humans we are able to use language for articulating our conations and for describing objects of the world. Human beings, thus have consciousness in the first sense of the word.

Animals also lack consciousness in the sense that they only know of the conative relevance of objects to the individual. Thus the animal only knows an object as object–for–the–subject. It does not know an object as an object–in–itself, i.e. as an object existing independently of the subject's cognition.

Human cognition is not limited to knowledge of the personal conative relevance of objects. Human cognition, beyond infancy, comprises knowledge of objects as objects–in–themselves. Human cognition comprises knowledge of objects as existing independently of the subject's cognition. And it comprises knowledge of objects having other properties than the properties perceived or known of by the subject or presently of interest to the subject.

As pointed out by Leontiev (1978), humans perceive and know the "objective meanings"[6] of objects. Human beings who live in societies, and

---

5   There are reasons to believe that chimpanzees constitute an exception from this rule.

not just in social groups, sustain themselves by using tools and institutions which they have, to a great extent, received from the preceeding generations. These human tools (in the widest sense of the word) are not only produced for use in one specific activity or task, nor only for the use of the person who has made the object. Human tools are generalized in relation to tasks and users, and they are produced in culturally–determined, standardized forms. Each new generation has to be introduced to the life forms of its culture by learning, in practical and theoretical upbringing and training, the "objective meanings" of such objects – that is, their general uses (functions) and the prescibed, adequate modes of use.

The objects to be "appropriated"[7] – like axes and bicycles, institutions and language – have their "objective meanings" independently of whether the subject needs objects with such meanings, and independently of whether the subject is actively linked with the objects.

Man's knowledge of objects as objects–in–themselves extends, however, further than to knowledge of the generalized, culturally–determined meanings of objects. The nature of this extension has been pointed out by Mammen (1983) in his analysis and critiqe of Leontiev's account (see also Mammen, this volume).

We know that the objects we relate to with mental and motor activities are more than what they are to us. We know that an object is not only an object for us, but also for other people. We know that the object has an infinite number of properties which are not given to us in our ongoing activities. We know that, were we given the possibilities, we could come to know much more about the object – although we cannot come to know everything about it.

Properties of objects fall into two categories: Natural properties and historical properties (see Mammen, this volume). Natural properties such as, for example, an object's weight or colour, or its "affordances" (Gibson, 1979), are not dependent on the history of the object. This mean that whether or not the object has the property in question may be determined by sensation, with or without instruments of measurement or other tools. It can be determinded without any knowledge of the object's history. The object's being a coffee–cup, for instance, is a property of a different kind. It is a property linked to the object's history – in this case to the fact that it has once been produced by human beings with a certain generalized function in mind.

The cognition of "objective meanings", as pointed out by Leontiev, is cognition of historical properties, but there exist many other historical properties than "objective meanings". We perceive or think of historical properties of other people when, for instance, we perceive or think of them

---

6 German: "Bedeutung"; Danish: "betydning".

7 German: "angeeignet"; Danish: "tilegnet".

is cognition of historical properties of a thing when we perceive or think of it as being our property, as being an object we have inherited from our grandfather, as something belonging to our neighbour, or as plants I have myself planted in my garden.

It holds in general for cognition of historical properties (and not only for cognition of "objective meanings") that, in order to know of an object as an object with historical properties, it is not enough to perceive it by sensation. We must by necessity also be able to know the object as a particular object with numerical identity (as identical with itself) independently of its natural properties, that is, independently of its sensory similarity to other objects in some respects (its qualitative identity).

Mammen has illustrated this necessity by the following example:

When we find a piece of flint-stone in the field, this stone is a tool from the stone age if, and only if, it has in fact been produced by a person from this period as a tool, with a certain function intended. Another flint-stone, with the same natural properties of size, form, weight, and affordance, is not a scraper from the stone age if the properties have been produced by forces of nature, and not by a person from the stone age. It may not be possible for us to determine whether the stone has, in fact, been produced as a tool by a person from the stone age. But if, on the other hand, the flint-stone was found in a grave of a certain type, this may furnish us with good reasons for claiming that it is a tool from the stone age.

The numerical identity of an object is independent of its natural, sensory properties. It is independent of its having changed, and of its having lost former properties or having accuired new properties. A thing may have become frail or corroded, and a person may have become wise, arrogant or senile.

Awareness of the numerical identity of objects is not only our foundation for cognition of their historical properties. It is also our foundation for cognition of objects as subjects of change, and is the foundation for our emotional object-relations to persons and to things (Mammen, 1986; Poulsen, in press).

Human consciousness comprises an understanding of the world as filled with objects with numerical identity, and thus it is a consciousness of objects as objects-in-themselves. This capability makes the human mind quite different from the mind of the subhuman mammals. But different as they may be, humans have still preserved ways of relating conatively and cognitively to the world which are characteristic of the subhuman mammals.

References

Engelsted, N. (1989): What is the psyche and how did it get into the world? In N. Engelsted, L. Hem & J. Mammen (eds.): *Essays in general psychology. Seven Danish contributions,* Aarhus, pp.13–48.

Gibson, J.J. (1979): *The ecological approach to visual perception,* Boston.

Leontiev A.N. (1978): *Activity, consciousness, and personality,* Englewood Cliffs, N.J.

Leontyev, A.N. (1981): *Problems of the development of the mind,* Moscow.

Lewin, K. (1926): Vorsatz, Wille und Bedürfnis, *Psychologishe Forschung,* 7, pp. 330–385.

Lorenz, K. (1977): *Behind the mirror,* New York.

Mammen, J. (1983): *Den menneskelige sans* (The human sense), Copenhagen.

Mammen, J. (1986): Erkendelsen som objektrelation (Knowing as object-relation), *Psyke & Logos,* 7 (1), pp. 178–202.

Pick, J. (1954): The evolution of homoestasis, *Proceedings of the American Philosophical Society,* 98, pp. 298–303.

Poulsen, H. (1991): *Conations,* Aarhus.

Poulsen, H. (in press): *Guds kærlighed og menneskenes.* (God's love and man's).

Prinz, W. (1992): Why don't we perceive our brain states? *European Journal of Cognitive Psychology,* 4 (1), pp. 1–20.

Taylor, C. (1983): Hegel's philosophy of mind, In G.Fløjstad (ed.): *Contemporary Philosophy,* Vol. 4, pp. 133–155, The Hague, Boston, London.

THE ELEMENTS OF PSYCHOLOGY

Jens Mammen
University of Aarhus

Activity as a unit of analysis in psychology

A recurrent theme in scientific human psychology is the problem of defining the basic "units of analysis". In this short paper I shall offer a blueprint of such a unit, or "element" in Fechner's terms.

My point of departure will be the theory of activity conceived primarily by A. N. Leontiev, and I shall make no attempt here to give an outline of this theory, but rather refer the reader to Leontiev's works (1978, 1981, 1982), to Engelsted (1989a, 1989b), Poulsen (1991), and to my own elaborations on the theory (Mammen, 1983, 1986, 1989).

In a fundamental sense "activity"[1] is the basic unit of analysis in human psychology as well as in animal psychology. It is the aim of this paper, however, to point out some minimal complexity of structure in human activity that is necessary for the analysis of specific human psychic phenomena, such as "consciousness", "sense" and "meaning".

Before picturing this complexity we must focus on the concept of activity itself. If activity is understood as mechanical interaction between pre-established subjects and objects we are missing the point, that we are talking about the activity of a subject. One way of understanding this very general and abstract statement is to conceive of activity as an act of "abstraction", as a subject abstracting or extracting an object from the infinite pre-existing matter, making part of the material world an-object-for-the-subject (Leontiev, 1982; Mammen, 1989). In the case of humans, this abstraction can be practical and be an act of selective attention, not necessarily perceptual but also an intention of thought.

Objects of activity

In this interpretation activity is basically characterized and distinguished by its object. To ask what can be objects of human activity is to ask about

---

1 Russian: "deyatel'nost'". German: "Tätigkeit". Danish: "Virksomhed".

what is in the world, and is as such an ontological question. But to say that anything existing in the world can be made objects of human activity, is on the other hand a postulate of the materialistic theory of knowledge which could be categorised as "practical realism" (Mammen, 1986).

Just to give examples, objects could as the one extreme be the after-image I see after staring in my lamp. In this case the object belongs to my body, but only exists for me as a subject. If others wanted to make it an object for them, they would have to go "through" me. Such objects only existing in one activity or relation ought rather be called "phenomena". Objects like "my favourite dish" or "my home" are also necessarily related to me in an activity, but could also, after being identified, be reached by others, who for instance could disagree with me on, respectively, its nutritive value or its distance from the central station. On the other extreme, objects like "Mozart's symphony no. 40" or "The planet Mars" are in no way dependent on being objects of my activity.[2]

Now, looking at objects that are not just phenomena, it is a characteristic of human consciousness,[3] that we know that what is an object for me is not just that. It is also an (in any case potential) object for other people, and has an infinity of features or properties, that are not objects for me in this particular activity, but of which any one could be an object for another activity, for instance one mediated by the object's interaction with other objects, etc.[4] This knowledge is not necessarily itself in the focus of consciousness, but rather in the "fringes" of consciousness. But it can be focussed on, when an object surprises us, is problematic in other ways, or just excites our curiosity.

It is characteristic for human consciousness to be open and humble towards the object's infinity and to be confident that it is possible, given the means, to know more about it, although not everything. This is true of animate as well as inanimate objects, and especially of our fellow human

---

2   In the above examples objects are "entities". But they could as well be present or past situations or episodes, as studied by Larsen (1983), processes, states, etc.

3   When speaking of human consciousness, I am referring to the specific human cognition as the highest level in the human psyche, co-existing with other levels of psychic life, also found in the animal psyche. This is in accordance with A. N. Leontiev's definition of consciousness as specific human psychic "being". I am not exclusively referring to what is conscious in a more narrow, phenomenological sense, what we are "conscious of", i.e. what is subjectively given with a certain clarity, being accessible to verbal formulation, implying self-awareness, being "reflexive" etc. I have discussed the very intricate concept of reflexivity in earlier publications (Mammen, 1969, 1982).

    In fact, as I use the concept of human consciousness here, it includes both "focal" and "fringe" consciousness, or tacit knowledge. It might also include parts of what psychoanalysis would name the unconscious.

4   Properties of objects may themselves be objects of human activity. So, the term "object" may appear in different senses in the paper. However, the meaning should be clear from the context.

beings as objects of our activity. This is also the basis for our capacity for reclassifying objects, as was demanded for instance in Duncker's well-known experiments on "functional fixation" (Duncker, 1935). And it is the basis for our capacity for a certain amount of simultaneous multiplicity of classifications.

It is possible for me at the same time to see the coffee–cup on my balcony–table as a coffee–cup, as an "ad hoc" paper–weight preventing my manuscript from flying over the roofs of Aarhus city, and as a physical body describable in terms of form, colour, and chemical composition. And still I know in the fringes of my consciousness, that this is just a selection of an infinity of possible properties of the cup, that it could manifest in an infinity of possible relations with other objects and with active subjects.

The natural and historical properties of objects

To make things simple, initially, let us look at that kind of objects, which are "things" with "substance" like the coffee–cup. And let us look at the properties, that are "objective" in the sense, that they are not dependent on any particular subject and his or her activity.

These properties could be the cup's weight, which is a manifestation of its mass in relation to terrestrial gravitation. It could be the cup's suitability for containing liquids, for containing soil and serving as a flowerpot, i.e. its "functionalities" in relation to other objects or substances. It could be its being "liftable" or "throwable" by normal grown–ups, i.e. what J. J. Gibson (1979) named its "affordances". And it could be its being a coffee–cup, i.e. that it among all its possible functionalities, by virtue of this particular object's history, has been constructed to serve as a coffee–cup, and in this case also has been used as such.

As is seen, these properties fall in two distinct classes. We could call them "natural" properties and "historical" properties.[5] The weight, the functionalities and affordances are so to say natural properties of the cup. They are relational, or "contextual" in the sense, that the properties are manifested in relation to gravitation, other objects etc., but still they are independent of the history of the cup. They are products of natural or cultural history, as is everything, but the properties are what they are now, and just now. Like the Moor, history has done its job, and may go.

But the cup's being a coffee–cup is another kind of property. It is not a natural property, but a historical one. This statement would indeed be

---

5   In a discussion of this distinction, Hem (1980) used the terms "universal" versus "local" properties, applying the concepts of universal versus local perspective characteristic of natural sciences and historical sciences, respectively. This distinction is parallel to the present one, and to the distinction between what was called "sense–categories" and "selection–categories" (or"categories of choice") in Mammen (1983, 1986).

problematic, or even nonsense, for the reader only recognising natural properties as real properties. But what is the reason for not recognising historical properties as real? It could refer to the historical properties being "contextual". However, the reference to memory, to habit, is not a good reason, because natural properties are also "contextual" or relational, as demonstrated above. The more fundamental reason is that the context is the cup's history, and that history, i.e. the past, is considered non–existent as an objective reality.

If history is considered as non–existent, the non–natural properties are also non–existent in the objective sense, and are just subjective "descriptions" rooted in the memory or habits of the individual subjects. And memory and habits are not history, but present products of history. Or the "descriptions" are rooted in language, in a system of "meanings" or the like.

However, both the reference to memory, to habit and to language still leaves the question unanswered, what properties manifested by the cup distinguish it as something that should be remembered or treated or named as a coffee–cup. We are left with the alternatives, that being a coffee–cup must either be a natural property after all, or it is just an idea kept in the realm of language or subjective, habitual "schemes" or the like, without objective reference. This is the traditional point of view, whether the "schemes" are called "scripts" (Abelson, 1981), "theories" (Neisser, 1976) or "Idealized Cognitive Models" (Lakoff, 1987).

In opposition to this "nominalistic" view, I claim that being a coffee–cup is an objective property belonging to the history of the cup. This has the ontological implication, that history is considered part of objective reality, and not just "passed" or "gone".6 That is, that events in the past can

---

6   When analysing mechanical phenomena in physics, all causes or conditions remote in time are seen as acting through a "chain" in time of infinitesimal, "immediate" causes. The behaviour of objects is explained from integrating differential equations describing the infinitesimal time "surroundings" of the objects. The equations have no "memory", so to say. They are *"time–local"*.You could even say that this analytic principle of "immediacy" is defining not only the subject matter of mechanical physics but of all natural science. When, for instance, biological objects are said to have "memory", what is meant, is only that certain relatively stable inner states are strongly correlated with remote causes, not that the principle of immediacy has been violated.

The properties of objects taking part in the above mentioned natural, immediate interactions are referred to as "natural" properties. *Natural properties are associated with the object in an infinitesimal interval of time.* This does not mean that they could not be lasting or invariable properties, that they have no history, or that natural scientists are not interested in for instance the history of the universe, or the history of the species. Only that the principle of explanation of natural science is the integration of a chain of immediate causes acting between natural properties.

What is referred to as *"historical"* properties are accumulated properties associated with the *"life"* of the particular object till now. Only if the universe is considered one big clockwork following laws that in principle would let it run exactly back to its beginning if

be objects of our attentive or intentional activity and not just the remote causes of the activities, as is the case in "natural" interactions.

As human conscious beings we can make the world's historical "deep structure" an object of our activity. Not to say that we can interfere with the past, or reverse the arrow of time, but to say that we can know about, ask about, be interested in and investigate our past. When I say that my great-grandfather was a master builder, I am referring directly to this late forefather of mine, not to some present effects of his being a master builder, as for instance somebody remembering him, or the content of some left documents. The truth of my statement is not dependent of any of these effects, although they may be what I take as evidence. But it makes sense to ask if the evidence is false or misleading, even if I am not able to answer the question.

If I had a fiancée and asked her where she spent last night, I was not just interested in the possible traces left by her adventures but in what really happened. And this still holds good, even if I cannot help making my own interpretation of whatever she tells.

So "things" in the world have these two types of objective properties, the "natural" ones, and the "historical" ones, and as conscious human beings we can make both kinds of properties objects of our activities.

There is, however, a substantial difference in the way we relate to these two types of properties in our activity. When relating to the natural properties, the basic act of discriminating the object and its properties from other objects and properties, is sensory. Not necessarily just sensing and perceiving with our native sense-organs, but as modern human beings also sensing through instruments of measurement, through optical or electronic devices, through tools as extensions of our body, etc. Of course we are doing a lot more than discriminating sensory properties to understand natural properties. To see "what they are", we are using the whole bulk of knowledge of the world. But still, the basis for discriminating "what is what" is sensory. What else?

When relating to an object's historical properties, the situation is more complicated. First, we must be able to discriminate and recognize the object's natural properties. We cannot recognize the cup as a coffee-cup without being able to see or feel its form rather accurately. However this necessary condition is apparently not sufficient as a basis for discriminating

---

the arrow of time was reversed, should it be possible in principle to map historical properties onto natural ones. Today no competent physicist believes this (see Prigogine & Stengers, 1984). And even if it was possible, some sort of "universal" knowledge would be needed, possessed by no living subject or entity (Mammen, 1969; Sørensen, 1985).

This ontological understanding of the "historical" properties as distinct from the "natural" ones is metaphorically expressed by Leontiev (1982) as the historical properties defining an objective "fifth quasi-dimension" in the world, besides the four dimensions of space and time.

historical properties. Of course we also need a lot of "theory" to recognize historical properties. But this is not what I am referring to. What I mean is, that the objective basis for being a coffee–cup is not just natural properties. Therefore the discrimination of natural properties is not sufficient as the primary objective basis for what the theories are to discriminate in the world. The theory of coffee–cups could be very elaborate and detailed, but it cannot itself decide when it is to be applied at a concrete object, if there is no objective discriminating difference to link with the theory. So, we have a problem. What more is to be discriminated than the natural properties?

Our 'pocketing' of individual objects

My answer is, that what is to be discriminated is what philosophers call the object's "numerical identity", its "individuality", "particularity", "singularity", "uniqueness", apart from its properties. It is not the properties of an object that have a history, it is the object itself. Two objects can have the same natural properties except for insignificant differences, the one being a coffee–cup, and the other one a tea–cup, if we can believe the labels in the museum. The director would turn rather emotional, I am sure, if we interchanged the labels with the argument, that there are no significant differences between the cups.

Two pieces of flint–stone found in the field might be practically identical, the one being shaped by nature, the other one being a scraper made by a stone–age hunter. There is no sign left in the stones' natural properties of which one is the scraper. But one of them is by a continuous thread in space and time connected with the hunter, the other one is not.[7] Perhaps this thread cannot be identified, and we shall never know which stone was the scraper. But perhaps the one was found in the hunter's grave, giving us good reasons for recognising it as a scraper.[8] We can give a detailed description of this stone. But we cannot give a description that would exclude all other stones, of which some would not be scrapers. What makes this stone a scraper is not the description, but the continuous thread to its

---

[7]   In natural interactions, described by physics, these "threads" play no role. The physical interactions are so to say "blind" for the numerical identity of objects. What counts is the natural properties.

[8]   The significance of location and material context for the identification of archeological material's meaning is convincingly elaborated by Larsen (1987) in a discussion of archeology and human memory.

     Archeology is not only a good example of our active investigation of the cultural world, but also serves, according to Larsen, as a useful metaphor for the "uncovering" of memory in psychoanalysis and other psychological inquiry. This interesting point of view lies beyond the scope of the present paper.

maker, which we can secure by keeping the stone under lock, not by describing it. What we "keep" in this way is not the stone's properties, but its "numerical identity" with itself. And this numerical identity is so to say our "handle" to its historical properties.

As P. F. Strawson (1964) has argued convincingly, no finite description of natural (or "universal") properties can single out an individual object from the world's infinity of objects. And as our practical sensory discriminations have the same finite "channel capacity" as our verbal descriptions, the conclusion is the same in respect of our inability to single out individual objects exclusively from sensory discriminations. If we still tried, we would be like paranoid schizophrenics who according to Mogensen (in press) engage all their energy in a futile project of ordering the world from natural properties, perhaps based on a fundamental "distrust" of the historical properties.

But why are we not all like these schizophrenics? And why are we not like lower animals who are also unable to discriminate the objects' history, but unlike the schizophrenics don't care? What is this human ability to go "beyond the senses", i.e. beyond sensory discriminations?

To understand this we must realise, that our active, practical contact with the world is not just a series of sensory discriminations. If I have two new coins, one in each hand, perhaps I am not able to discriminate them from differences in their natural properties. If, however, I put the coin in my right hand in my right pocket, and the coin in my left hand in my left pocket, I can still tell which one was in which hand without discriminating the coins, if I am only able to discriminate my pockets. The sensory discriminations are not to be viewed as isolated. They are embedded in a practice, just as they are known to be embedded in motor activity, as it has been studied under the heading of "re-afference" (von Holst & Mittelstaedt, 1950; Held, 1965; Gregory, 1966). Impairment in motor activity, for instance, dramatically disturbs sensory discrimination of movement. Correspondingly Goldstein demonstrated severe consequences in orientation following disturbances of body-image (see Merleau-Ponty, 1962).

In our practical contact with the world we so to say make and fill "pockets". If we just have unbroken lines to the "pockets", their contents can be discriminated unless somebody or something is replacing things. Usually we have some chance of telling this, or basically trusting it if we have not been cheated too much in our early career.

You could say that this "pocketing" practice with its embedded sensory discriminations is an expansion or generalisation of what J. J. Gibson (1966) would call a higher-order variable in perceptual discrimination. And as such it is itself a generalised perceptual system in Gibson's terms and a manifestation of a human "sense", which in fact was what I called it in an earlier paper (Mammen, 1983).[9]

The "lines" to the pockets can be "chained", i.e. the pocketing–relations can be combined or "nested",[10] thus defining a complicated ramified system of orientation in the world. Examples would be my possessions, my relatives, and their possessions, etc. It could be my ancestors, and their possessions, of which some may now be mine.

The orientation in this interwoven system of relations of "belonging", of lines to present objects, and "roots" to past objects, is just as automatised as is our orientation towards the world's natural properties. If, however, it becomes articulate in our experience, it is as a rule with a certain feeling, an "affection" or "sentimental" value. Perhaps this is just what we have these feelings for. There are clinical indications, that in some cases a severe disturbance in this sort of feelings is accompanied with a break–down of orientation in the world's historical "deep structure" (Mogensen, in press).

The structure of human activity. A model

To understand this system of double relations to the world, i.e. to the "natural" and the "historical", we must look a little more detailed on its structure. In figure 1 the minimal complexity in the structure of human conscious activity is outlined:

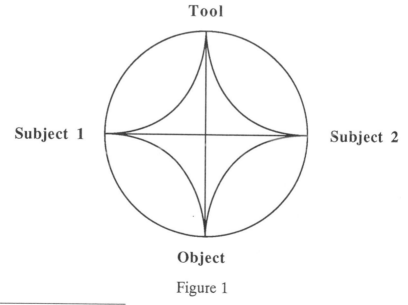

Figure 1

---

9   It can be debated if "perceptual" covers these acts of discrimination, as the memory or recollection of past episodes of activity is involved (see Larsen, 1983).

10 The relation of "pocketing" thus being a "transitive" relation: If A pockets B, and B pockets C, then A pockets C.

Figure 1 is a model of the specific human conscious activity of "Subject 1". In Leontiev's analysis of conscious activity, with human work as the paradigm example, this involves a subject engaged in an activity towards an object mediated by tools and in co-operation with other subjects. What makes this activity "conceptual" in the specific human sense is that Subject 1 in his or her activity is not just interacting but is abstracting and classifying in a specific way.

The Object (e.g. a tree) is not just recognised in its immediate appearance for the Subject, but also, at the same time, recognised in its relation to the Tool (e.g. an axe). For instance the tree is seen as too hard for the axe. The Object is also seen in relation to other Subjects. For instance the tree is seen as suitable for the carpenter but not for the boat–builder.

The Tool is at the same time seen not just in its relation to the Subject. For instance it could be rather heavy to handle. It is also seen in relation to the Object. It may be too dull for this tree. And the Tool is seen in relation to other Subjects. As it is a "standard axe", I see "in it" that it could also be used by other normal grown–up men in my community, but that it could not be handled by my little daughter.

And Subject 2, the other subjects in my community, are not just immediately appearing subjects. They are actual or potential consumers of Objects, and they are actual or potential users of Tools. The Objects and Tools mediate my relations with my fellow human beings.

You can say that the different "instances" in figure 1 are not just interacting but are also each others' yardsticks, thus producing new generalisations or "abstractions". Axes being sharp or dull wood–axes, trees being hard or soft timber, people being good or bad artisans, are examples of this.

It ought to be said, also, that the same object could in some relations be Object, in others Tool, and that even subjects can be Objects or Tools. The instances are "logical positions" for concrete objects. Also, the instances could be a plurality of objects, tools or subjects, again connected with each other, etc.

Now, let us focus on the "lines" connecting the "instances" in figure 1. The circular, peripheral line connecting the four instances should symbolise their "natural" interactions. These interactions are between the instances' natural properties and are independent of what were the historical remote causes of the instances and their properties. For instance the Object's natural properties is interacting with the Subject's sense organs.

The crucial point concerns the other six, "radial" lines, i.e. orthogonal to the peripheral line, connecting the instances. They symbolise the relations between the historical properties of the instances. What made my coffee–cup a coffee–cup was not just its natural properties and their actual or potential interactions with the table, the coffee, my hand and my lips. In addition to that, my coffee–cup should have a specific history, being produced by other Subjects (of whom I might be a special case, if I was in the pottery–branch) who perceived this object in relation to other Subjects potentially using the cup for drinking coffee. And what made it my coffee-cup, and not anyone else's, is also a property of this singular cup's history, in this case that I received it from my daughter as a birthday present.

My relation to the coffee–cup is thus not just interactions, but a "thread" connecting me with the cup and its past, which again is connected with "threads" to the producers, the sellers, buyers, givers and receivers of the cup. And to complete the picture, for the producer, the cup also has a relation to other coffee–cups in the past, to a tradition of producing coffee-cups in our society. All this makes it a "cultural" object.

My relation to a Tool like my axe is also not just interaction. The tool is also an Object like the coffee–cup, being produced in a tradition. But it is even more than that. To be an efficient tool not just for felling one tree, but for my general knowledge of which trees are hard and which ones soft, it has to be kept or "pocketed" in a lasting relation with my body. That could be a relation of ownership. If I used a new axe every time I felled a tree I could not know if the differences in efficiency were due to variations in dullness of the axes or hardness of the trees. And I could not interpret the gradual decrease in efficiency with the same trees as a result of wear and tear, thus giving me an insight in the laws of nature, which I could not reach without this lasting connection with the axe. The axe is as a tool an extension of my body.

My relations with other Subjects are, above all, not just interactions between natural properties. What makes my children my children is not at all their natural properties, but our common history, including the fact, that they were born by my wife having specific relations with me. My feelings towards my children are not just towards their natural properties, but towards those historical properties that are just an expression of their being mine. That they in some respects are like me, is not what I love them for (see also Poulsen, in press).

In figure 1 the Tool and the Object is also connected by a "radial" line, although none of them are Subjects. Without human subjects, Objects are so to say "blind" for their own and other objects' history. The remote causes do not participate in the present interactions. But embedded in human activity the relations between objects are historical in the sense, that they play a role in and mediate historical relations to subjects. Objects and Tools can "pocket" each other and in a chain of pocketing be pocketed by us.

What is interesting about a certain tunic button in a museum show–case is neither its natural properties, nor its relation to the insignificant Subject who used it as a bullet, but the fact that it was this button which hit Charles XII of Sweden (as an Object) and killed him.[11]

---

[11]   For a short account of the dramatic history of this button and its importance for revealing, in 1940, the assassination 1718 of Charles XII by one of his own men, see Carlsen (1948).

Less exotic examples of the "pocketing" relations between Tools and Objects, or between Objects, could serve as demonstration of the coupling between natural and historical properties, and to generalise the latter beyond cultural history.

When Gregor Mendel did his far–reaching experiments on plant breeding, what was new, was not just a detailed study of the plants' natural properties, but that this study was embedded in a practice which followed the "threads" of descent of every single plant, not by recognizing its natural properties (this would be "circular", and bring nothing new), but by pocketing the plants, using their positions in the beds as a Tool. It is thought-provoking when Bronowski (1973) tells us, that what was Mendel's exceptional quality, was not his scientific training but his affection towards his plants.

The above example illustrates the implications of man's "double–relations" not only with the natural and historical properties of cultural objects, but also with other objects of labour and experimental investigation. When working with a particular stone, making it a stone–axe, the producer is both recognising the stone's numerical identity, its being identical with it–self, defining a historical "thread" by its continued pocketing relation with his body, and at the same time, with his senses, recognising the differences in its natural properties. This joint observation of identity and difference, makes it an act of recognising change or process, thus yielding insight in the laws of nature, not being accessible to passive sensory observation.

Not until the renaissance is this aspect of labour united with scientific thinking, in the scientific experiment (Lewin, 1931).

The model as a unit of analysis

After giving this short explanation of the relations in figure 1, let me go on looking at the figure as a psychological "unit of analysis". As mentioned above, the "instances" in the figure are "logical positions" to be filled in by concrete subjects and objects. Until now the examples have been concrete, substantial "things", like myself and my coffee–cup. And in a certain sense these examples are fundamental as they define the interwoven tissue of historical "threads" or "pocketing" relations functioning as the practical basis or "context" for all other less "substantial" examples. But the figure could easily be applied to the latter kind of examples too.

Let us illustrate the above point with the example of my axe as a Tool. As mentioned, my axe, besides being my special axe, was a "standard axe" in the sense, that it fitted in a standardised practice for its use by other

---

(continued). For a related but more peaceful example used by the German sculptor Joseph Beuys, see Hermann & Gregersen (1978, pp. 155–158)

Subjects on a range of Objects, and that it was produced by Subjects in a tradition. This is just what Leontiev means by saying that the axe has the "meaning"[12] of an axe, i.e. that it is comprised by the concept "axe". The concept is a unit connecting the meaning with the word "axe". This word is neither creating the concept nor the meaning, but it is a necessary condition for maintenance of the meaning. Or a necessary Tool for the meaning as an Object.

So the figure is applied as a unit of analysis on two levels here. First in analysing the meaning of the axe as a Tool. Then in analysing the concept "axe" with the word as a Tool for the meaning. But the analysis can go further, seeing the concepts as Tools for communication (Fog, 1986), and as Tools for each other, in the development and transmission of theory, of metaphorical reference, of ideology etc. (Bertelsen, 1988).

The figure could also be used as a unit of analysis of what Leontiev calls personal "sense".[13] The personal sense of the axe is what it means to me besides its standard meaning as an axe. This could for instance be a feeling of affection, motivated in my relation to this particular axe's history. It could have been passed over from my father, and it could have saved my life helping me out of a burning house. So what I am relating to in this case is also the axe's "historical" properties, its past relations to other Subjects and Objects, and to myself as a Subject.

Leontiev is referring to the personal sense as "subjective", and the meaning as "objective". This is only justified in the respect, that the sense is personal, and the meaning is standard. Both sense and meaning is both subjective and objective, as it is a subject's activity abstracting certain objective relations, as depicted in figure 1.

The difference between sense and meaning is not the difference between the subjective and the objective, but is the difference between the Subject's personal life–history and its Objects, and the history of the society or the culture and its Objects. It is a difference of the small and proximal context of the Subject's individual life–history, and the large and distal context of society and history.[14]

Seen as such, it is apparent, that sense and meaning is not just a duality. It is rather a polarity with the smallest and the largest context for activity, and the historical properties of its objects, in each pole.

Between the poles is for instance the context of the family, of the generation, and of all kinds of sub–cultures. These contexts are embedded in each other, and are in certain respects also in conflict with each other.

---

12 Russian: "znachenie". German: "Bedeutung". Danish: "betydning".

13 Russian: "smysl". German: "Sinn". Danish: "mening".

14 This analysis has been further elaborated in Torben Østergaard Christensen's investigation (unpublished) of the life–world of young people attempting suicide.

This generalisation broadens the psychological implications of the analysis far beyond Leontiev's conception of conflict or non–coincidence between sense and meaning, and correspondingly between the individual and subjective on the one hand and the "societal", cultural and objective on the other hand.

To take the family as an example, the reality of a two–year–old boy in a family with parents and an older sister is not just his personal sense or the cultural meaning of objects. The objects' history in the family may be more important. The puppet on the shelf is not just nice–looking (sense) and some puppet (meaning). It is above all the older sister's property and her object of affection. This is a reality to be respected if the boy is to have good relations with his sister, and his parents. And what is to be respected is not the puppet's natural properties, it is a reality beyond these. The little boy has to learn that whether he finds the puppet attractive or not, new and shiny or worn and ragged, doesn't matter. He must learn to be open and humble towards objects, realizing that they may be much more than is immediately seen. On the other hand, to learn this, requires that he can trust the sister and, above all, the parents when they mediate this reality to the boy. So, humbleness, openness and faithfulness are not only ethical or "motivational" concepts, but epistemic ones as well.[15]

When appropriating the meaning of Tools and Objects in his world, aided by grown–ups and peers, the child not only learns what they are and how they are used in the relevant context, but also what they demand and how they should be used. The meaning is both descriptive and normative.[16] And after having appropriated the meanings, his acts towards Tools and Objects in many cases need no explanation for himself or his relatives. To ask what was your motive answering the phone, or calling the fire–alarm when your neighbour's house was burning, usually makes no sense, while it might require some motivational explanation if you did not.[17] No individual "motives" are needed for every conscious act except in psychology books.

To conclude: One advantage of using the same basic "unit of analysis" in all these different cases, is that some of the traditional distinctions between cognitive and "motivational" psychology, or psychology of per-sonality, vanish.

The development of early object–relations, as studied by psychoanaly-sis, the development of interests in adolescence, and scientific activity as an

---

15 For another, more elaborate example, see Bertelsen & Hem (1987, pp. 402f).

16 This has been stressed by Chris Sinha (1988) in his discussion of the concept of 'canonicality'.

17 Poulsen (1991, p. 101) makes this point clear. The perception of the demand character of meanings in the different large–scale and small–scale contexts of life also appears to unite what Katzenelson (1985) calls the in–side and out–side of morality.

attempt to reveal "deep" structures in the world, are variations of the same theme, and all incorporate the basic structure of human conscious activity.

To understand these different phenomena and their diversity within the same general dimensions will be a step in the direction of making psychology a "Galilean" science in the terms of Lewin (1931).

References

Abelson, R. P. (1981): Psychological status of the script concept, *American Psychologist,* 36, pp. 715–729.

Bertelsen, P. (1988): Kategorier, modeller og metaforer i kulturpsykologi (Categories, models, and metaphors in cultural psychology), *Psyke & Logos,* 9 (1), pp. 23–59.

Bertelsen, P. & Hem, L. (1987): Om begrebet: Klientens model af verden (On the concept: The client's model of the world), *Psyke & Logos*, 8 (2), pp. 375–408.

Bronowski, J. (1973): *The Ascent of Man*, London.

Carlsen, P. S. (1948): Karl 12, In H. Møller (ed.): *Nordisk Konversations Leksikon,* Vol. 8, pp. 23–24, Copenhagen.

Duncker, K. (1935): *Zur Psychologie des produktiven Denkens*, Berlin.

Engelsted, N. (1989a): *Personlighedens almene grundlag* I & II (The general foundations of personality, Vols. I & II), Aarhus.

Engelsted, N. (1989b): What is the psyche and how did it get into the world? In N. Engelsted, L. Hem & J. Mammen (eds.): *Essays in General Psychology. Seven Danish Contributions*, Aarhus, pp. 13–48.

Fog, J. (1986): Adskilt i forbundethed (Separated in unity), *Psyke & Logos*, 7 (1), pp. 86–108.

Gibson, J. J. (1966): *The Senses Considered as Perceptual Systems*, Boston.

Gibson, J. J. (1979): *The Ecological Approach to Visual Perception*, Boston.

Gregory, R. L. (1966): *Eye and Brain, The Psychology of Seeing*, London.

Held, R. (1965): Plasticity in sensory–motor systems, *Scientific American,* 213, 84–94.

Hem, L. (1980): *Empiriproblemet,* II (The Problem of Empirical Knowledge, II), Copenhagen.

Hermann, J., & Gregersen, F. (1978): *Gennem sproget* (Through Language), Copenhagen.

Holst, E. von & Mittelstaedt, H. (1950): Das Reafferenzprincip (The principle of re–afference). *Die Naturwissenschaften,* 37, pp. 464–476.

Katzenelson, B. (1985): Moralens inderside (The in-side of morality). *Psyke & Logos,* 6 (2), pp. 354–377.

Lakoff, G. (1987): *Women, Fire and Dangerous Things. What categories reveal about the mind,* Chicago.

Larsen, S. F. (1983): Erindringens natur og historie (The nature and history of recollection). *Psyke & Logos,* 4 (2), pp. 277–307.

Larsen, S. F. (1987): Remembering and the archeology metaphor, *Metaphor and Symbolic Activity,* 2(3), pp. 187–199.

Leontiev, A. N. (1978): *Activity, Consciousness, and Persona. ·ty,* Englewood Cliffs, N. J. (Russian edition, 1977).

Leontiev, A. N. (1981): *Problems of the Development of the Mind,* Moscow. (Russian edition, 1957).

Leontiev, A. N. (1982): Psychologie des Abbilds (Psychology of the perceptual image), *Forum Kritische Psychologie,* 9, pp. 5–19 (Translated from a Russian manuscript, 1975).

Lewin, K. (1931): The conflict between Aristotelian and Galilean modes of thought in contemporary psychology, *Journal of General Psychology,* 5, pp. 141–177. Reprinted In Lewin, K.: *A Dynamic Theory of Personality.* New York, 1935, pp. 1–42.

Mammen, J. (1969): Menneskets frihed – det frie menneske (Human freedom – the free human), *Dansk Psykolognyt,* 23 (20), pp. 295–299.

Mammen, J. (1982): Epistemologisk refleksivitet (Epistemic reflexivity), *Psyke & Logos,* 3 (2), pp. 255–59.

Mammen, J. (1983): *Den menneskelige sans. Et essay om psykologiens genstandsområde* (The human sense. An essay on psychology's subject matter), Copenhagen.

Mammen, J. (1986): Erkendelsen som objektrelation (Knowing as object-relation), *Psyke & Logos,* 7 (1), pp. 178–202.

Mammen, J. (1989): The relationship between subject and object from the perspective of Activity Theory, In N. Engelsted, L. Hem & J. Mammen (eds.): *Essays in General Psychology. Seven Danish Contributions,* Aarhus, pp. 71–94.

Merleau-Ponty, M. (1962): *Phenomenology of Perception,* London (Translated from *Phénomenologie de la perception,* Paris, 1945).

Mogensen, J. (in press): *Sanse- og udvalgskategorielle strukturer i den skizofrenes erkendelse – og i psykiatriens* (The structures of sense-categories and selection-categories in the cognition of schizophrenics and of psychiatry), Aarhus.

Neisser, U. (1976): *Cognition and reality,* San Fransisco.

Poulsen, H. (1991): *Conations.* Aarhus.

Poulsen, H. (in press): *Guds kærlighed og menneskenes* (God's love, and man's).

Prigogine, I. & Stengers, I. (1984): *Order Out of Chaos. Man's New Dialogue with Nature.* With a foreword by Alvin Toffler, New York.

Sinha, C. (1988): *Language and Representation. A Socio-naturalistic Approach to Human Development,* London.

Strawson, P. F. (1964): *Individuals,* London.

Sørensen, T. S. (1985): Kaos og orden i natur og samfund (Chaos and order in nature and society), *Slagmark,* no. 5, pp. 43–66.

THE CONSCIOUS BODY: BIRTH OF CONSCIOUSNESS – A THEORETICAL SYNTHESIS

Mogens Hansen
Chief school psychologist
Lyngby–Taarbæk

Abstract: This paper deals with the development of consciousness. Part I presents human cognition with its five forms of experience, the double architecture of the mind with its automatized skills and reflective thinking, and its seven kinds of intelligence with their distinct competencies. Part II describes the development of human consciousness based on the inborn readiness or preprogramming in the human infant: 1. Focusing on 'the world'; 2. Synchronicity; 3. Indication; 4. Attention; 5. Intentionality; 6. Reciprocity. They have a common developmental history in the individual child and are interwoven in the person's activity, but each one has a specific influence on consciousness.

The complete unfolded structure of cognition is presented prior to the developmental principles and processes. Then the individual developmental project for constructing one's own conscious awareness is described. This could seem to be a reversed order of presentation, but instead it elucidates the human infant's inborn goal for development in an almost teleological sense. Human cognition unfolds itself in both structure and functional systems built on a broad spectrum of inborn possibilities or pre–programs, but no basic readiness in the genome unfolds without active interaction between the infant and its world: its body, perceptions and cognition, and its material world and world of persons. The same is true for the principles of development: in the genome the human development is mapped out in stages. Without the child's active focusing and reaching out for his or her world, and without interactions – and transactions – with competent adults, growth and development are inhibited or impaired.

Therefore, it is crucial to have knowledge of the goal before the journey starts – both for the human infant and the reader.

I. The structure of cognition

The evolutionary history of the brain

The human brain has through its evolutionary history unfolded a capacity for five distinct forms of experience. The mind's house can therefore be described as a house with five stories, many apartments and rooms, and even cellars and a top–storey.

These qualitatively different forms of experience are:

- attractions and repulsions,
- emotional and social,
- cognitive,
- metacognitive,
- creative.

In the evolutionary history of living organisms no apartment or room in the brain's structure – not even the smallest closet – has been renovated, closed or locked. We have the total evolutionary history since the time of the reptiles 300 million years in the anatomy of our brain. At one and the same time we perceive, categorize and act as reptile, cat, chimpanzee, as well as human being.

Emotions, thinking and activity cannot be separated. Attempts to formulate the goals and means are never separated from affect and emotional relations to fellow human beings. Lev S. Vygotsky (1987) stated it in this way: "Thought ... is not born of other thoughts. Thought has its origin in the motivating sphere of consciousness, a sphere that includes our inclinations and needs, our interests and impulses, and our affect and emotion. The affective and volitional tendency stands behind thought. Only here do we find the answer to the final 'why' in the analysis of thinking".

The double architecture of the mind

In a simplified model the human mind can be described as having two levels: a level with automatized skills and a level with conscious methods or strategies and symbolic knowledge.

In this paper, only the latter will be elaborated upon.

A skill is a complicated and automatized piece of knowledge to be exercised with precision and plasticity in routine behavior. You have specific and uncomplicated skills, for instance, for many motor routines – they are task–specific, and you have broad and complicated skills consisting of a lot of more specific and narrow skills. These broad skills or competencies are, for example, driving a car, reading the newspaper or preparing a tasty meal in the kitchen. They are all based on a heavy load of tacit knowledge – knowledge without symbolic representation in for example words; you can also call it the knowledge of the body. Skills are executed rapidly and with no reflections, and therefore run the risk of being both 'impulsive' and 'stupid'. In the daily routines, as for example driving a car, preparing a meal in the kitchen or swimming at the beach this skills level is nonetheless effective.

In many life situations, however, quick routines are not enough. In new or unexpected situations you have to think, i.e., use all your reflective capacities, as a condition for understanding, planning and activity. It is time–consuming and therefore a slow process compared to the automatized skills.

In cognitive psychology this 2nd floor is called metacognition, i.e., conscious thought and strategies in problem solving. In conscious thinking, in order to realize your plans, strategies and beliefs, you have to find answers to the questions: why? – when? – and how?

The 'why?' is about becoming consciously aware of your goals and intentions.

The 'when?' is about being consciously aware of selecting methods, strategies and tools in the broadest sense on the basis of thought, instead of automatized routines.

The 'how?' question is the last and most important. It is about conscious awareness of the process itself in an activity, i.e., the ability to ask questions relating to one's own 'inner world' with both feed forward, activity and feed back. This is the conscious task awareness.

At its best human activity is thousands of functional systems or integrated capacities with a balance between automatized skills and reflective thinking interwoven with intentions, emotions, attitudes and social interactions.

The seven intelligences

The human intellect is not a single and uniform force as postulated in the nearly 100 years old global theories of intelligence, by for example Alfred Binét, Louis Terman or David Wechsler. All brain research, research in pathology and pedagogical experience with children in the teaching–learning process points to intelligences instead of one global intelligence. In one of the most influential theories on the edge of year 2000 (Gardner, 1983, Hansen, 1992) the human intellectual potential is described as consisting of multiple intelligences or modules. Human beings have at least these five modules of intelligence:

- linguistic intelligence,
- musical intelligence,
- logic–mathematical intelligence,
- spatial intelligence,
- bodily–kinesthetic intelligence.

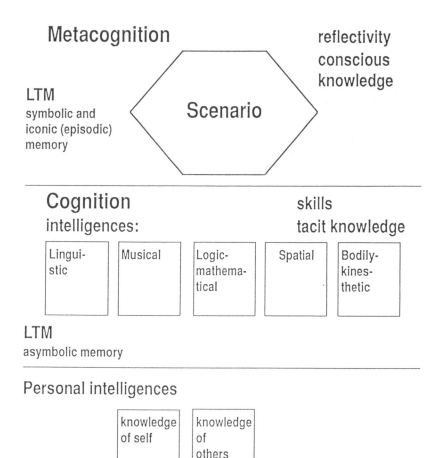

Figure 1. The double architecture of the mind with the seven intelligences (LTM = long term memory)

Each of these intelligences has its own symbolic representation. The linguistic intelligence 'listens to' and 'talks' in the verbal code; musical intelligence 'listens to' rhythm and melody, and has its own written language; logic–mathematical intelligence 'listens to' and 'talks' in, for example, classifications, seriality and in numbers and mathematical symbols; the spatial intelligence 'listens to' and 'talks' in, for example, pictures and images; and the bodily–kinesthetic intelligence expresses itself in dance, facial expressions, movement in space and all the fine movements and gestures with hands and fingers.

In this way each intelligence has its own specific competencies or complex skills. In fact, a module defines itself via its competencies. In lingui–

stic intelligence the fundamental and critical capacities are phonology, syntax, semantics and pragmatics; in musical intelligence they are rhythm and melody (pitch); in the mathematical–logical intelligence they are sequential and relational thinking, seriality and classification, and ultimately abstract thinking and recognizing, and problem solving tasks; in spatial intelligence they are the capacity for precise visual perception, to perform transformations, modifications and inner manipulations of percepts, and the ability for reconstruction of percepts – all on the inner scene. The ability to form vivid, visual imagery is central for growth in spatial intelligence; for the bodily– kinesthetic intelligence the critical competencies are skilled use of the body, and skill in the manipulation of objects in the world.

Inside these modules you also develop and keep your tacit knowledge – all your automatized skills.

Besides these five modules of intelligence, the human being has two more intelligences: intelligence for knowledge of self and intelligence for knowledge of others. The first comprises knowledge of one's own emotions, consciousness and self (intra–psychic intelligence); the other, knowledge of other people's temperament, emotions, and intentions (interpersonal intelligence). These two intelligences are the basis of all other functions.

Metacognition

Metacognition is a general and comprehensive term for a person's ability to observe his own planning, problem solving, evaluation, language, emotions, intentions, etc. This 'reflecting on one's own thinking' depends on the development of an active and engaged self. The role as observer of one's own mind is an active and involved role. It is not the passive role of an audience witnessing what happens on the stage. Reflective thinking is to be able to reflect or 'mirror' the thoughts in the mind.

Reflective thinking is learned in school via the interaction between teacher and child, and via activities in the teaching–learning process in the classroom. It is a cultural product. To become reflective is to learn to look at oneself from the outside: 'I'm myself, looking at my mind'.

Metacognition is also the person's capacity intentionally to focus and maintain her attention on her own activity, on objects, persons and the inner world of her thinking, imagination and emotions. In this way metacognition is the capacity to have conscious awareness. Metacognition is in this way the self–regulatory aspect of the mind. The concept of metacognition is a heavily loaded term. It represents the awareness of self and identity, consciousness, reflective thinking, monitoring and control of both thinking and activity, short term memory (the working memory), intentionality – and the scenario itself with its capacity for powerful imagination.

Metacognition is a classic topic in psychological theory and research. The Swiss psychologist Jean Piaget used the term *decentration* to describe the development of the child: Until the age of 5–6 years, the child is 'the center of the world' (egocentric), then the child moves from the center of the scene to occupy the role as his own active observer. The Soviet psychologist L. S. Vygotsky described this process in the development of language using the metaphor of the window–pane in 'the glass theory'. The 'glass theory' tells us that children see the world as through a window (glass), and at a certain point in their childhood they become aware of the glass itself. Up to a certain age the children do not see their own language, but at an age of approximately 6 years they are able to learn to observe both the contents and the form of their own language. The American psychologist C. H. Cooley coined the term 'the looking glass self' for the child's conscious awareness of self. This self–identity grows out of social and linguistic interaction with other people. Without this interaction with other persons – or with meager interaction – the conscious awareness of self will not develop fully. The observations of Piaget, Vygotsky and Mead are all examples of metacognition in broad areas of development. All three psychologists agree on this: that development of conscious awareness or metacognition is dependent on learning – and paradoxically also the other way round: that genuine learning is dependent on conscious awareness.

One further comment is justified. Conscious access to the modules or intelligences depends on their 'bubbling up' into consciousness. This bubbling up depends on the modular development of each module's symbol–system or language so that they are able to 'speak' to each other. This metacognitive access to the seven modules and their specific competencies results in a drastic increase of the richness and possibilities of the mind's planning, monitoring and reflection on diverse programs and ends. However this metacognitive function is domain specific. Metacognition is not one single function. It seems to have to be learned over and over again throughout life from task to task, level to level, from module to module. For example trained metalinguistic awareness does not transfer smoothly to other metacognitive functions (Brown, 1987).

The scenario functions and consciousness

In the center of the metacognitive capacity is the scenario. The capacity of the scenario at a certain moment is to 'look at' and 'use' 5–6 items at a time. It is a rather limited capacity for reflective thinking. The items on the scene, however, can call or attract new items from the long term memory (LTM) and recombine items by using chunking, so one single item on this inner stage can represent a large amount of information.

The scenario is multi–dimensional and has a richly faceted cognitive capacity. At least these functions are facets of the scenario:

- consciousness (conscious awareness) of the outer and inner world, 'the eye in the mind',
- reflective thinking, i.e. 'reflecting on one's own thinking', thinking in both images (iconic symbols, for example pictures and diagrams) or in serial symbols (verbal, mathematical, arithmetical),
- intentionality (the free will) which is heavily dependent on the inner manipulations of items in–and–out of the scenario,
- work memory (short term memory, STM),
- monitoring, control and evaluation of thinking (feedback or revising approach and feed forward, anticipation or 'looking into' the zone of proximal development, etc.) and monitoring the automatized skills and competencies,
- awareness of self (the personal experience of identity), and
- the scenario's functions (see figure 2).

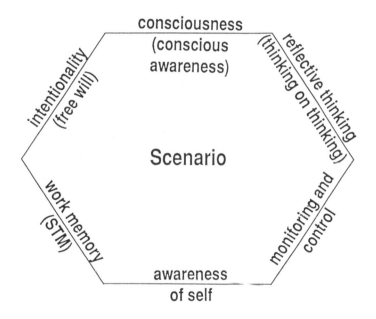

Figure 2. The scenario with its primary functions: consciousness, reflectivity, monitoring, self, work memory (short term memory, STM) and intentionality

One of the dynamic functions of the scenario is imagination. The imaginational power is not only visualizations, but also auditive and kinesthetic images, images of surface and the hands, manipulative images of form of objects, smell images, etc. Imagination is a creative function developing from infancy to adulthood. One part of the power of imagination and creativity is based on experience and knowledge. The more knowledge (tacit or symbolic) you have, the better your possibilities are for creative activity. L.S. Vygotsky (1990) has described this line of development as early as 1930:

> We know that the experience of the child is less rich than the experience of adults. We know, further, that his interests are simple, more elementary, poorer in quality. Finally, his relation to the world does not have the complexity and diversity that distinguish that of the adult and which are important in the work of the imagination. It is clear from this, that the child's imagination is not richer, but poorer, than the imagination of an adult.

But this statement is only one side of the matter. The capacity for imaginations in young children is in many ways enormously vivid and rich, though restrained by their lesser experiences compared to adults (Gardner, 1980, 1982).

The scenario is fundamental for interaction with and understanding of other humans. The capacity to 'mirror' other people's scenarios in one's own scenario is a basic condition for empathic understanding. It is also this ability to reflect on other people's minds that gives us (our subjective) knowledge of their intentions. This ability the child learns from the start of life in social interaction with the adults in its world. The mediation is asymmetric as the grown-ups have something to give to the child in the interaction process. In this way the child builds a reciprocal identity with the capacity to 'mirror' other people's scenarios in his own scenario. Intentionality is growing out of reciprocity as a forecasting of wishes, activity and inner planning (Engelsted, 1990). This reciprocity is basic for the teaching-learning process as a shared and social process – learning is fundamentally 'social in nature' as said by L. S. Vygotsky.

The body in the consciousness

Imagination and thinking in the scenario are spatial. When reading a novel, we create in our inner space a world of persons acting, feeling, loving and fighting in the space of the story. We create our own inner movie. This is a fact not only for such episodic material but also for abstract, mathematical-logical and theoretical thinking. All sorts of thinking have an imagined form in the three-dimensional inner space. Humans don't think in pure concepts, as in words or formulas. Thoughts are given shape and mental existence as they move around like things within the scenario. The physicist Albert Einstein puts it this way (Einstein, 1973):

> The words of the language, as they are written and spoken, do not seem to play any role in my mechanisms of thought. The psychical entities which seem to serve as elements in thought are certain signs and more or less clear images which can be voluntarily reproduced or combined ... The above mentioned elements are, in my case, of visual and some of muscular type.

This first phase of thought is followed by a meticulous translation to conventional words and other symbolic systems in a second phase. Thoughts are based on bodily activity – are internalized movements.

Human consciousness is created by verbal language, inner pictures or images and the body. Verbal language is basically metaphoric. A large part of our verbal language is created out of the tacit knowledge of the body itself, its movements and activity, the body in its space and time. Verbal language is not in itself a tool for defining concepts and fixing minor differences between this and that. Verbal language is heavily loaded with metaphors which we use to explain and understand ourselves and the world ("the world is at his feet"), and pictures we use about unknown things and situations as analogous to something well known ("the brain is as telegraphy", " ... a computer", "... holograms"). We use the metaphors as analogous to ..., and in this way we understand. The metaphorical verbal medium creates our insights and experiences. The metaphorical character of verbal language gives man the possibility of analogical thinking as a basis for creativity. Analogical thinking sometimes gives you totally new knowledge by combining hitherto incoherent facts with new coherences; the double helix as a picture of the DNA molecule is just one such example.

The body is a reservoir for metaphoric creativity. Head, face, eyes, ears, mouth, lips, teeth, arms, elbow, hands, fingers, nails, et cetera, are the raw material, which we can use in our understanding ourselves and the world. The 'arms' of the chair, the 'legs' of the table, and 'teeth' of the comb are metaphors, though we hardly recognize the fact. Almost every object or situation can, however, be a useful metaphor that opens our eyes for fresh new insights and emotional experiences, as poetry shows us.

Metaphors also contain seduction and deceit – both in experiencing the 'world' and in communication. Verbal language has many facets – both dark and light sides that you will meet in teasing, irony and sarcasm, and in jokes, riddles and puns.

The conscious body

The body is quite a different sort of object from any other object in the world of the person. Any other object than our own body can disappear, but our own body is always present from the same angle – with the words of the French philosopher and psychologist Maurice Merleau–Ponty (1970):"... its permanence is not a permanence in the world, but a permanence from my point of view (p. 90). The body is an integral part of activity; not a motor vehicle for it. It is via the body in activity that man creates his/her bodily consciousness and imaginations, not from an object but from a situation. It is in action that our body learns its spatiality.

Our body gives significance both to the objects in the world and to cultural objects like for example words:

> If a word is shown to the subject for too short a time for him to be able to read it, the word 'warm', for example, induces a kind of experience of warmth that surrounds him with something in the nature of a meaningful halo. The word 'hard' produces a sort of stiffening of the back and neck, and only in a secondary way does it project itself into the visual or auditory and assume the appearance of a sign or a word. Before becoming the symbol of a concept it is first of all an event which grips my body, and this grip circumscribes the area of significance to which it has reference. One subject states that on the presentation of the word 'damp', he experiences, in addition to a feeling of dampness and coldness, a whole rearrangement of the body image, as if the inside of the body came to the periphery, and as if the reality of the body, until then concentrated in his arms and legs, were in search of a new balance of its parts. The word is then indistinguishable from the attitude which it induces, and it is only when its presence is prolonged that it appears in the guise of an external image, and its meaning as a thought. Words have a physiognomy because we adopt towards them, as towards each person, a certain form of behavior which makes its complete appearance the moment each word is given. (Merleau–Ponty, 1970, p. 235–6 – refering to: Heinz Werner: Untersuchungen über Empfindung und Empfinden, I and II: Die Rolle der Sprechempfindung im Prozess der Gestaltung ausdrücksmässig erlebter Wörter, 1930).

The specialized hemispheres

The human brain consists of two relatively symmetric hemispheres (halves). The right hemisphere controls the left side of the body, and the left hemisphere controls the right side. The nervous system crosses the center line of the human body from hemisphere to body, limbs, eyes, ears, et cetera. In man the brain has developed a specialization of the information processing of each hemisphere. The two forms of processing are the analogous and the digital processing both of perceptions and expressions in activity. For most right handed persons the analogous processing is performed in the left hemisphere, the digital in the right (for left handed persons the picture is more blurred: left handed people have their digital abilities either in the right or in the left hemisphere or distributed in both).

Analogous information processing results in perception and expression in wholes, for example in icons (picture–like gestalts), perception of the face and its finer expression of emotional details – one of the most complicated wholes you meet, and perception of the body scheme (the body in the spatial world), i.e., simultaneous information processing in 'more–or–less', with gradual transition between objects instead of distinct borders.

Digital information processing results in perception and expression based on analysis of details, breaking wholes into parts, and expression based on thorough analysis and construction of synthesis, for example in decoding and coding the verbal language (discourse). The digitalized approach is a sequential processing in contrast to the analogous approach with its simultaneous processing. Digital processing results in perception and expression based on understanding of distinct differences and borders between objects, or in expressions, for example 'yes–no'.

The two specialized hemispheres always work in unison as they are coupled via the corpus callosum.

Functional systems and knowledge

Competencies, complex skills, behavior and activity are all functional systems consisting of systems of brain functions in their relations to the outer world. Functional systems are always goal–directed and, therefore, a relation between the organism and its environment.

A functional system has at least three dimensions of mind: experience, intelligence and processing strategy (see figure 3, p. 56).
The experience dimension is from an evolutionary point of view very old (the oldest level, that of attraction and repulsion is approximately 300 million years old, as old as the reptile brain). The human mind always reacts and acts with all five levels of experience, with a complex of the seven intelligences, and with both analogue (holistic, simultaneous) and digital (in parts, serial) processing. Human knowledge (or functional systems) is therefore: *experience x intelligence x processing*, as shown graphically in figure 3.

II. Development of consciousness

It begins with the body. The body is there before consciousness. The cognitive apparatus gets comprehensive impressions from bodily activity and perception. The newborn child is born with no consciousness of itself as a human, a person or a personality. Nor is the child on the other hand born as a 'tabula rasa' on which the stimuli print themselves as experiences.

The child begins life with a heavy luggage of knowledge of what you have to do to become human, a member of society; not knowledge in the conscious or reflective sense, but the inborn readiness to reach for the world of persons and objects. This inborn knowledge is in the human genome as the genetic pre–programming for interaction. In upbringing and education parents and teachers have to dog the developmental footsteps of the child.

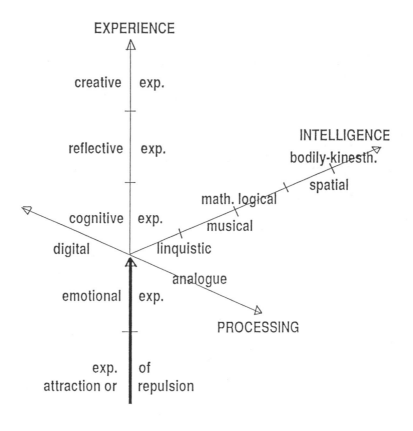

Figure 3. The mind's capacities with its experience of the world (how to perceive and experience the outer and inner world), its intelligences (how to learn skills and competencies and how to code and symbolize the two worlds) and its processing strategies (how to comprehend). Below the three-dimensional human mind you have emotional experience and experience of attraction or repulsion, which are evolutionary fundamental and very old structures in the brain. In this model KNOWLEDGE = experience x intelligence x processing. At the reflective and creative levels of experience knowledge becomes representational, i.e. to symbolize and "use" at the scenario in an iconic or serial form.

1. Focusing on the world

The child is born with an active attention for the world surrounding it. This ability for active focusing is ready just a few hours after birth. It is not a conscious and intentional function as with the older child or the adult.

This pre-programmed focusing on the world has a precise, selective capacity and therefore a biologically high value of survival.

In the beginning the child is much more attentive to persons than to objects – both the gestalt of the human figure and human speech. The most selective focus is for the human face, especially the surroundings of the eyes and the mouth. Precisely here, humans express their emotions of love, pleasure, joy, anger, distress, anxiety, fear, et cetera. The surroundings of eyes and mouth are among human beings the medium or channel for expressing and understanding emotions, moods and attitudes. The newborn child is equipped with solid (tacit) knowledge about where to focus – on face and voice – to initiate and to receive social and emotional contact.

The communication is facilitated by the gaze between infant and mother. They both unconsciously seek each other's eyes and gaze – and the mother's eyes are looking at the child's eyes long before the child can track anything with its eyes. When the child is ready to look for its mother's eyes there is a good chance that the mother's eyes are there already – in the child's zone of proximal development, so to speak. The gaze as contact and monitoring of communication is active from the second month of life (Trevarthen, 1979).

Early in life the child smiles to caring persons. This reflective and unconscious smile provokes positive reactions from the caring adults: they smile back at the child, react with rhythmic movements, with their voices, et cetera. It all acts as a psychic snap and secures continuous interaction between infant and adult. Both parties are spontaneously and unreflectively attracted by this game. The biological value for survival is obvious.

The bodily–kinesthetic contact is presumably an inborn readiness for both mother and baby. When the mother takes her baby up and places it so that the child's head is close to her shoulder and the side of her head, the child will, as its first reaction, explore the space by looking around (so it seems from an observer's viewpoint) and then place its head close to the neck and head of the mother and move its body to obtain the closest and most direct bodily contact possible. The mother reacts with an immediate bodily answer both in body and breast, so mother and child together build a communicative base (Brazelton, 1979). In many other situations the mother places the child close to her body, near the heart, to facilitate (so it seems) their joint experience of nearness through synchronicity, supported by the mother's rhythmical movements and sounds.

Discrimination between persons and objects develops at a much later time in the infant's life. For a long time it has no biological value for survival or growth.

Next in this line of development is the child's experience of the body as a separate object. Step by step the body becomes 'my' body. This body-experience functions as 'landing ground' for the consciousness in the body. It is a lifelong project to get and maintain an awareness of identity based on personal integrity.

The psychogenesis (the evolution of the psyche) will not be treated in this ontogenetic sketch; see for example Engelsted (1984, 1989), Jaynes (1976), Katzenelson (1989), Leontiev (1977), Popper & Eccles (1985), Schultz (1988).

2. Synchronicity

The interaction between infant and parent depends on a synchronous activity. This going after synchrone interactions is another aspect of the tacit knowledge, which the infant brings along into life as a prerequisite for development. The medium of synchronicity is rhythm, melody (pitch) and pauses, which give 'musicality' to social and emotional contact.

When observing a mother and her baby, you will see a complex pattern of mutual interactions, literally they perform a 'dance' together. The mother's invitations with her body, head, face and voice elicit the baby's movements with body and head, so it also smiles and looks intensely at the mother. The baby's smile, its babbling and movements with body, arms, legs and head elicit further reactions and invitations from the mother. It is fascinating to observe this on video played in a reduced tempo.

Often the child is satiated before its mother. After less than 10 minutes of this 'dancing' with the mother, the child needs a pause. If the mother continues, the child will show more and more signs of satiation and at last turn its head away in discomfort and cry. Small children need to alternate between open periods and closed periods, open periods where the child is ready for interaction and closed periods for rest and getting order in the social and emotional impressions so that they become personal experiences. This alternation between open and closed periods is lifelong and not limited to early infancy. At school age and among grown ups we often forget this alternation between openness and closeness when people meet. In school we talk about unmotivated pupils or narcissistic children with no interest in learning to become competent. In the kindergarten we talk about children with attentional deficits or the like. Among adults we talk about people without intellectual energy or interests. In many cases the manifest reaction represents satiation instead of lack of interest in the topic or activity.

If the child is born with insufficient or even lacking abilities for perceiving and expressing musicality in social and emotional interaction, it has a risk for loosing the basic and necessary contact. The mother experiences her own child as refusing her invitations, which is extremely rarely the case; child and mother cannot find a common melody for interaction because the child has no ear for the musicality that is basic for social and emotional contact and growth. In extreme cases the child will become an autistic person. The autistic child is a child with extensive communicative difficulties both with rhythm, melody and pauses in interaction with the mother but also extensive language problems, dysphasia. Until recently these unhappy mothers were described as the causal factor to autism in their child, as emotionally cool and inhibited personalities. Updated research has shown that causality often goes the other way round: the experience that it seems impossible to reach one's own child in the very basic emotional contact, with a rather high certainty leads to disappointment, insecureness about own feelings and fear of emotionality, for 'maybe something in me is wrong'.

These unmusical and dysphatic infants need a thorough diagnosis and direct and active training. The child and the parents need to find a common musicality, even if it has an unusual tune and almost unpredictable pauses and invitations. Parents, kindergarten teacher and school teacher must learn this child's special rhythm, melody and pauses.

In other cases, the parent is lacking in musicality, emotional openness and the ability to establish the social and emotional contact.

Synchronicity uses both analogous and digital processing. The analogous processing is rhythm and melody; the digital processing is seriality in interactions and time–structure with pauses. Musicality is based on mutual processing for simultaneousness (spatial structure) and activity in time (temporal structure).

This interactional synchrony is developed together with self–synchrony. The child's bodily–kinesthetic activity with fingers, hands, arms, body, legs and its sounds, babbling, mimics, winks and gaze are synchronized with pauses, alertness, drowsiness and peaks in activity (Condon, 1986). This synchronicity consists in a complicated totality united by the waves of many rhythms in unison. Without this orchestration of bodily, psychological, social and communicative function, human activity will end up in disintegration. The orchestration secures timing, sequencing and coordination.

When this emotional and social 'dance' unfolds, expectation is born – in the start with a rudimentary experience of a 'now', a future and a past. Expectation is interwoven in the mother–child interaction. The situation with joyous expectation at the same time involves basic experiences of a self.

3. Indication

Indication is a gesture with the purpose of directing someone's attention to something. When the mother with her infant points with her index finger at a red ball, at the same time looking at her child and then turning her head and focusing her eyes on the ball, moving the child's body in the direction of the ball saying: "look here, yes here – it is a ball, a red ball", then she acts with a whole complex of indicative gestures.

Just as mother and child are interwoven into a close relationship in the 'dance' concerned with social and emotional contact, they have a joint project in focusing on certain objects, persons and incidents. Together they look and listen to what happens in the child's 'world'.

This project starts in early infancy with the mother using much time and energy to show and tell her child about persons, objects and what happens around them. Objectively she initiates their joint project long time before the child is able or ready to understand anything of her indications. She starts before the child is able to look at or listen to, or to identify objects or incidents, or understand spoken language, but she, the mother, continues with optimism and expectation. The mother has an unrealistic trust in her child's actual possibilities and maturity, but in this way she is always some steps ahead of the child. In this way she is almost always ready in the child's zone of proximal development. This overoptimistic interpretation of the child's actual cognitive competence secures a constant 'ready–to–go' interaction. The biological and developmental value is obvious.

The mother points and looks at what she wants her child to focus on. She builds their joint focus. When the child reacts with a glance or by moving body, head, legs, arms or hand in the expected direction, she over-interprets the child's behavior as an expression of meaning and under-standing. When her child moves reflexively a little in the direction of the red ball she is sure that the child tells the mother that this is a ball, that the ball is red and that "I want the ball" or "give me the ball". In the long–term perspective of development, intentionality and symbolic activity are launched in this joint project. The reaching for the ball becomes stepwise a communicative activity with intentionality in the child's mind and a sym-bolic gesture in its reaching and pointing. All this also depends on the joint musicality and synchronicity of mother and child.

The indicative gesture or *deixis* represents a perceptual and cognitive scaffolding for the child; this structuring activity includes: 1) *framing*, i.e., giving situational boundaries to situations or objects, for example via pointing and language symbols, 2) *selecting*, i.e., discrimination between critical and distinctive stimuli and unimportant stimuli, 3) *focusing*, i.e., joint attention, 4) *duration*, i.e., focusing for longer and longer periods of time, 5) *naming*, i.e., talk about, refer to, comment, emphasize and giving names to objects, 6) *importance*, i.e., that this, exactly this, is essential, has meaning.

The newborn child is pre–programmed to listen to the spoken language. Words are 'ready' to become indicative – they are figures on the back-ground of all other sounds. Words have indicative functions not least dur-ing the period of growth when they are still a property of an object and not yet representations separated from the object. In school, through the teach–

ing–learning process, words become more and more indicative: they indicate just as the pointing index finger for the infant, the rapid glance from the spastic child.

4. Attention

In early infancy the child's attention is attracted by any powerful stimulus or situation. Its attentional shifts are determined by change in stimulus intensity, so that the child is a slave, so to speak, of the stimuli impinging on its senses. Sudden movements, loud noises or voices, powerful colors are all unavoidable stimuli to which the child's attention is turned.

Shortly after birth, the mother starts the joint project of assisting her child to overcome its inborn attentional impulsiveness. Spontaneously and unreflected she tries to establish a joint attention to certain objects and situations by pointing and talking. This indicational activity is a comprehensive and joint communication project between mother and child in the preparation for selectivity and duration of the child's attentional development.

This joint focusing and selectivity of attention is basic for the child's development of an autonomous, attentional function. An integrated part of this is the simultaneous development of consciousness, intentionality and reflectivity. Selectivity is the basis for reflectivity.

The stimulus–bound and impulsive attention, where the child is attracted by immediate changes in the visual field, and by high or sudden sounds, are a hindrance to reach for and experience the important cues in its 'world'. The essential objects or situations are, of course, what the adult considers to have essential meaning or value. At the same time the child learns autonomous attention, and it learns what is most important and what is beautiful, has value, is fascinating. For one child, this meta–learning will be an attentional focus on order and cleanliness, another child will learn to notice little and beautiful flowers in the grass, birds and insects, and another child still will notice even minor changes in his or her mother's face expressing rejection or acceptance and love.

This is also true in the teaching–learning process in the class room in the school. What the teacher finds essential, beautiful or valuable is basic for what he or she directs the children's attention to. In this way the teacher – just as the mother and father – is moving around in the zones of proximal development of the pupils in the class.

Metalinguistic awareness training in preschool illustrates this. Children up to an age of 5–6 years have no conscious awareness of their own spoken language. Listening to and using language is at this age an automatized skill. The metalinguistic awareness is learned from the teacher in the teaching–learning process via the teacher's pointing to the elements in the children's language: that they use words, phonemes, sentences, syntax, pauses, semantics, meaning and pragmatics, with specific intentions, in certain situations, with a certain form.

In school, children learn in cooperative activities with teacher and class-mates in the teaching–learning process to select among different activities and possibilities in the classroom. They learn to absorb themselves in cer-tain activities and push aside other activities. This intentional attention on own activity gives the children from 8–9 years of age the capacity to dis-criminate between social gathering and the teaching–learning situation in which you are a pupil working towards specific goals via specific methods, materials and learning strategies.

From 5–6 years of age children are ready to become consciously aware of their own consciousness. They can say: "I am myself". At this age they become the engaged and involved audience of their own thinking and activity. They become 'the conscious body' with intentional attention directed to both the inner world and the outer world.

5. Intentionality

The personal and subjective experience of being a 'self' with a 'free will' means: the open possibility to choose between goals and to initiate an activity towards the goal 'from the inside', rather than be triggered by an outside stimulus.

This experience unfolds more and more from the age of 5–6. Is it illu-sion or reality? The self is there, phenomenologically and subjectively, as an aspect or function of the scenario, as an active part on this inner scene in the human mind. But the question is: is the self a clown in the play, running around and believing itself to have influence without in fact having any?

I see it this way: We experience our own plans and intentions for acti-vity before we actually perform the intended action. We see free will or intentionality behind the behavior in other people. We ascribe to their behavior wishes (from interest to desire), convictions (from belief to knowledge), hope, annoyance, shame or disappointment. The free will is in this way a reality of the mind.

Intentions are about future activity. It has a built in arrow of time from now to a nearer or more distant future. The intentionality contains expecta-tions about a goal or purpose. There is a 'free choice' just here, where the person in his mind can choose between different means to an end. Even though activity planning needs not involve consciousness, it is potentially a conscious matter, and in this way consciousness is the extra possibility to interfere by weighing and choosing different possibilities in the behavioral repertoire. All this is performed in the light of consciousness of the sce-nario.

The scenario *in toto*, therefore, in this argumentation, serves as bridge and interface between mind and body, provides a causal link between 'pilot' and 'plane'. The scenario functions can in this way be understood as a human speciality: you can try with 'free will' if you decide to, but you can act in your social context almost without it.

Not unusually, humans therefore produce the reasons and explanations for certain behavior afterwards instead of producing them before they act (Gazzaniga, 1985, Jaynes, 1976).

6. Reciprocity

Consciousness develops out of interactions with other people, between adult and child. In other words: consciousness is a product of humans reflecting their minds into each other. This is a central function of the reflection theory in the cultural history school in Russian psychology. Paradoxically you also have to say that consciousness is a condition for interaction and dialogue between people. It is exactly this paradox that the mother overcomes by ascribing to her child much more awareness, intentionality and understanding than is the child's capacity in infancy. She communicates as if the child is reflecting back to her. This illusion creates reality: a child with his or her own reflectivity. In this one sided interaction, the mother hands over to the child the reflective capacities.

Contact between people is dependent on the basic development of reciprocity, i.e., a reciprocal reflectivity. My assumptions about you as a human being with a consciousness are a reflection into my scenario, where I perform a play showing me how your scenario looks like. And you create in your mind a scene invested with what you suppose is in my mind. Feelings of social and emotional contact are based on this endless reciprocal mirroring between people.

This line of development gives the child 'a theory of mind', i.e., a competence to have and to construct beliefs about other people's intentions, wishes and emotions – with a fundamental belief that other people have minds like oneself. Autistic individuals lack (more or less) this competence, and they don't experience other people's activity directed by intentionality. An autistic boy of 5 years often goes into the supermarket with his mother. He likes this routine. One day his mother turns around to go back to the shop after they came out. The boy cries in anger and emotional chaos. For him the behavior of his mother was a total breakdown of the daily routine, but for her it had a simple meaning: she had forgotten her sales ticket. She bases her daily activity on 'meaning', he has to base his whole life on routines and rituals to obtain predictability.

This 'theory of mind', or metacognitive awareness of reciprocity, is an indispensable precondition for complicated communication.

In school, children need to be trained in discourse. They need to learn communicative awareness by asking questions and constructing answers, they need to learn social standards in an optimally clear social setting, they need to learn cooperation in practice with negotiation, control and giving and asking for help from classmates, and they need to be trained in role–

taking, i.e., to be the one who initiates, takes the lead, tries to cope with situations. All this they need to learn, both on a skills level and on a reflective level. In their minds they develop an image of reciprocity, of a continuous shift of focus from 'me' to 'you' to 'me', on and on. This inner frame of reciprocity is supposed to be one of the cornerstones of writing and reading. With an awareness of language as a communicative medium the child has in his mind an internal dialogue with the author when he reads, and with his reader when he writes (Nystrand, 1986, Tudge & Rogoff, 1989).

The mental processes in the human being are dialogic both in their ontogenesis and in their developed structures and functions. They have their roots in discourse in the social setting. The mind developed from social dialogue which became psychological.

Conclusion

The six developmental lines are not perfectly distinct functional systems. They are distinct in some respects, therefore they each have their developmental story in the text, but in other respects they are so interwoven that they seem more alike than different from each other. The development of one of the six lines will also be a development of the others; so in a theoretical way they are distinct, but in interactions during upbringing and in the teaching–learning process they are woven into each other. The unfolding of capacities is dependent on the social and cultural context which must offer guided participation involving children and grown–ups in culturally valued activities (Rogoff, 1990).

All the six developmental lines from early infancy and onwards are based on the fundamental stages in human development; as Vygotsky said it: you learn everything twice: first inter–psychologically (socially) then intra–psychologically (individually).

Together the child and the grown–up pass the bridge from nature to culture, via joint activity and spontaneous experiences to individual activity and systematic learning. This developmental move towards internalization of outer activity, and thus to functional systems, takes place in the child's 'zone of proximal development' (Davydov & Zinchenko, 1988).

Productivity or work in human society depends both on understanding (sign meaning), on activity (skills), and on an awareness of purpose (consciousness). These three themes in development are also the three key concepts in the 'double architecture' of the mind.

References

Brazelton, T. B. (1979): Evidence of communication during neonatal behavioral assessment, In Bullowa, M. (ed.): *Before speech. The beginning of interpersonal communication*, London, Cambridge.

Brown, A. L. (1987): Metacognition, Executive Control, Self-regulation and other more Mysterious Mechanisms, In Weinert, F. E. & R. H. Kluwe (eds.): *Metacognition, Motivation, and Understanding*, N.J.

Condon, W. S. (1986): Communication: Rhythm and Structure. In Evans, J. R. & M. Clynes (eds.): *Rhythm in Psychological, Linguistic and Musical Processes*, Springfield, Ill.

Davydov, V. V. & Zinchenko, V. P. (1988): Vygotsky's Contribution to the Development of Psychology, *Soviet Psychology*.

Einstein, A. (1973): *Ideas and Opinions*, New York.

Engelsted, N. (1984): *Springet fra dyr til menneske*, Copenhagen (The jump from animal to man).

Engelsted, N. (1989): What is the psyche and how did it get into the world? In Engelsted, N., L. Hem & J. Mammen (eds.): *Essays in General Psychology. Seven Danish Contributions*, Aarhus.

Engelsted, N. (1990): Forsøg på en profan tilnærmelse til det sakrale. *Psyke & Logos*, 11(2), pp. 237-250 (Attempt on a profane approach to sacredness).

Gardner, H. (1980): *Artful Scribbles*, New York.

Gardner, H. (1982): *Art, Mind and Brain. A Cognitive Approach to Creativity*, New York.

Gardner, H. (1983): *Frames of Mind. The Theory of Multiple Intelligences*, New York.

Gazzaniga, M. S. (1985): *The Social Brain. Discovering the Networks of the Mind*, New York.

Hansen, M. (1992): Intelligens – om hjernen, tænkningen og erkendelsen. Horsens, 2. ed. (Intelligence – on the Brain, Thinking and Knowledge).

Jaynes, J. (1976): *The Origin of Consciousness in the Breakdown of the Bicameral Brain*, Boston.

Katzenelson, B. (1989): *Psykens verden, i verden. Et naturevangelium*. Aarhus (The World of the Psyche, in the World).

Leontiev, A. N. (1977): Problemer i det psykiskes udvikling, Copenhagen (Problems in Development of the Mind).

Merleau-Ponty, M. (1970): *Phenomenology of Perception*, London.

Nystrand, M. (1986): *The Structure of Written Communication. Studies in Reciprocity between Readers and Writers*, Orlando, Florida.

Popper, K. R. & J. C. Eccles (1985): *The Self and Its Brain*, Berlin.

Rogoff, B. (1990): *Apprenticeship in Thinking*, New York.

Schultz, E. (1988): *Personlighedspsykologi på erkendelsesteoretisk grundlag eller mysteriet om personen der forsvandt*, Copenhagen (Personality psychology based on the theory of knowledge).

Trevarthen, C. (1979): Communication and cooperation in early infancy: a description of primary intersubjectivity, In Bullowa, M. (ed.): *Before Speech. The beginning of interpersonal communication*, London, Cambridge.

Tudge, J. & B. Rogoff (1989): Peer Influences on Cognitive Development: Piagetian and Vygotskian Perspectives, In Bornstein, M. H. & J. S. Bruner (eds.): *Interaction in Human Development*, Hillsdale, N. J.

Vygotsky, Lev S. (1987): Thinking and speech. In Rieber, R. W. & A. S. Carton (eds.): *The Collected Works of L. S. Vygotsky*, New York.

Vygotsky, Lev S. (1990): Imagination and Creativity in Childhood, *Soviet Psychology*, 28 (1), pp. 84–96.

RELATING SUBJECT AND SOCIETY
IN ACTIVITY – A CRITICAL APPRAISAL

Erik Axel & *Morten Nissen*
University of Copenhagen

Clots in the Activity Theory brew?

This paper will discuss some theoretical reasons for the disparate and incongruous reception of Leontiev's Activity Theory. The discussion will only be concerned with the central concept of activity. According to our materialistic position we will sketch an history of Activity Theory in relation to its practical functions in order to trace its inner inconsistencies. Our aim is to indicate possible directions for the further development of Activity Theory.

When a theory has made a very widespread impact one often finds that continued work within the tradition disperses into different schools, each with its own characteristics. This dispersion should be considered fruitful, even though the consequence might be a complete dissolution of the theory into many disparate approaches. We think that Activity Theory is in the middle of such a dispersion.

Still, we consider it important to identify the reasons for the dispersion. Through the identification of the social functions of the theory one can specify the reasons for the theoretical problems concerning the activity concept. Hereby the dynamics of the lines of dispersion can be identified, and only those lines taken which will lead to an enhancement of the materialistic approach and not to its dissolution.

Nowadays Russian psychologists talk of Activity Theory as having had two functions in the Soviet Era. They distinguish between its scientific and ideological functions. The ideological function is characterised as a common protecting umbrella under which many psychologists could work. To us such a description must imply that in a society where people were supposed to organize themselves according to common principles psychologists could relate to the needs of actual practice supported by Activity Theory as a general psychology: They could transform the general theory into applied psychology in such a way that they were given opportunities to work according to the local interests of the studied field of practice, without making contradictory interests too explicit. This could be a reason for allowing ambiguous or unfinished concepts in Activity Theory to remain instead of relentlessly pursuing the problems in order to make proper distinctions within the whole. But having ambiguous or vague general concepts is like brewing on a poor font: It tends to allow specific viewpoints to congeal around specific contradictions in actual practice. Such a natural "clotting" process will mirror the contradictions in practice in the sense that it will not be easy to stir the clots back into the Activity Theory dish.

In order to explicate this point of view we will first demonstrate one of the ambiguities in the notion of activity. Then we will sketch out how a Soviet application of Activity Theory sought shelter in the ambiguity and thrived on it. We will hint at the implications this had for the dispersion of Activity Theory. Lastly we will discuss the reasons for the ambiguity and suggest a solution.

The ambiguity in the notion of activity

It is common to discuss the concept of activity by using two examples provided by Leontiev, the example of the primeval hunt, and the example of reading a book to take an exam. Most often the hunting example is discussed, with the reading example drawn in to shed light on some difficulties surrounding the concept. We will therefore proceed in that order.

The hunting example is from "The Origin of Human Consciousness", published in 1947. In the text (Leontiev, 1981, pp. 210–214) activity is introduced as a sociological category, derived from the division of labour: To understand the actions of the beaters, one must look at their relations to that of the hunters, and to the social need for the prey. The characterization of activity by its motive appears as a secondary characteristic. Through the hunting example one gets the impression that the essential thing to do in order to delimit an activity is to look at the interrelationship between the actions of human beings cooperating. One can even say that the theoretical construct surpasses the problems of sociological functionalism in an interesting way: In functionalism, society works because its institutions realize their goals through the acts of human beings. As a consequence, the individual is reduced to a mere appendix to the supraindividual institutions. In Activity Theory, on the contrary, human beings perform motivated activity and the so-called goals of social institutions are mere expressions of how this activity is organized; and the setting of these goals come about as a negotiated result of revisions more often than prestructurings of this organization. The stressing of cooperation as an essential element in human social life is what could be expected from a historical materialistic point of view. The hunting example is thus used to characterize fundamental aspects of human activity in any historical stage. It clearly belongs to the general psychology of Activity Theory.

The status of the example of reading a book to take an exam is more complex. It is an everyday example and more historically specific, although Leontiev (1981, pp. 229, 400f) does not state this explicitly. It belongs to that area of applied psychology, besides general developmental psychology, where Activity Theory has had the greatest impact in the west, namely educational psychology. However, it is used to call attention to general features of human activity, and thus it belongs in the discussion of the general theory. On closer analysis, one discovers that in the book–reading example, activity is not at all a sociological category, but a psychological one (though one could perhaps talk of it as belonging to social psychology): If a student is reading a book and puts it down when he is told it is not needed for the exam, his activity is an exam taking one; if the student keeps reading, his activity is part of the scientific community. It is a question of my motives, whether I am in scientific or school activity. The motive of the individual is the characteristic of activity by which you differentiate the one from the other. One thus differentiates between kinds of activities on a purely psychological basis, even though the concept of motive is not purely psychological.

There are several reasons for this strange state of affairs, in which activity is alternatively to be understood as a sociological and psychological concept. We can identify these reasons by comparing the two examples.

The hunting example is based on the social organization of production for the satisfaction of a basic or primary need. As it is easy to identify a primary need or motive, it seems possible to delimit what belongs to the activity. Whatever is more or less immediately relevant to the satisfaction of a primary need must be included: The making of tools, the hunt, the distribution of the game, the preparation of food and other objects from the game, their use in satisfying needs. In this example, activity can be considered a sociological concept – activity is all the acts bound together to satisfy a primary motive – as well as a psychological concept: Psychologically, it is the motive which defines my activity. The motive is created when my desires find their object, and the goal of my action can appear to be in contradiction to the motive; therefore I participate in the activity if I can see the relation between my action and the activity.

Matters are quite different in the reading example. It is based on the social organization of education, which is a recent historical phenomenon within Western culture and which includes teaching, learning, and examinations as a control measure. But it is not self evident what keeps these institutions going. To claim – in accordance with a defining characteristic of activity – that motives keep them going, is to psychologize sociological phenomena. We find ourselves without criteria of relevancy for the delimitation of sociological aspects of educational activity.

We suddenly see that we are not equipped with a clear method for identifying the sociological aspects of the activity concept. We only thought we were when we investigated an example based on primary motives. Only when we moved to an example with derived motives complexly intertwined in a complex society did we discover this deficiency in our theory. When we cannot identify its sociological aspects, we are left with activity as a psychological concept. The motive of activity can now be understood as a projector from the individual consciousness onto social processes, determining the scope of participation in a social process, which on the given principles remains unidentifiable. If the student reads the book because he wants to take the exam, his scope of consciousness is narrow. The action is reading the book. The goal is finishing it. The activity is exam taking. The motive might be the prestige of having passed the exam. If the student reads the book because he is interested in its contents, then we have three matriushka dolls: Two actions – reading the book, passing the exam; and one activity – participation in the scientific community (for now as an informal member, later – on the condition that he will be admitted to it – as a formal one). The motive of the activity might still be getting prestige, now through participation in the community. However, it is clearly not the intention of Leontiev and other activity theorists to conceive of activity as a purely psychological concept.

This state of affairs arises because of the unfinished nature of the concept of activity. Activity is conceived of as a mediator between society and consciousness; society and its development is meant to be constituted through activity, as is consciousness and the personality of the individual. Defining the concept of activity by its motive does not capture these aspects of its meaning. Perhaps you can differentiate between kinds of activity by reference to their motives. But in scientific discourse you cannot differentiate between an activity theory and other ways of conceiving human praxis based on motives. To say that a need finds its object in the motive does not necessarily give us a materialistic concept of activity which overcomes the theoretical rift between inner psychic phenomena and the external material world inherited within Western thought since the philosophy of Descartes (Leontiev, 1981, p. 269 ff). Using a concept with a defining characteristic which cannot differentiate, means using a blurred concept. Using a word for a blurred concept, means using a word which contains many different concepts. The road is open for a dispersion of the word "activity" into many conceptions, some of them overcoming the Cartesian rift, others reinstating the split between human being and society from before Leontiev.

Any element from the unified and concrete understanding of the social human being may also, as was done before Leontiev, be exalted to a general notion explaining most of the phenomena pertinent to a distinction between society and human individuals. If we go back to talking about drives, we could find ourselves on the way to a psycho–analytical conception with its ideas of patricide as the foundation of society and enculturation as a burdensome limitation to the free play of our drives. Falling back to interaction, we are on the way to a conception of the social contract as an instrument to the fulfilment of our individual biologically developed drives. A retreat to social functioning – and we could be on the way to a functional sociologism, where institutions are conceived of as primary a-gents with goals of their own, and individuals are seen just to fit in.

Paradoxically, then, the attempt to unify social and individual activity by the category of motive opens the road to separate options: Determining activity by its motive, we are caught oscillating between the two poles in a dichotomy in the theoretical functions of the concept of motive. At one pole, motives depict how the individual merges into societal activity; at the other, they depict how the individual regulates her individual and not necessarily societal activity.

Furthermore, defining an activity by its motive paves the way for subjective arbitrariness in research. Deciding whether an object of investigation is an activity or an action is a matter of what sort of motive configuration the researcher sees or reads into the individual under investigation. He will not always be able to test his interpretations in the way we are able to with the reading example.

With the help of commonly discussed examples from the works of Leontiev, we have seen that it is inadequate to define an activity by its motive. First, because derived motives cannot be defined as simple, identifiable entities. Second, defining activities by their motives leaves out their social organization. Third, the definition cannot, as intended, in itself bridge the gap between subject and object: "A biological drive finding a social object" is a conception which could also involve distinctions between unlimited biological needs and realistically limited social satisfaction, thus reestablishing the distinction between subjective and objective phenomena. A similar critique has been presented by H. Osterkamp (1977).

It is now time to look at the consequences of this state of affairs. We will give an example of how the blurriness of the concept of activity in the general theory has been useful in application. We will attempt to demon-strate how the general theory was transformed into the applied area of educational psychology in such a way that the contradictions in the studied field could be absorbed by functionalistic and structuralistic theoretical elements. This will be exemplified by the approach of V. V. Davydov.

From Activity Theory to an application –
what follows from the equivocal concept of activity

An ambiguity in a basic theoretical concept such as the one postulated here would be no problem if it were considered, as indeed Leontiev himself seems to have, a temporary formulation of a theory in development. Indeed, in this case, the very contradictions inherent in the concept could provide a springboard to further theoretical inquiry, leading perhaps to theoretical reflection of the concrete relations of the opposites.

In our view, however, this is not what happened in the development of Leontiev's theory of activity into the theory, empirical research and practice of Leontiev's followers (and to some extent of Leontiev himself). Instead, we find that the ambiguous concept of the concrete relations of the individual to society acquires theoretical and practical implications. Theoretical development on the general level has been halted. Contradictions in practice have been blurred by giving rise to reductionist theories of activity on the empirical level.

Among many others (e.g.,. D.B. Elkonin (1980), W. Hacker (1980), Y. Engeström (1987), W. Volpert (1974)) the theory and practice of V.V. Davydov and his collaborators are considered the most prominent and unfolded example (e.g.,. 1988). We will substantiate the above general characterisation with a brief review of Davydov et. al.'s version of Activity Theory. We quote primarily from the English presentation in Davydov & Markova (1983), with references to Davydov (1967) in German translation.

During the 1960's and the 1970's, Davydov, basing his work on Leontiev's theory of activity, developed a practicable theory of educational psychology, which has experienced widespread reception in many countries, including Denmark.

Davydov refers directly to Leontiev's theory of the structure of individual activity – the two parallel sets of activity–action–operation, and motive–goal–constraint. He proposes that it is these structural links which must be re–worked in the learning process, which is to be investigated in the actual course of its formation (1983, p. 55). We aim to explore the necessities in educational practice, which lie behind such a conception of learning as a "re–working of the structural links of activity".

In this way we hope, first, to identify the progressive elements of Davydov's approach and then to analyze the problematic aspects in relation to the general concept of activity.

The project was begun in Soviet Pedagogical Psychology at the end of the 1950's (1983, p. 55), paralleling the intensified interest in educational matters in USA exemplified by Project Head Start. In the Soviet Union, under the heading of the Scientific Revolution, the overall task was to design theoretical guide–lines to support the utilization of what came to be seen as "large reserves of cognitive possibilities present in young school-children" (1983, p. 55). Evaluating Soviet schooling of the day, Davydov accumulated data that indicated that considerable time could be saved by presenting the learning material in a way different from that normally used (1983, p. 72). He obtained his results by educational experiments, where he and his collaborators worked with the presentation of the subject matter as well as the integral characteristics of the mental development of the children (1983, p. 64). This double scope of the experimental work was based on the general materialistic principles of Activity Theory. According to these, the development of children must be seen as constituted by their historically specific activity. Therefore there can be no universal developmental phases. The question then becomes: What forms of activity in education will optimize the mental development of children?

An activity approach to the problems of education will necessarily be opposed to the behavioristic approach which dominated much of the thinking in Project Head Start. Davydov's point of view is interesting. He summarizes the American method in two points (1967, p. 257): The learning material was supposed to be organized in small steps (based on Skinner's principles for programmed instruction), and instant reinforcement of correct responses was supposed to facilitate learning as well as its controlled progression. Davydov then argued (1967, p. 260ff) that this method is based on a static conception of the actual performance of the child and his empirical everyday thinking, and that the teaching will only lead to categorization and rule learning, which characterizes empirical thinking whether found in science or childhood. He therefore concluded that the behavioristic procedure can only be understood as a method of organizing material for an educational presentation. It is insensitive to the specific way of thinking of a particular science, and therefore fails to develop the scientific thinking of the child. Developing such thinking requires understanding that a particular science is organized through a fundamental concept, according to which all the other 'moments' can be put in relation to each other (1967, p. 266f; 1983, p. 66). In order to set-up a curriculum, one must therefore identify the specific structure of the particular science. Then, maintaining this structure and with a developmental purpose, one must project the structure into an educational presentation, while paying respect to the general developmental background of the children (1967, p. 256). This was a strong position to maintain in the 1960's, because it insisted on the child's development taking its course from his activity, which in school is organized around the presented material. Thus the position provided a more comprehensive understanding of the child's development than did the behavioristic conception of a step by step progression motored by the teacher's reinforcement – or than did dynamic psychology's conception of biological phases constrained by restrictive teaching or activated by stimulating teaching.

According to the general theory of activity, a human being develops through its activity. Therefore it is only by being an active subject that a human being can learn. Furthermore, Activity Theory conceives of childhood as the development from the spontaneous, social infant to the conscious, working adult. One can look at Davydov's concept of educational activity as a reworking of the structural links of the notion of activity on the basis of these general principles. In this regrouping he transforms the general theory to its applied version. He sets up the structure of the educational activity: It consists of educational tasks, educational acts and acts of control and evaluation (1983, p. 61 f.).

Expanding this structure, we can identify a more comprehensive under-standing of the learning process in the activity approach: The child is seen as developing by actively appropriating the learning material. This also means appropriating both the theoretical thinking of the particular science and the evaluative aspects of education. The student incorporates these in his autonomous activity. Thus development can be described as moving towards more and more comprehensive relationships – towards reflection, analysis and internal plan of action (1983, p.67); and from selection of specific means and methods of educational activity, – over conscious choice of ways of doing things, assisted by the teacher – towards becoming a subject of one's own activity (1983, p. 68f), thereby transforming educational to creative activity.

In this short summary we already have hints that something has gone awry. To consider educational activity as a necessary tool for a transformation of the structural links of activity is surprising: To what extent does the practical re-working of activity imply a re-working of the theory itself? How does this shift from understanding activity according to its level of consciousness or societal impact (activity–action–operation) to a semi-temporal classification, task–act–control, retain an activity–oriented perspective? Is Leontiev's theory in fact reduced to a set of structural elements to be put together, not according to the general theory, but according to the necessities of an empirical process out of which a distinct applied theory emerges? It seems easier to identify the behavioristic elements of common pedagogical concepts: The educational and controlling acts as components of educational activity seem closely related to the learning steps and their reinforcement from the control technology of programmed instruction. We get into even more trouble when we notice that the control of educational activity is supposed to be appropriated with no fuss by the student.

Incorporating Davydov's discussion of appropriation and development compounds the problem. He introduces the concept of educational activity by claiming that it is unique in its endeavour to analyze the transformation of activity into its subjective product (1983, p. 55). This transformation takes place through appropriation and development. Appropriation is the reproduction by the individual of historically formed methods of trans-forming objects, while development takes place through appropriation by the individual of sociohistorical experience (1983, p. 58), in short, you appropriate actions and develop psyche.

This distinction has serious consequences, which gives the impression that the reworking of the structural links of Activity Theory in pedagogical psychology may be better understood as a substitution of fundamental elements.

First the distinction takes acts and psyche apart in ways which are inim-ical to Activity Theory. This reinstates the Cartesian mind–body dualism (where thinking is spiritual and acting is physical) which Activity Theory was supposed to overcome. This dualism can be found in many pedagogi-cal theories, and has many consequences. One is that it opens up for some kind of perception of thought structures as external bodies in the realm of logic, which can be analysed and understood in isolation. Davydov seems to be moving towards a variant of this in which activity and thought struc-tures can be analysed as one independent body, to which individual sub-jects later become added as appendices – to put it bluntly. This variant seems implicit in the following description of the teachers cultivation of educational activity:

> A thorough, controlled process of education always presupposes that each component of educational activity has been developed in the child, that they are interrelated, and that there is a gradual transmission of the com-ponents of this activity from the teacher to the pupil himself, for his inde-pendent action without the aid of teachers (1983, p. 62f.).

The appended individual can dream of harmony as its highest achievement:

> Educational theory is a theory that sheds light on the conditions that best ensure all–round development of a harmonious personality (1983, p. 70).

Furthermore, the singular direction of appropriation – and perhaps even of development – from society via activity into the child, belongs to a widespread pedagogical way of thinking. It can be summarily characterized by the metaphor of the child as an empty vessel to be filled with substance. This way of thinking can be identified in common pedagogical func-tionalistic conceptions of learning, which work as part of the selective and controlling function of schooling. A variant of this thinking mode can be detected in statements by Davydov like:

> Through activity it is possible to go on to control of the process of mental development of the child, and this, essentially, is now the chief task of developmental and educational psychology (1983, p. 57).

What has happened? Why is it that the control aspects of the pedagogical praxis and the subject object dualism have crept into Activity Theory when reorganizing it in order to move into an applied psychology?

One essential condition for this to occur was the theoretical ambiguity present in a concept of activity understood as a societal structure of actions, yet with each activity defined by its individual motive. From this point, it is all too easy to shift the theoretical focus, as Davydov claims (1983, p. 56) from the transition "subject–to–process–of–activity" to the transition "activity–to–its–subjective–product". The way this shift is implemented implies an abstraction from historical and concrete social conditions: Edu-cational activity is not, in fact, determined by its motive, but instead by its so called content, which is an anonymous appropriation and development process. The substitution of motivation with anonymous appropriation and development poses motivation as a problem, makes it external to activity. The anonymous and ahistorical character of this conception of educational activity makes it, by the way, well–suited for export: The same characteristics which make particular educational problems incomprehensible make it easy to transfer the theory to other nations, as the wide–spread reception of Davydov's models testify.

The general point that we wish to make is how well Leontiev's concept of activity is suited to precisely this sort of hybrid construction, housing as it does the ideological paradoxes of institutional ordering of subjective activity. The dichotomy in Leontiev's concept of activity presents itself in institutional discourse in a manner well–known to Western pedagogical psychology: The normal practice of schooling as the structuring of the activity of children is founded theoretically on the assumption of a general harmony in the relations of individual motives to societal goals, while setting these aside as essentially irrelevant or even disturbing. In the face of motivational problems or individual abnormality, the psychologism of interpreting individual motivation, as (i.e. insofar as it forms) a deviation from social norms, comes into place to organize the specialized practice of psychologists.

As one pedagogical psychologist using Davydov's theories – Ole Bredo – unbluntedly concluded at the proceedings of the conference which is the occasion of this paper: The less motivated educational activity proceeds, the more successful the outcome!

Conclusion – sketch of a remedy

Paradoxes such as the one just mentioned seem to support a conclusion that is much in vogue: That Activity Theory has failed the test of logic and should be laid to rest in the museum of communism. In our opinion, though, rumours of its death are rather premature. We will even conclude by suggesting that a remedy can be found, which will enable it – if not to prevent further clotting of the dish, since catalysts to this process remain outside of scientific discourse – then to continue to be a rich font for theoretical brewing; and that this remedy is to be found precisely by returning to the original tradition of historical materialism.

We find that detecting a contradiction in the core concept of Activity Theory must lead to a review and restatement of the fundamental issues of psychology according to the general principles of dialectical materialism (for a discussion along these lines, see Axel, 1992). Since such a programme can only be briefly outlined in the present context, we will limit ourselves to pointing to a scientific tradition which represents this position vis á vis Activity Theory, the so–called Critical Psychology, and to outlining how certain key features of the problem can be approached in this tradition (for a general introduction, see Tolman & Maiers, 1991).

Going back to Marx' "General Introduction" to the "Grundrisse" (Marx, 1973) we find clues to the overall structure of human activity in the deliberations concerning the intertwined 'moments' of productive and consumptive praxis. Human beings socially produce their life conditions in the form of generalized meaning, thus guided by an anticipation in a generalized form of the consumption of the produce. This means that the unity in societal relations originates in the break between producer and consumer, which is mediated in a generalized form. This conception of human activity has implications much more profound than the notion of a, however mediated, joint activity, from which Leontiev, as we have seen, derived his general concept of activity (the cooperation of the hunter and the beater).

Firstly, a general conception of human motivation can no longer be founded on a theory of primary, consumptive needs, not even if this need is thought to meet a socially produced object; such an idea would clearly tear apart the two sides in a unitary social relation, thus reopening the possibility of a Cartesian dualism. At this point, a theory of productive needs proper is called for. The task is to show how the motives of the individual are grounded, not only in societal necessities, or social structures, but – relating to these – also in the potentials of human nature. As demonstrated by H.–Osterkamp (1975–77), one can trace the phylogenetic emergence of a category of needs not directly related to physiological reproduction of the species or of the individual organism. This category of needs develops with the emergence of learning (which Leontiev did not directly incorporate as a significant step in his description of the phylogenetic development of the psyche). These needs are involved in the organization of activity around those aspects of the organismic world which change faster than the evolutionary adaptation can keep pace. They are called control needs and appear in learning as curiosity, interest, anxiety. In the genesis of human nature, these control needs are transformed into a general need system directed at individual appropriation and development of the generalized societal control of life conditions, the need for action potency.

The important feature of the concept of action potency – in this context – is that it cannot be reduced to either purely individual control or individual integration into society. Rather, it is construed in the concrete dialectic of the two, as this unfolds in ontogeny. The concept thus captures the emotionally charged criteria by which the individual engages in social activity, in a way which does not in itself lead to a polarisation between individual and society once the question of individual motivation is raised.

Secondly, the breaking of immediacy in the societal relations which constitute human activity facilitates the overcoming of the nature/nurture dichotomy in the Activity Theory of ontogeny. When conceived as a distinctly motivated appropriation of generalized meaning, ontogeny must, from the outset, supersede the mere reproduction of cultural experience. The individual subject confronts cultural experience as sets of generalized action possibilities and makes use of them in an inherently creative process. The concept of action possibilities implies at the same time that the societal processes can go on without this subject, and that subjects can realize the possibilities according to their interests. As outlined by K. Holzkamp (1983), the hallmark of an Activity Theory of the individual subject is its ability to understand how the "possibility relation" of the individual subject to society, in one and the same process, both mediates the social necessities and forms the basis of development of the individual subject as a person relating consciously to her societal conditions and to herself. This includes the option of "resistance", as well as integration, as two deeply intertwined 'moments' of the same general notion of developing into society. With this conception, any opposition by the individual subject to societal demands is not psychologized as deviance or signs of immaturity, but may be well-founded in the individual's appropriation of and – throughout ontogeny, in-creasingly conscious – relating to contradictions in societal meaning struc-tures.

Such a conception has far–reaching consequences for psychological investigation and practice: It follows that one simply cannot "structure the activity" of a person, or understand a psychological process in a matrix of logic. Nor need one, however, settle for subjectivist interpretations of "experience phenomena" as unquestionable entities. Rather, the concept of subjectivity facilitates theoretical reflection of a process in which these two sides are concretely interrelated: The reflective praxis of the subject herself. Structure, as well as experience, are turned into the objects of an inquiry in which the involved persons are subjects (i.e. agents) in the framework of an activity on which they have good reason to reflect, and sufficient action potency to alter accordingly.

This brings us to the anchor point of any such science of the subject: It could not develop in the context of a body of knowledge built to support one system of state power in catching up with another. And it will never grow out of a commodified psychological practice. It is called for and unfolds where what is demanded of people is no longer only "motivated activity" or "theoretical thinking", but increasingly also a subjectivity con-sciously developing its own social contingencies.

For this reason, the development of a science of the subject remains an unfinished project, closely affiliated with as yet quite tender movements toward democratization of the societal institutions that generate and prac-tice knowledge of the human individual.

References

Axel, E. (1992): One Developmental Line in European Activity Theories, *Quarterly Newsletter of LCHC*, Volume 14, 1, pp. 8–17.

Davydov, V.V. (1967): Beziehungen zwischen der Theorie der Verallgemeinerung und der Lehrplangestaltung, In Budilowa et al. (eds.): *Untersuchungen des Denkens in der sowjetischen Psychologie*, Berlin.

Davydov, V.V. (1988): Problems of Developmental Teaching: The Experience of Theoretical and Experimental Psychological Research, Parts I–III, *Soviet Education, XXX*.

Davydov, V.V. & Markova, A.K. (1983): A concept of educational activity for Schoolchildren, *Soviet Psychology*, 21:2, pp. 50–76.

Elkonin, D.B. (1980): *Psychologie des Spiels*, Köln.

Engeström, Y. (1987): *Learning by Expanding*, Helsinki.

Hacker, W. (1980): *Allgemeine Arbeits– und Ingeniörpsychologie*. Berlin.

Holzkamp, K. (1983): *Grundlegung der Psychologie*, Frankfurt, New York.

Holzkamp-Osterkamp, U. (1975–77): *Grundlagen der psychologischen Motivationsforschung* I–II, Frankfurt a. M.

Leontiev, A. N. (1978): *Activity, Consciousness, and Personality*, Englewood Cliffs, New Jersey.

Leontiev, A.N. (1981): *Problems of the Development of the Mind*, Moscow.

Marx, K. (1973): *Grundrisse*. Translated by Martin Nicolaus, London.

Tolman, C. & Maiers, W. (eds.)(1991): *Critical Psychology, Contributions to an Historical Science of the Subject*, Cambridge, New York.

Volpert, W. (1974): *Handlungsstrukturanalyse als Beitrag zur Qualifikationsforschung*, Köln.

ON MIND AND SOCIETY

THE PSYCHODYNAMICS OF
ACTIVITIES AND LIFE PROJECTS

Preben Bertelsen
University of Aarhus

The questions I, as a psychotherapist ask my clients, are: "What is your life project? – Which kind of human life is meaningful and important to you? – and by which sorts of activities do you try to realize this life?". Maybe I do not ask exactly in these terms – but they are the questions that characterize my therapeutic projects in the therapeutic process. The concept of life project is the concept by which I can understand my client as a human being engaging in a partly troublesome life – and by which my client can become conscious of him self. And perhaps even change, by changing his life project.

The life project should be understood as being in connection with the life world in the same way as intentio should be understood as being in connection with intentum in intentionality. This paper deals with the question of how the life–project/life–world intentionality, regarded as the psychological essential of human being, comes into existence, and by means of which forces. This is a question of psychodynamics.

Psychodynamics in a broader sense concern all psychological perspectives upon these forces: The cultural–historical (diachronic) perspective, the cross cultural (synchronic) perspective and the personal life historical perspective. Psychodynamics in the narrow – and traditional – sense of psychodynamic theory, concern human motivating forces in the perspective of the personal life history. The concept of the unconscious is an integrated part of psychodynamic theory. It deals with motivating forces which are not conscious, and which may appear to the person concerned to be alien forces not belonging to himself.

The criticism that activity theory has nothing useful to say about psychodynamics and clinical psychology simply is not correct. On the contrary – and for the sake of both activity theory and clinical psychodynamics – we must find a way of unifying them, that is: find a way of explaining psychodynamics and clinical phenomena in terms of activity theory.

1. Activity theory

Activity theory's proposition to anthropological psychology

Nothing at all exists without connections. Activity is a special sort of connection. To be in activity is not just to be striving for contact with the surroundings. The striving itself must be understood as already being a connection.

Thus activities can be defined as vital connections with biological, sociological and psychological aspects. In this paper I shall deal only with the psychological and psychodynamic aspects.

The psychic contribution of the individual to creating and sustaining his active connections, or just, his human beingness I shall call *the project of human life*. The life project of human beings is one pole or position in the active connection. Or, in other words: the connection is seen from the subject perspective. The life world is one and the same connection seen from the object perspective. Life project and life world are epistemologically the same connections seen from two different perspectives, and ontologically they are the two positions of a connection reflecting each other.

Human activity can then be characterized on the one hand by the project of human life by which it is *initiated*; and on the other hand the life world can be characterized as a system of culture and society historically created by the lived lives of mankind. The life world establishes the conditions for the realization, through activity, of the life project. Thereby it *orientates* the life project and the realizing activity.

Different living beings relate to the same surrounding world in different particular ways, and so these same surroundings become different life worlds. Not different just in the manner in which they are experienced, but also in the manner they are related to through different activities.

If activity is fundamentally a dynamic connection, then the life project – the psychological essentials of man – must be understood on the basis of an understanding of the lived life and the life world. This is a very important methodological point: 1) In fact we can become knowledgeable about the essentials of the human psyche/life project by identifying the very characteristics of the lived life and the life world. 2) The essentials of the lived life and the life world, which we identify, always force us to make corresponding assumptions about the life project. If for instance we identify aspects of the lived life and the life world that cannot be decomposed into independent factors, then the classical factor–analytic approach to the person reflecting, involved in, creating, sustaining this life/life world, would then be a misleading approach to the understanding of the person and his life project.

The cultural–historical topography of the activity theory

Elsewhere[1] I have tried to outline the cultural–historical development of mankind from hominids to modern human beings. The main concepts in this outline is centered activity, decentered activity and individuated activity.

Centered activity (emerging with the first hominids and lasting to about 30.000 B.C) is – seen at large – characterized by the identity of the group's activity and the activity of the individual. All individuals are doing almost the same things at the same time although division of activity and labour occurs. Centered activity is initiated and orientated relative to the ongoing activity patterns of the group. This form of activity, therefore, is based on spatial and temporal closeness amongst the individuals. They must be able to see, to hear and to feel each other. What we have to notice here, is that centered activity demands neither consciousness nor will–power, to be initiated and orientated. The only precondition is the capacity for imitation and for rhythmic coordination of action patterns between individuals.

The next cultural–historical leap in the development of human activity (and with it the development of the project of human being and life world–conditions) is the occurrence of decentered activity (from about 30.000 B.C to about 2000–1000 B.C). Decentered activity is characterized by a qualitatively different sort of division of activity and labour. The individual activity gradually begins to differentiate from the group activity as such. One individual is good at manufacturing stone tools – an other one goes hunting, etc. Decentered activity is based on spatially and temporally detached individuals. Specific activities are now often performed out of other's sight and hearing, but they nevertheless depend on each other (one is making a fishing net, one goes up the river to fish, one is making tools out of the fish bones). Decentered activity, then, cannot anymore, as could centered activity, be initiated and orientated by the perception of the group activity. The conditions for the evolution of this higher level of activity are to be found in the products and artifacts of the activity. The tools, the fishing nets; the standardized activity forms and cooperative fishing from the shore become meaningful: in the fishing net itself and in the standardized fishing activity, lies a meaning that calls for just that specific use and activity. The products and artifacts become meaningful action indicating symbols and gradually these symbols become independent of immediate use. The most effective and independent sort of action assigning symbols at all times is language.

These detached meanings (products, artifacts, words) constitute the possibility of dividing the superior group activity into individually performed, spatially and temporally detached, activities. Such meaningful products, artifacts and languages enable the next generation to learn from the former.

Once again, notice that decentered activity does not require 'modern' forms of the human psyche like consciousness or will–power. It only requires the

---

[1] Bertelsen 1990.

capacity to be initiated and orientated by the artifactual meanings in the cultural–life world.

The last leap in the evolution of modern human activity is the leap to individuated activity (about 1000 B.C.). The very complex city states that had evolved in the previous 5000 years increasingly required individuals who were able to make decisions on their own (on trade journeys, on mining expeditions); individuals who could see the society in their own perspective (how to plan and administer water channels for the fields, and how to plan and administer the building of a trade fleet); individuals who were able to initiate a whole series of activities in cooperation with or in conflict with other people, interests and other activities in the city state. Individuals who could bear in mind these complex activities, make decisions and then act. With the onset of all these activities, the qualitative new and modern human capacity of consciousness and will–power was required and evolved. These capacities then became the conditions for the evolution of the modern human personality characterized by self–consciousness, will–power and free choice.

The evolution of modern human activity is a history of increasing organization from centered to decentered activity, the latter then subsuming the former. In the same way, individuated activity subsumes the decentered activity. Modern human activity thus has a topography, as have our life projects. On the highest level we have the modern, individuated, personal, active form of being. But this activity form is based on the fact that our projects of human being come to existence in and with the life world–conditions of the common human society – however complex they are, and however spatially and temporally divided they may seem. However detached we as personally acting individuals may seem, on a deeper level we are acting in common simply because we a rooted in the same decentered and centered kinds of human activities and artifactual meanings.

The organizational logic of activity theory

The grounding humanism of activity theory is a confrontation with functionalist materialism, the latter reducing the human to a mechanism of psychic functions. This functionalism considers consciousness, will–power, and free decisions as by–products of psychodynamic functions, independent of and outside consciousness, will–power and decision. Let us have a quick look at the ontological possibilities for such a humanistic view of activity. The ontological condition for a modern nonfunctional psyche to come into existence is that phenomena in the world can be organized on ever higher organized levels.

We have to differentiate between mechanical and non–mechanical organized systems. A mechanical system is a system, whose behaviour can be understood and predicted from the knowledge of the elements and their behaviour of which the system consists. Any variations in the elements and their behaviour will have a definite and predictable consequence for the system as such. An organized, non mechanical system, on the other hand, would advance beyond this elementary ground and evolve its own laws on a higher and more complex level.

We have to differentiate, then, between what is an element of a mechanical system and what is element of a complex organized system. The complex organism with its high level laws and organization has on the one hand advanced from these elements. But, on the other hand these high level laws and organizations reflect back upon the elements subsuming them and determining *a new order* in which they work and function together. Thus these elements no longer function in terms of low level order, but are *high-level organized* in what we could call *elementary forms*[2]. The behaviour and functions of elementary forms cannot be understood, nor can they be predicted unless we are able to take the higher level in account. The biological cells can, maybe, to a certain degree be described and understood on a biochemical level as biological elements. But as elementary forms in a biological organism they can never be understood or predicted unless we understand the organism itself.

The relation between the two levels is as follows: Looking 'bottom up' the lower level *constitutes* the higher level. Looking 'upside down', the higher level *organizes* the elements of the lower level in elementary forms.

The higher level is freed from, but not detached from, the constituting lower level due to the evolved high level laws and organizations. We do not have to assume a mystical detached 'ghost in the machine' (nor a 'machine in the ghost') to argue against functional materialism. On the contrary we are working with a concept of 'degrees of freedom'. The high level organized system has more degrees of freedom in relation to the lower levels, because the high level with its own evolved organizing logic to a higher or lesser degree can organize its own constitutive elements in elementary forms.

In short: there is a fundamental difference in proposing that the higher level is constituted by *elements*, and in proposing that it is constituted by *elementary forms*. The former denotes the mechanically deterministic point of view, leaving no freedom, no choices, no will-power; the latter denotes a humanistic point of view.

It is by the activity of man, that the process of creating still higher levels of organization (cultural life world, lived life, life project, conscious being, consciousness), comes into existence. It is this actively created, highly organized process, which is reflected in the cultural-historical topography of centered, decentered and individuated (self determining and self creating) activity.

---

2   See also the concept of 'org' by Gerard (1957), and the concept of 'holon' by Koestler (1981). Functional double-faced units: Top-down they act as wholes, bottom-up they act as parts

The macrostructure of activity

Activity theory shows us that human activity is structured by such mutually constituting and organizing levels. And this is what makes the activity theory a deeply humanistic project. This organizational thinking is sustained in the model of the macrostructure of human activity.

Let me give an example. One of my daily actions is to take my children to the kindergarten on my bicycle. I kiss them good–bye, and ride to my office. But the reason why I take my children into the kindergarten, and spend my own day at a totally different place can only be understood by taking into account the high level activity by which I live, and form my life. I must take in account my whole personal, and social lifestyle by which I organize my own and my children's lives in a way that places us apart from each other.

This series of actions and many other daily series of actions must be understood as organized by the higher level of activity by which I realize my personal being in the world. To take my daughters to the kindergarten is a situative project among other daily situative projects. But the objective of these situative projects can not be found if we consider them as elements on their own level. The objective can only be found, if these situative projects are seen as elementary forms that (bottom up) constitute my life project and (top down) are organized by this life project. Corresponding to this, my action can only be understood when seen as an elementary form, organized by and constituting my very activity. The other pole or position, the reflection of the situative project is the situative goals (e.g. to take my daughters to the kindergarten). It orientates my action, by making it a goal–directed action. And again: we cannot identify and understand the situative goals on the level of the action alone. We have to look at them as elementary forms, organized by the human life world and constituents of this life world.

So far the levels are given by activity and actions (and their mutual reflecting poles or positions). Let us elaborate on the example. To perform the action of taking my children to kindergarten I take out my bicycle, I put my left foot on the pedal, I push the ground with the right foot, I mount the bike, and I press down the other pedal, etc.[3] Given this we can see that each action or each part of an action on a lower level, contain and is realized by an enormous series of functional operations, which are orientated by the elementary material conditions of the world. Again we see the same connectional structure: the two poles or positions of the functional operations are the elementary conditions, reflecting and reflected by the other pole or position. We can then call this pole or position the elementary project, which is initiating the functional operations. The functional operations can be properly understood only

---

3   There is no lower level for analyzing operations: we can analyze the physiological principles for riding a bicycle – furthermore the mechanical principles, biochemical principles, subatomic principles ... The point is that one cannot deduce from subatomic principles the principles of riding a bicycle, because the elementary forms simply do not exist on this low level. These forms are organized from the level of actions.

if they are seen as organized by the action which they constitute. And the same can be said about the two positions: the elementary projects are organized by and constituting the situative project, and the elementary conditions are organized by and constitute the situative goals.

The operations make up the functional level of human life and activity. This functionality is transcended in two steps reaching to still higher degrees of freedom: Firstly by being organized by the higher level of action – secondly by these actions being organized by the higher level of activity. The more complex the actions, the more degrees of self organizing freedom from the functional level. The more complex the organizing of the actions in elementary forms, the more degrees of self–organizing freedom on the level of activity.

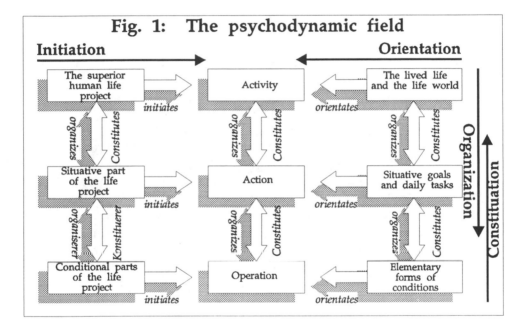

As a whole, the macro–structure of activity is reflected as a non mechanical organized and complex system. This is illustrated in Figure 1. Horizontally viewed it illustrates the monistic connectionistic point of view in the activity theory: the active connections on the different levels between the two positions reflecting each other as initiating and orientating the active connection. Viewed vertically, the figure illustrates the organizational and humanistic point of view, the lower levels constituting and being organized by the higher levels.

The methodological point that can be derived from this model of the macrostructure is: 1) Human actions must be understood as constituted by the operational *forms* which they organize, and the action–forms are the markers

of human activity, which they both constitute and by which they are organized. Thus human activity can be identified by these action–*forms*. To really
get in touch with these complex organized forms is no simple task. 2) By
identifying the actions (as markers of activity) we can identify the particular
humanistic aspects of life projects, and thereby the essentials of being human.

Psychodynamics in terms of the macro structure

The macro–structure of activity so conceived, shows us a field of interdependent forces through which human beings are becoming involved in a self
organizing process of becoming.

Psychodynamics can now be defined as the vital human creating forces,
which evolve in activity when initiations meet with orientations, organizations
and constitutions.

The vertical organization of activity is not static. A much used example
(e.g. by Leontjev) concerns car driving. For the young man who is engaged in
learning to drive a car, car–driving may be the predominant life project.
While learning, this car driving activity is divided into a series of actions
requiring a great deal of awareness: clutching, shifting gears, turning the
wheel, etc. After some time the novice driver has grown rather skilled and is
on his way to a date. All the car–driving skills which only recently required
his full attention and will–power are now automatized functional operations.
He doesn't give his driving much thought – he is much more concerned with
his dating. In fact the dating is the activity and driving the car is only one of
several organized actions which constitute the whole dating activity.

In other words, what formerly was activity is now action, and what formerly was action is now operation. This is the case both for personal life
history and for the history of mankind.

Life is realized through a set of activities. Each activity can be realized
through one of several actions: Project Dating can be realized through car
driving, but the young man might just as well have walked or ridden his
bicycle. In turn, the same action can constitute one out of several activities:
for one young man car driving only is interesting as means for realizing his
dating activities. For an other young man car driving constitutes a life style
driven by fascination with cars and technology. The same can be said about
the relationship of action and operation. The same operation (e.g. clutching)
can be an elementary form of either changing gear or checking if the clutch
works.

2. Meaning and sense as basic concepts of psychodynamics

Meaning versus instincts

By which unit can the essence of human psychodynamic forces be identified?[4] In place of Freudian instincts the activity theory proposes meanings.

As we saw previously in our brief exploration of the cultural–historical topography of human activity, it is artifacts and meanings (of artifacts and activities) which constitute human life as we know it. It is meanings, as the psychic aspect of the activity connections, which constitute the particular human forms of psychodynamics. Meanings, and not instincts (triebe), are the particular human essence of the psyche, and are thus, in a historical sense, self–creating aspects of human activity.

Meanings as implicate order

There are three aspects of a meaning (as a psychodynamic connection with two positions or poles). From the Late Middle Ages the following three aspects of meaning have been distinguished: the emotive, the cognitive, and the conative aspect.

When an object is meaningful to me it has an emotional meaning to me. My life project gives it an emotional meaning, and thereby my life project reflects the range of emotional meanings this object culturally–historically and life–historically *has*.

Correspondingly, this same object of my activity (the object pole of my activity) on the one hand *has* a range of cognitive meanings and on the other hand is given a specific cognitive meaning. Finally, this object has a conative meaning aspect as well: With my efforts, will–power, wishes, attempts, etc. I am – with the conative aspect of my life project – striving for the realization of the connection to the object. The life project pole of my activity connection gives it a conative meaning – the life world pole of this connection *has* a range of cultural–historical meanings.

Life, then, *has* an emotional, a cognitive and a conative meaning – or is given such a three sided meaning – depending on the perspective in which the activity is seen: given, seen from the life project pole or position and *having*, seen from the life world pole or position.

And note: man is not *either* in an emotionally connection or in a cognitive connection or in a conative connection. Man is always *both* emotionally, cognitively and conatively connected. Something can only have an emotional meaning to me, if I in some way have recognized it (even if only as: 'something'), and when I am in some way striving for it (even if only in 'opening my eyes', striving for awareness connections). And further: if I am

---

4 See also Mammen's paper about the basic unit in this volume.

striving for something in its conative meaningfulness I have also already recognized it as being in some way cognitively and emotionally connected.

Thus meaning in itself (as an aspect of activity) exists in what I shall call an implicate order[5] . Only in the specific and concrete situations given by the specific and concrete activity realizing actions and operations, the meaning explicated in emotional, cognitive and conative meanings. For example an emotion orientated therapy may let the emotional aspect of the meanings of life and life–projects of the client come to the fore–ground, while the cognitive and conative aspect will stay in – and as – the background. A cognitive therapy may let the cognitive aspect be realized in the foreground, etc.

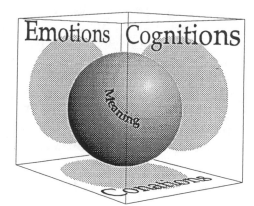

Fig 2: The implicate order of meaning

But most skilled therapists, not restricted to a single school of therapy, will follow the client in his process and now let one aspect come to the foreground and now the other.

The implicate order of human meaning systems and their unfolding in the three perspectives is represented in Figure 2 representing the dimensions of meaning. This model shows that cognitions, emotions and conations are not parallel elementary functions as classically conceived. On the contrary: in the modern human psyche they are explications of a complex phenomenon.[6]

Sense and meaning

Meanings are super–individual and individuals possess them in a personality creating and individuating manner. Sense, then, can be the term for this personal possession of meanings.

Within the same cultural region 'father' has the same meaning to all, because fathers, seen at large, are meaningful in the same ways. But nevertheless 'father' has a unique life–historically given meaning to each of us. 'Father' has a general meaning and a unique sense. The sense of something

---

5   Corresponding with Bohms concept, see Bohm (1983).

6   Of course this modern meaning structure has its evolutionary history, and it can be shown that historically, conations have to be seen as more fundamental than cognitions – and that these two together have brought modern emotions to existence. See Poulsen 1991 for further elaboration of this point.

meaningful is given by the concrete life–historical method of internalizing the given meanings.

The more ways in which the same meaning has been internalized through life history, the more senseful it will become to the individual. The more concrete, and the more differentiated, the interactions with my father, the more senseful he will become as being just my father.

This personal and unique sensefulness exists only as meaning, but it reflects the way in which one has created one's own life projects and life world, thereby creating and sustaining one's own life.

The concepts of meaning and sense, and not of instinct and need, are the basic concepts of a psychodynamic activity theory of the psychological aspects of the vital forces of the modern human mind.

We are now ready to elaborate the concept of psychodynamics with these basic concepts: we shall deal in turn with the basic phenomena of motives, consciousness and will–power.

3. The basic phenomena of motives

Motive explanations

Motive explanations are about the psycho dynamics of a person's life, activities and experiences. Seen from a Cultural–historical perspective a motive is a meaningful 'piece' of life. In the example above such a 'piece' of life is the meaningfulness of becoming a car driver. In psychology of personality, explanations of motives are about the meaningfulness in the young man's cognition of, emotions of and striving to become a car driver.

Psychodynamic motive explanation will not be complete unless it – at least – includes all the three perspectives we have indicated:

1. The implicate/explicate order of meanings: cognitions, emotions and conations.
2. The macro structure of activity: activity, action, operation.
3. The cultural–historical topography of the modern psyche.

The meaning perspective on motives

Emotions – being an aspect of what is meaningful and senseful – reflect reality. Emotions are the reflections of the emotional meanings that something *has*, and thus emotions are one aspect of our reality testing.

In activity theory, feelings cannot be understood as apart from action and they do not come from 'within'. Like every other mental phenomenon, feelings can only be understood in terms of the concept of action. Feelings becomes motivating when they are parts of an action directed towards an object, which has emotional meaning, and when the goal of this action is to create a connection with this emotionally meaningful object, e.g., to be near the beloved. This is a matrix for the understanding of every determination motivating phenomena. Needs for example become human motives only by being a part of the goal directions of actions.

Emotions are high level forms of meanings, and as such creations of culture and history. One can speak about a person with a strong sense of duty, or speak about the feeling of love for one's family, the love for one's profession, etc. These high-level emotions – or basic phenomenological phenomena – exist in the form of phenomenological feelings, e.g., the sinking feeling when a piece of a life project suddenly seems to be in danger of being obstructed.

Feelings are signals. The phenomenological experiences tell whether a certain goal is reached or not. E.g. the lustful tension the young man experiences the first time he drives his car to his sweetheart, and then the confusing feelings, when he realizes that she hardly notices the car, and does not even comment on him being a car driver.

The same considerations can apply to the relationship between the two other psychodynamic aspects of meaning and motives: cognitions and conation.

Cognitions are motivating when they are embedded in an action – directed toward a cognitively meaningful goal (the goal being the creation of an acknowledgment of a connection). And in the same way as feelings, cognitions can also be seen as signals. In fact, as a signal, about whether a connection and a life project have succeeded, many people only have confidence in the product of acknowledgment, the cognitive reflection of an activity. And this to such a degree that the signal function of feelings fades out of awareness. The young man may believe that his 'project dating & she being impressed by his car' has succeeded: he has confidence in her being with him in his car. But she hardly remarks on his car and car driving. The confusing feeling, he hardly notices, may have been a signal, telling him that there has to be more in it for her than driving in his car, before she will join in the realization of 'project sweetheart'.

Finally about the conations. They too become motivating when embedded in actions directed towards the goal strived for. When the conations are transformed from being strivings for the *creation* of connection to the striving for sustaining the connection, this in itself is a signal of success. For our young man healthy jealousy can be a complex signal of success constituted by emotions, cognitions and conations, telling him to sustain his new beautiful connection to his sweetheart. A rigid repeating of the striving for creating a connection (as in neurotic transference and neurotic jealousy) on the other hand would be a signal of non-success regarding the desired goal: the connection.

Emotional motivations can be the foremost psychodynamic force in constituting a certain activity. But this never occurs without the cognitive and conative aspects of the motivations being embedded in the background. The cognitive and conative aspects too can be in the foreground but never without the two others as co-motivations in the background. We have to refer to all three aspects:

> He did what he did because he had the feelings he had; because the case was emotionally meaningful in exactly this way...

> He did what he did because the case had exactly that cognitive meaning to him, and because he did not recognize the case in another way.

> He did what he did because he strived for, hoped for, wished for the case to be realized.

The macro structure perspective on motives

As mentioned, an action can only be incompletely understood on its own level. We have to take in account also the levels of activity and operations in our motive explanation. In terms of the macro structure a motive explanation can be formulated as follows:

> He did what he did, and was goal-directed in just this particular way, because he (bottom up) had the required operational capacities, organized by the actions, and because he (top down) was engaged in this particular activity, qualified by this particular life project.

On each of these motivational levels we find each of the three aspects of meaning (cognition, emotion, conation) as aspects of the level specific motivation. For example the conative aspect on the activity level is the superior striving for or wish for a specific kind of life, and on the action level it is the situative striving for a situative goal (as a microscopic constituent of life as such).

The topographical perspective on motives

The causes of actions then on each macroscopic level have several meaning aspects. Furthermore this macroscopic structure – and with it the three-sided meaning structure, has a topographic structure: centered, decentered and individuated activity. In terms of the topographic structure the motive explanation can be formulated as:

> He did what he did, because his activity basically is centered: it is deeply embedded in human culture and society. He did what he did exactly because the center of his action is the identity of sociality and individuality.

> He did what he did because his activity furthermore is decentered, motivated by the meanings of his life-world.

> He did what he did, finally, because his activity is individuated: because the meaning of the life world has become meaningful in a life–historically unique way, that is, in a senseful way.

The subject of the highest motive–explanation is the individuated life project with personal meaningfulness: He did what he did just because this sort of life was meaningful to him. Corresponding with: He did what he did just because of the givenness of a cultural–historical meaningful life world.

On the high level of individuated activity motives cannot be understood as external causal factors. On the contrary: on this level man with some degree of freedom, creates his motives himself. In other words: motives on the highest level of organization are not to be understood as causes but as reasons.

In so far as man himself – with some degree of freedom – creates his motives, he also on some occasions creates motives which give him reason to deny some other motives of his. He can deny them, repress them, make them unconscious. Let us have a closer look at that.

4. The basic phenomena of being conscious and of consciousness

Being conscious is the form of meaningful and senseful activity in which a person lives his life. Consciousness is the experiencing phenomenological reflection of this conscious being (in the world). Consciousness is the highest level of psychic organization of activity. From the Cultural–historical point of view the change in the range of possible life–worlds implies a change in the reflecting consciousness. Seen from a personality–psychological point of view consciousness initiates life–creating and life–changing activities (and life–worlds). An image of man as being conscious, and of consciousness as life–project (consciously capable of creating and changing the way of life) is basically a humanistic image of man. In this materialistic sense we must agree with the phenomenological–existentialist image of man as a self–creating and self–sustaining being.

Preconsciousness and unconsciousness

Preconscious being is defined as a way of being conscious, that is, as a reflection of the meaningfulness and sensefulness of life, which has not yet advanced to the high organizational level of focused and reflected consciousness, but which is at any time capable of this higher organization. As an example one can be aware of the whole atmosphere and psychological settings in being together with a group of people without being conscious of it – one only senses a puzzling sort of uncomfortableness. Another example is our young man and his confusing sense of being together with a girl who ignores his car. He has a preconscious feeling – a signal to him which he *could* (and maybe *should*) advance to consciousness.

In general both the highest level and the lowest level of the macrostructure of activity are preconscious. When I take my children to the kindergarten in the morning, I seldom reflect on which life project I thereby am realizing. And similar I am not conscious of the single operations constituting the act of taking my children to the kindergarten. I would fall off my bicycle and hurt myself if I tried to be conscious of every little step in this operation.

Only the situative actions are immediately conscious, being initiated on the basis of a reflected phenomenological model of the situation, the situative act and the situative goal.

When a person turns his awareness away from something, this something does not cease to exist as meaningful and senseful. Therefore this something is not an alien force outside volitional conscious being. At least it is not an alien determination in the mechanical sense of *elements* or *representations* on one hand existing in a space or system outside the reach of consciousness, and on the other hand causing consciousness and human life. The preconscious always has the *elementary forms* (please see: 'The organizational logic of activity theory') of consciousness – only it is not focused and reflected upon.[7]

However, as is well known there also exist forms of being conscious which cannot easily be organized by consciousness. Let us turn to our young friends: The young man and his date have been driving downtown in the car and have now arrived at Sartre's Café.[8] We shall let Sartre tell us what happens now:

---

[7]   I am aware that these notions about alien and alienating forces and causations can be misunderstood. When I say that preconsciousness and unconsciousness do not cause human conscious being and consciousness, and that they can neither be understood as alien forces, nor can be understood as systems giving 'room' for such forces, I thereby try to say something in the terms of what in this paper is called the logic of organization. On the other hand we know from therapy, that the preconscious and the unconscious in a phenomenological way can be experienced as an alien force coming to one from the 'outside' (this is really not me – I do not understand myself). We also have to distinguish the above–mentioned formulations of the logic or organization from the clinical notions of repression, which can be understood as alienating something – making it alien regarding ones desired self–understanding. The whole matter becomes additionally troublesome when one tries to compare the concept of uncon-sciousness in this paper with Freuds concept of unconsciousness (the unconscious), because the dualism, determinism and pessimism of Freud made him believe that unconsciousness consists not only of formerly conscious material but also of alien mechanical determining forces, the instincts (triebe) and representations of instincts, which can never advance to consciousness. Not to be able to advance something to consciousness must be distinguished from not to be willing to advance it to consciousness. I shall not here try to come to a decision whether there is something in our human essentials that we will never be capable to let come to our knowledge (but I doubt it). If this is the case it would belong to the necessary conditions of our existence. But in therapy – and in our elaboration of therapeutic and clinically mean-ingful concepts – we have to concentrate on what we in principle could, but are not willing to make conscious (to this belongs also our not being willing to come to insight regarding our fate). Therefore I will maintain that a clinically meaningful concept of unconsciousness is not about what we are not capable of but what we are not willing to advance to consciousness. And therefore the remarks about preconsciousness and unconsciousness not consisting of alien forces.

[8]   The following is a paraphrase of Sartre's famous example.

She is *completely* (!) preconscious of his flirting overtones and undertones. But she won't let the erotic come in between them. They can freely and in a platonic way talk about highly intellectual things, and thereby let the erotic over- and undertones give the conversation its own magic. But now the young man goes a step further: he takes her hand. She, then, can choose either to withdraw her hand from his, but then she will destroy the magic in a radical way, or she can let him take her hand, but then the eroticism will be made explicit, realized, and come in between them, also in a radical way destroying the magic for her. As far as Sartre sees it from his table, she finds a third solution. She lets him take her hand, but with reluctance, she turns her conscious awareness away from the holding hands and the eroticism in it.

With our own words now, we can say that she, with the will power of conative reluctance locks her consciousness, preventing it from returning to focused and reflected awareness of the holding hands. She continues talking in the same platonic way, but it is as if the magic is fading away. A puzzling feeling of something missing now – but she will not (!) let the missing something be conscious.

Unconsciousness, then, is the aspect of being conscious, that *one actively and with an act of will–power prevents from being advanced to the high-organized conscious level by focused and reflected awareness.*

Unconsciousness is the person's very systematic, very energetic non-awareness of something that nevertheless is personally very meaningful (and very senseful) – and thus it is an important moment in activity at large. It is the part the person cannot not allow himself to contain as a part of his self-image.

This part of our life project not only is preconscious but also unconscious. Remember how our young woman in Sartre's Café has a life project which initiates her active withdrawal from consciousness of the sexual aspect of life.

Like preconsciousness unconsciousness is not an alien force. On the contrary, unconsciousness is a particular meaningful (and senseful) part of a person's conscious being, which he will do a lot to disown, but which nevertheless is a way in which he actively performs parts of his life project. In exactly this sense meanings, motives, acts and life projects can be unconscious. Motives are always the psychodynamic aspect of the conscious being of man, but they do not always reach the high–organized form of consciousness.

5. The basic phenomena of will–power and neurosis

Conscious and nonconscious acts

Consciousness is a meaningful anticipatory instruction for an action directed towards a situative goal, and so consciousness is a phenomenological model of action (not of activity), where motives and goals are focused on and reflected upon.

Conscious actions with the quality of will–power are actions characterized by determination and resolution: 1) They hold on to a goal even if they have to take a long way round to reach it. 2) They hold on to a goal in spite of resistance, both resistance from without (troubles one has to overcome, the counter–interests of others which one has to take into account, etc.) and resistance from within (counter–motives corresponding to actions which have goals contradictory to the first goal). But with the act of will–power one motive and one goal is enforced despite resistances, problems, and contradictory motives and goals (e.g. goals embedded in the life project 'professional career' versus goals embedded in the project 'family life').

Conscious being with will–power and contra–willpower

We are now able to invoke a more precise concept of unconsciousness. Unconsciousness is the aspect of being conscious, that one actively and with an act of will–power prevents from being advanced to consciousness. I withdraw my attention from the full meaning of my unconscious actions.

Let us once more turn to Sartre's Café. Within the young woman there are conflicting motives regarding the first factor of will–power, organization of conscious being. She wants to appear both as a woman with sexuality, and to appear as a noble and virginal decent girl. But then, regarding the second factor of will–power, things go wrong for her. She doesn't manage to integrate these motives, they remain contradictory. She cannot integrate and advance them into a single high–level life project where educative talking and eroticism can melt together somewhere in between Plato and Aristotle.

In other words: she has a will–power directed against the noble and virginal self–image, and this will–power is at the same time a contra–willpower turned against the will–power of being a 'floosie'. So once more: what is she doing? She splits the full meaning of the situation in two. Only one side of the meaning, the platonic side, is allowed to advance to consciousness, the other side, the sexy side, is in activity too motivated and governed by will–power but in an unconscious way (note that she in fact lets him take her hand). If later in the evening, she should be making love to him, one of two things can happen: Either she discovers that it is not that bad. Or she remains in a stronger neurotic split–condition. She is in despair over her actions, she doesn't understand herself, feels that she was driven by alien forces, what happened was against her will (!), and she might blame him for dishonoring her. Maybe she even feels seduced – either by some 'mysterious alien forces' in her–self, or by him. It therefore is not instincts (triebe) that scare her. On the contrary, it is high–level organized aspects of her self as a person, that scare her.[9]

---

9 In fact the phenomenology I deal with in this paper is not based upon instincts, impulses and needs. Neither is this phenomenology based on idealistic self–actualizing tendencies as we find in Rogers and 'Humanistic Psychology' (Maslow, Bugental, Bühler). It is a phenomeno-

Let us try to understand this with the methods, that the parts of the phenomenological–existentialist psychology have in common with activity theory: an activity has to be understood by its goal. And further: an action/experience has to be understood by the situation in which it exists. A life project has to be understood on the basis of an understanding of the lived life, and the particular life world to which it is connected. Certain situative characteristics will force us to propose certain characteristics of the life project (and the essence of human beings). We can in a valid way conclude: these objectively identified essentials of the situation could not exist unless certain human essentials exist. For example: the characteristics of uncertainty and of ambiguity of a situation – we do not know into which new situation it will be transformed – requires us to take into account a human being, who has a free will and responsibility for his actions and his life and the consequences of these for others. If we had a knowledge of human situations, which only could be unfolded in pure mechanics, we would have to propose man – as the situation–maker – as a nice piece of mechanics. As did the behaviourist who never came to an understanding of human situations going deeper than finding a pathway through a labyrinth.

So far the methodological approach. In the examples above we have a situation (a bit of lived life) with the following characteristics: a) a Platonic way of being together – b) spiced with eroticism – c) with a *not to be touched and realized* sexuality, which nevertheless is there (in the form: not to be touched).

The situation, manifested in the young man (as a tiny part of her life world), has the meaning of a platonic connection, and he of *not* being a *male* with sexual attractiveness, whereby he, exactly for the same reason is a human being with a sexual meaning for her. But there is something more to say about these meanings: To the meaning of sexuality the meaning is connected: 'not to be touched!' – and to the meaning of platonic intercourse the meaning is connected: 'stay away from the sexuality'!

Therefore, we are forced to take into account a life project – here the concrete human essentials of the young woman – with the following characteristics, or meaning and sense: It is a life project split in two (or more) parts: 1) One part of the life project (the Platonic one) is partly allowed to be advanced to consciousness and is in a senseful way initiating an activity which is orientated by a goal with the connotative meaning: 'can be touched, is allowed to be conscious'. Partly it is not allowed to advance to consciousness, it is directed against the other split of the life project (the sexual one) initiating an activity which is orientated by a goal which for this second split of the life project has the meaning 'this I really desire', and which for the first split (the Platonic one) has the connotative meaning of 'keep away'. 2) The other split (the sexual one) of the life project is thereby actively prevented from being

phenomenology based upon the concept of meaningful and senseful activity, and upon the concept of life–projects.

advanced to consciousness, because it is the reflection of a connotative meaning of 'not to be advanced to consciousness', given by the first split (the Platonic one).

The central point here is that both splits of the neurotic life project, conscious, or not, have the characteristics of volition. None of them stem from outside causing forces – both of them essentially have their reasons, given by a responsible person. Both of them are well–motivated high–organized acts of will–power. Further more one of them has the characteristics of double-directed motivation and will–power: 1) initiating a connection with the meaningful piece of life world (the 'Plato' in the young fellow, the young woman is dating) – 2) preventing the other split from realizing how much it is strived for and how much it too has the characteristics of volition. In other words: The one side of the split has the characteristics of volition and of contra–volition, both being realized, but only partly advanced to consciousness, the other side has the characteristics of volition, but is not allowed (by the first one) to be advanced to consciousness.

In Figure 3 I have tried to outline these characteristics of what could be called a one–sided neurosis. Such a life project can be found on two levels of organization of conscious being in the world: on the level of consciousness and on the level of unconsciousness.

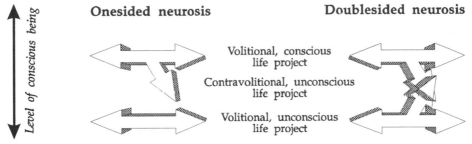

Fig. 3:   Neurosis

The phenomenological distance between the two levels lies on a continuum: From total blindness of the higher level, regarding the activities and life projects of the lower level, nevertheless being very energetic, determined in preventing the low–level activities to be realized. And through a gradually decreasing self–hating rejecting of certain sorts of activities and life projects, which are experienced more or less as disturbing and more or less as strange parts of one self.

This sort of organization can be regarded as a one–sided neurosis. It is one and the same part of the life projects which captures the high–level-organizational position, or: which is conscious, and which consequently and with an act of will—power is turned against the other part of the life project, holding it in unconsciousness.

In a double sided neurosis, the two splits can change organizational levels. Maybe one evening we find our young lady in Sartre's Cafe having a virginal contra—project turned against sexuality, and the next evening we find her at the discotheque being a sexy beauty, and feeling only contempt for every sign of Victorian virginity in the behaviour of others. In turn then part of the life project is banished to just that margin of conscious being, which we call unconsciousness.

Let us then turn back to Sartre's Cafe. Her style is a closed self—containing style and a closed containing style regarding certain aspects of the situation. It is outside her self—image and what she is capable of containing, that she wants their date to have a broad range going from the Platonic conversation to cheerful love making with each other. Only unconsciously does she want sexuality to come in between them. And so she in a self—contradictive way, full of will and contra—will pulls in additional projects from his side. He has to identify[10] with both the platonic and the sexual aspect of their being together.

One of the preconditions for a happy end of the evening and for a happy common future is that his containing style is more open than hers. First he has to have a more open containing style regarding himself and his sexuality. Secondly he must be able to contain her closedness. And he must be able to contain the complex contradictory life project of hers, turned against him and their dating.

Maybe he goes just too far, in the moment he takes her hand, going beyond her 'zone of proximal development' regarding a more open containing style. But maybe that little sensitive action was necessary to show her, that he is capable and willing to contain the whole range of her − and his − projects with the evening. And when he, sensitively and cautiously, contains the whole range of what is meaningful for her, then he has literally given her a hand, helping her to enlarge her containing style and self—image.

---

10   Projective identification is a developmental relation (Klein 1946, Ogden 1979). In terms of psychotherapy, the relatios can be described in thi way: 1) The therapist feels a faint irritation and contempt. It shows up that these feelings are directed against the client. Maybe he finds himself perceiving his client as lazy. 2) Giving it a second thought, it shows up that these faint feelings are corresponding with a project of the client directed at the therapist: 'do you want to deal with me when I am so lazy?'. This project of the client on the other hand corresponds with the client's closed self containing style: 'I reject the same sides of my personality as my mother did. Now one of two things can happen: 3a) When the therapist himself is not capable of containing a lazy lifestyle he also will reject this side of his client (as did his mother). 3b) But if the therapist is capable of containing this side of the client, it will be the first step for the client to be self containing regarding this side of his personality.

6. Clinical psychology and psychotherapy

The fundamental life project

The image of man which can be deduced from what has been said so far, is an image of a being with the fundamental life project of *making a culture of the surroundings and of making human beings of each other*.

Let us have a look at the second part of that project. In every life project of man the deepest sensefulness, at the level of centered activity, is that a person as a social being always already *re*cognizes the other in himself and himself in the other. On the higher level of decentered organizing of activity the meaningfulness of life and the life project regards human beings as communicating beings, caring for others and working together with each other. And on the highest level of organization, on the level of individuated activity, the meaning of life and life projects is characterized by human beings as being intending persons, giving personal contributions to humanity, society and culture. This is the topography of the life project of 'being a human and being a person'.

It is this topography in the human sensefulness of the life world that the little newborn encounters – at first as the topography of the project of upbringing with which the parents meet their little newborn. In this givenness of a topographically meaningful life world the child gradually will come into existence as a being with a centered, with a decentered and finally with an individuated activity and life project. The child becomes human, and it becomes a person with exactly that sort of topographic life project with which it can relate to us as a person, thus being recognized as a person; as one of us. It is in this way that the human topographic organization reflects the cultural-historical topography of meaning and sense.

Clinical psychological problems and the topography of the life project

Above we saw an example of how the neurotic life projects of the client again and again are realized in neurotically split life forms. But nevertheless: exactly in this way the client repeatedly *tries* to realize certain connection with another person. A connection which would be the condition of possibility for that other person, if his containing capability is open enough, to reflect the client in such a way, that he can internalize exactly this containing capability (and the integrated personality lying in this) as his own. The client would then develope and organize his being in the world, his life project and his personality and overcoming his neurotic splits.

Basically, clinical psychological problems have to be understood as problems with the topographic organization of the life project. Each of the levels has its own organizational law and its own developmental laws pointing to the next higher level. Therefore, a clinical problem has to be understood firstly on its own level, and secondly not only as a disturbance, but also as a curative possibility of higher level of organization.

The process of psychotherapy, therefore, has to be understood as a developmental process regarding the topographic organization of the life project. And the effect of psychotherapy cannot be understood except on the basis of understanding the activity–connection between the client and the therapist. The client–position of this connection is marked by the client's level–specific curative striving for higher level organization through the connection. The therapist–position is – at best – marked by the therapist's capability to connect to his client, and to have the necessary openness in his containing project.

Topographical possibilities of (curative) development

On the level of the centered activity, the developmental and organizational possibility relates to basic trust, and the fundamental experience of belonging to the fellowship of man. The more fortunate developmental and organizational process takes its point of departure from a deep sense of belonging and trust. The less fortunate developmental path takes its point of departure in the opposite: basic mistrust, the experience of not belonging to any fellowship and the experience of being in a fierce, cruel and cold life world. Clients in that deeply ill–fated position is said to have borderline complications and the central curative aspect of *their* life project is sometimes a very subtle, very sensitive, form of activity, which goal is a trustworthy and psychological symbiotic connection with a good and containing adult/therapist.[11]

Such unfortunate people cannot develop any further, cannot transcend their borderline level before they really connect with at least one other person who is *capable* of and *willing* to engage in such an activity – maybe for years.

On the higher level of decentered activity we find what can be called the narcissistic developmental and organizational and curative task. A good development here will take its point of departure in the creation of evident pride, care and sympathy, partly for the person himself (activity marked by mature extrovert engagement in life) and partly for other people (activity marked by mature admiring of others and mature goaldirectedness in the life project.[12] The developments and higher level organizations are disturbed if the child on this level is not responded to, by a parent with a sufficiently mature project: 'making a human being and a grown up person out of my little

---

11   It is necessary to distinguish between the topography of activity as seen in cultural–history and in clinical psychology. That the modern human being can have life projects fixated on the centered level, thereby suffering from borderline–problems, does not mean that the early hominids were 'borderlines'. In fact it prescribes a modern mother's/father's high organized but borderline–characterized upbringing–project to make it difficult/impossible for her/his little child to develop a mature and healthy human life–project himself (although he will never stop striving for a mature connection with a healthy and mature adult).

12   This view of the mature narcissistic aspects of the life project is based on the works of Kohut.

child'. The child then cannot perform the task of integration and maturation of the narcissistic psychodynamics and will be stuck on the deeper decentered level: On one side as the grandiose child we all know, striving for the parents admiration – and on the other side as the child we also know: admiring its parent as omnipotent and grandiose.

The life project and activity of a person who is stuck on this organizational level will forever be marked by demanding unconditional admiration and praise from other people – but also by demanding the other to be grandiose and omnipotent in a way which can fill out a deep emptiness. But a narcissistic life project is *also* marked by the curative longing for a person, who can contain these projects in an open and mature way and who can reflect them in a way that helps the narcissistic person to growth and high level organization.

At the top of the topography, on the level of individuated activity we find the classical conflict neurosis with splitting of the life project, and activity in contradictory parts.

And again: the curative task embedded in every action–realization of such a neurotic activity is to realize a togetherness with

Fig. 4:
TOPOGRAPHY OF THE LIFE PROJECT

Level of activity	Organizing themes	
INDIVIDUATED ACTIVITY. Evolved lifehistorical. Inititated and orientated by general meanings and personal senses.	**Personal moral** conscious, volitional,life projects	**Guilt** unconscious, volitional life projects
DECENTRED ACTIVITY. Spatiotemporal separeted activities. Initiated and orientated by general symbolic meanings.	**Self-/object constan.** normal idealization and self-assertion	**Shame** narcissistic idealization and self-assert.
CENTRED ACTIVITY. Being regulated by the action patterns of the group or parent-child-dyade	**Basic trust** The world is a good place to be in	**Mistrust** The world is a bad place to be in

another person (or in general with a life world) capable of advancing the splits to an integrated, noncontradictory level of organization.

Figure 4 shows the topography of the human life project. It shows how the developmental/curative theme regarding basic trust and feeling of belonging in the human world, is advanced to the higher level of the narcissistic developmental/curative theme regarding initiation (mature admiration of one's own energy) and orientation (mature goal directness and admiration of human life worlds). How the theme is developed on *this* level is conditioned by the degree of success of fulfilling the tasks on the level of centered activity. With a point of departure in basic mistrust and a basic feeling of nonbelonging and being thrown out in a cruel life world the development of self–confidence, goaldirectedness and appreciation of the social life world of man is obviously given a hard time, if not completely blocked.

Correspondingly the success of organizing on the level of individuated activity is preconditioned by the integration and organization of the level of decentered activity. If the motivations of reaching out, and of goalseeking is split apart then this will imply a basic split in all sorts of concrete motives resulting in the conflict neurosis.

7. Conclusion

Psychodynamics must be understood from the following points of view:

1) Psychodynamics lies in the dimension of activity. Activity is a special sort of connection. Seen from the subject–point–of–view: human life project. Seen from the object–point–of–view: life world.

2) The cultural–historical topography: On the deepest level man's activity is centered, on a higher level man's activity is decentered, and on the highest level, man's activity is individuated.

3) The macrostructure of activity: Psychodynamics can be defined as the vital human creating forces, which evolve in activity, when initiations meet with orientations, organizations and constitutions.

4) The organizational logic of activity theory: the constitutive elements are organized as elementary forms by the high level organization of the psyche. Therefore man, with a certain degree of freedom is self–organizing. As the phenomenological–existential psychologists would say: man *can have* and *has* his own life as a task. Psychodynamics, therefore, rather than being conceived in terms of external (estranging) causes, must be conceived in terms of man's own reasons. Advanced to its highest level, psychodynamics has the form of volitional consciousness.

5) Meanings, and not instincts (triebe) are the particular human essence of the life creating and self–creating aspects of human activity. Meaning is conceived as an implicate order, which unfolds in concrete situations with either the conative, the emotive or the cognitive dimension in the foreground.

It is from these perspectives, then, that psychological problems, psychotherapy and conscious activity must be understood.

Only a small part of activity, of the life projects and of the meaning and sense embedded in our life world is conscious. And so it has to be. To a certain degree and at certain times the life projects and the activities have to be unconscious, but not in a defensive, repressed way. On the contrary. The process of human life would be stiff, without playfulness and innocence, if it was totally reflected. We could not act, and could not be innocently involved in life if we had to reflect upon every situative action, figuring out in which way our actions reflect our superior and organizing life projects. This does not mean, that the macrostructure of activity does not unceasingly move, advancing to still higher levels of organization, thereby making formerly unconscious activity conscious high–level actions. At the actual top of the macrostructure of our psychodynamics, activity grows at best by being left in preconsciousness and unconsciousness. I – I myself – can let it be there, when it has this meaning for me – and when I choose to give certain aspects of my life project exactly the meaning of 'not–to–be–attentive–and–speculative–about'. And in contrast to what Freud thought, this necessary unconsciousness lies not at the bottom of the psychic organization of the mind, but at the top.

References

Bertelsen, P. (1990): Den villende bevidstheds evolution – en indlæsning af Jaynes' model i en kulturhistorisk teori, *Psyke & Logos*, pp. 89–126.

Bohm, D. (1983): *Wholeness and the Implicate Order*, London.

Engelsted, N. (1984): *Springet fra dyr til menneske. En argumentationsskitse*, Copenhagen.

Engelsted, N. (1989): What is the psyche and how did it get into the world. In Engelsted, N., Hem, L., Mammen, J. (eds.): *Essays in General Psychology*, Aarhus.

Gerard, R.W. (1957): Units and Concepts of Biology, *Science* (125; pp. 429–433).

Jaynes, J. (1976): *The Origin of Consciousness in the Breakdown of the Bicameral Mind*, Boston.

Klein, M: (1975/1946): Notes on some schizoid mechanisms. In: *Envy and Gratitude and Other Works, 1946–1963*, London.

Klein, M. (1975/1955): On identification. In: *Envy and Gratitude and Other Works, 1946–1963*, London.

Koestler, A. (1981): *The Ghost in the Machine*, London.

Kohut, H. (1977): *The Restoration of the Self*, New York.

Leontjev, A.N. (1981): *Problems of the development of the mind*, Moscow.

Mammen, J. (1989): The relation between subject and object from the perspective of activity theory, In Engelsted, N., Hem, L., Mam–men, J. (eds.): *Essays in General Psychology*, Aarhus.

Ogden, T. (1979). On Projective Identification, *International Journal of Psychoanalysis*, (64); pp. 357–373.

Poulsen, H. (1991): *Conations*, Aarhus.

Sartre, J.P. (1943): *L'etre et le neant*, Paris.

Winnicott, D.W. (1965): *The Maturational Process and the Facilitating Environment*, London.

Vygotsky, L.S. (1934, 1965): *Thought and Language*, New York.

METHODS, FOCUS OF INTEREST, AND THEORY IN HUMANISTIC RESEARCH

Erik Schultz
University of Copenhagen

For many years I have been working on basic issues in personality psychology. Some of the problems here are familiar themes in human science in general. This paper tries to present some viewpoints regarding the coherence between three elements in human research: The researcher, the phenomenon he investigates, and the methods he uses.

Terminology

In science we usually distinguish between subject and object. The subject is the scientist, that is the person who makes the observations and investigations. The object is the thing which is being observed and investigated.

This distinction works well in natural science, because natural scientists investigate objects. In human science the distinction becomes confusing, because human scientists often investigate subjects. In psychology the confusion is total.

In this paper I shall preserve the subject–object distinction but choose some more co–operative terms. The traditional "subject" will be *the observer*, and the traditional "object" will be our *focus of interest* or just *focus*. In this way misunderstandings can be avoided.

As to the concept *theory*, Popper has suggested that we use the term "subjective theory" when we speak of the observer's a priori knowledge about a certain focus of interest. If such a priori knowledge is written down, we are able to confront it as a special focus of interest, and Popper suggests we call this an "objective theory" (Popper,1972). A paper containing an observer's considerations about some facts in this complex world is an example of an objective theory.

For reasons that I have given elsewhere (Schultz 1988,p.109) and do not want to explore in this paper, I prefer to call subjective theory *implicit theory*, and objective theory *explicit theory*. These terms work exactly like Popper's. When Freud confronts his focus of interest (his analysand) with some a priori considerations about human nature, he employs implicit theory about mankind. If he, as he so overwhelmingly did, writes these considerations down on paper, we find Freud's explicit theory about human nature on the bookshelf.

Now something about *method*. The method is the direction the observer takes and the tool he uses in order to grasp some new knowledge about his focus of interest.

This paper will try to argue that the issue of methodology is misplaced. The problems of choosing right methods is a problem of having the right theoretical knowledge.

Methods follow from theories, whether they are of the implicit or explicit kind. Imagine an observer who wants to study the ears of elephants, and tries to use a microscope as a tool. We question his sanity, because we a priori know that this focus of interest is too big for this method. Here the correct method is observation by an unaided eye. Another crazy scientist might try to look at quantums in the microscope. Again we shake our heads, because this focus of interest is too small for this method. In both examples our a priori knowledge of method is strictly dictated by our theoretical knowledge of our focus of interest.

The focus of interest in human science

Let us shortly describe the focus of interest in different types of science.

In natural science the focus of interest is *objects* or, more precisely, it is the dead matter in the world.

Human science can be roughly divided into two categories. The first and largest category of humanitarian studies have *meaning and sense in man-made products* as their focus. A text is an excellent example. This focus of interest consists of earlier generations' explicit thoughts written down on paper or whatever they had to write on. The buildings, tools and institutions of earlier generations or of contemporary foreign cultures are other examples. Philology, archaeology, history and anthropology are examples of disciplines in this category.

The other category of human scientists has *mind in itself* as focus of interest. Psychology is the main example; – but some branches of philosophy might also be mentioned.

Popper divides the world into three categories, which he calls the first, the second and the third world. The first world is the nature that also existed before life emerged. The second world is mind, that is to say knowledge in the living substance. The third world is mind products. It is creations made by the second world. A spider's web might serve as a quick example of the third world (Popper, 1972).

It is obvious that natural science has the first world as focus of interest. Human science has *the human part of the second and third world as focus of interest*.

Epistemology and ontology

Imagine an observer who looks at the complex world surrounding him. Some of this world will be perceived or experienced by him.

Our imagined observer is able to choose something as his focus of interest. Let us suppose he does so. Now he is, in principle, able to do three things with his focus, and these can be done regardless of what the focus might be.

He may regard his focus as a form in it's own right, he may dissect his focus into the material parts that it is made of, or, finally, he may try to find out what bigger forms his focus of interest is a material part of.

An example will illustrate this issue. Let us suppose our observer is sit-ting at the beach and has chosen the sea as his focus of interest. He may choose the experience of the sea in its own right, he may dissect the sea, and find out that the main constituting materials are oxygen and hydrogen atoms, and finally, he may seek knowledge about the sea as a material part of a bigger ecological system.

Inspired by this example, we can see that it is senseless to ask a general question about which parts of the world are "material" and which parts are "formal". The answer depends on how we decide our focus of interest. If the sea is looked upon as a form, the atoms are the constituent material. If the atoms are looked upon as forms, something smaller (quantums) are material parts. If the ecological system is considered as a form, the sea is a material part.

This Aristotelian way of looking at the world makes it clear that it is problematic to have a "materialistic" world picture, because anything can be a material part in the constitution of something bigger and at the same time be itself a form made up of material parts. Let us therefore say that we have described a *realistic* worldview. Everything that we can experience exists, and the question whether it is a "material thing" is senseless. Of course it is material – when we are interested in the bigger coherence; and of course it is nothing but a form – when we are interested in its component parts.

Traditionally there are three ontological arguments against this realistic world description. Let us take them up briefly in turn.

1) One argument would be something like this: Our observer at the beach is an organism with sense organs and a brain. The sense organs are stimulated, and the brain is working something out as a consequence. Therefore anything the brain might construct (atoms, seas, ecological sys-tems, children, anxious children or whatever) is a perceptual entity, and the

observer has no chance whatsoever of knowing what are realities in the world. There thus exists no method of getting knowledge of the world in itself. Berkeley is known as a radical representative of this so called solipsistic viewpoint.

2) The second argument is that only the smallest parts of the identifiable world exist in reality. Our imagined observer uses the right method to grasp reality when he dissects the sea. He identifies the atoms that water is made of, and these are in reality what exists. The rest of the experienced blooming and blossoming world is something the observer creates in his mind. Democritus is known to be one of the founders of this way of thinking.

3) The third argument claims that the realistic description is correct, as long as we are dealing with dead substances, whether big or small. Mind qualities, on the other hand, do not exist in reality. They are something the observer, in interpreting organismic movements, is constructing. Our atoms are ontological realities, our water and even our ecological system are realities, but if our observer is looking at an anxious child and chooses the anxiety as his focus of interest, then we are told to consider the anxiety as simply an experience that the observer has. Anxiety is not a real focus of interest in an ontological sense. It is rather an observer–mind–creation in an epistemological sense.

This third argument is, although with some variation, the most popular viewpoint regarding the epistemological/ontological problem. For that reason it is the viewpoint that bothers human science most.

In this paper we shall stick to the realistic viewpoint. When an observer looks at the world, he is able to identify some of it. The higher his theoretical level, the more he can identify; but the real world will always be bigger than the part of it the observer is able to know. The ontological world is bigger than the epistemological, and the latter is contained in the former.

In our three counterarguments the opposite thing happens. The arguments are cutting bigger or smaller parts out of the perceptual world and are claiming that these parts are observer constructions. That leaves us with an ontological world that is smaller than the epistemological.

The first argument cuts away everything except experience per se. Everything you see around you is a mind creation. In a fundamental way this means that any old thing is epistemological.

The second argument cuts away most of the world except elementary particles. That gives us a nuclear world out there to be studied ontologically, and that makes room for a nuclear physics. The rest of the world belongs to the epistemological domain.

The third argument cuts away the mind part of the world. All the dead matter out there is ontologically real; – but mind phenomena are observer creations and thereby epistemological entities. This makes room for a natural science, because there is a dead nature out there to be studied. However, it makes no room for a mind science, because such a science gets into difficulties when it looks for its focus of interest. It is not out there in reality.

Although the cutting knife gets more and more modest down through the three arguments, *in all cases it removes the mind from reality.* That is precisely what bothers human science, and that explains why methodology often becomes an isolated problem. You have an observer, but you have no focus of interest and, for that reason, no theory about it.

A theory of mind based on a pure realistic position is, in fact, a rare thing in psychology. In a way, all explicit psychological and philosophical theories contain a lot of hypotheses about mind; but more often that not they are hypotheses about "how mind creates a picture of something", or "how the machinery of mind is working". It has been a major project in Danish psychology over the past two decades to work on this missing theory, and the present paper reflects some of this work, although the ideas presented here are my own. Beside my own work on this issue (Schultz, 1988) we can point to the work done by Mammen (1983), Engelsted (1984, 1989), Karpatschof (1985) and Katzenelson (1989). This Danish "trend" is mostly based on the works of Leontiev (1967, 1975) but Spencer (1881) and Popper (1972) have also been "discovered" as contributors to the realistic position.

Mind is intentional

Dilthey has provided a famous explanation regarding the difference between natural science and human science (Dilthey, 1913). In natural science we seek natural laws in order to *explain* the movements of our focus of interest. In human science we *interpret teleological* phenomena, and that is the same as *understanding intentions* in our focus of interest.

This tradition is further developed by Habermas (1968) and Apel (1968). They preserve the two Dilthcyan types of science, called naturalistic and hermeneutical, and add a third type, called emancipatorical, that is a mixture of the two. In our context we shall limit ourselves to the naturalistic and hermeneutical types, as they are sufficient for the purpose in this paper.

The naturalistic type seeks manipulative control over the focus of interest by means of knowledge of it. The hermeneutical type seeks to understand what intentions the focus is communicating.

Let us give quick examples to illustrate:

Naturalistic science: An observer looks at the moon and notices that it moves around the earth. He (let us call him Newton) tries to explain this movement by acquiring knowledge of celestial natural laws. What method does he use? – Well, he suggests certain laws as hypotheses and looks at the evidence at hand to see if it corresponds with the hypotheses. The evidence corresponds, and because we have not yet found an example that does not fit the hypotheses, we say, with Popper, that these laws are the best explanation. In other words, we try empirically to falsify our hypotheses. This is the right scientific method. (We disregard of course the objection about very high velocity; – it is not relevant here.).

Hermeneutical science: Now the observer looks at a man who most of the day is busy washing his hands. The observer (let us call him Freud) tries to understand this by finding the focus person's *intention* with this activity. What does he wish to achieve with all this hand–washing? The observer manages to discover that the focus–person is trying to wash dirty feelings and aggressive tendencies away. What method does our observer use? He communicates with the focus–person for a very long time, and little by little these intentions in the focus person become evident to both persons, observer and focus–person.

Notice the absurdity if we mix the methods. What would happen if we, for example, tried to understand the movement of the moon by getting insight into the moon's intentions. What intentions does the moon have in moving like that? Well the moon has no intentions, so there is no knowledge about intentions to be found.

The same absurdity would arise if we tried to explain the handwashing movements by finding the natural laws that determine them. I have dealt with these problems in much more detail in my research (Schultz, 1972, 1979, 1988), and I shall in a moment return to them.

As earlier mentioned, in many branches of human science we have the meaning and sense in human products as our focus of interest. *Meaning and sense in human products are intentions*, because they contain *intentional history of man*. Let us consider an example.

An observer is coming to a foreign culture and finds a long piece of wood with handles at both ends. The big piece of wood in the middle can turn around when rolled on something. If our observer is a human scientist, an anthropologist for example, he certainly will not try to explain this focus of interest by finding the natural forces that mingled with the wood to achieve this result. Rather, he tries to understand the *intentional history* of this piece of wood. If our observer succeeds in his investigation, he has discovered what this gadget is meant for. He has found the object's meaning. Let us suppose that the tool is a rolling pin. If the observer manages to understand that it is meant for treating dough in cooking activity, he has understood the meaning.

I shall elaborate on this example in order to define *sense*. Suppose that our anthropologist observer has managed to understand the meaning, but that he finds the rolling pin in a horse stable. Then he has a sense problem. What is the *intention* of putting the rolling pin into this context? If he, on the other hand, finds this tool in a kitchen, he understands the sense in having it there.

In short: Meaning and sense in manmade products are the focus of interest in many branches of human science. As in direct mind science *intentions* are the focus of interest. Consider language as a focus example. Words have meanings as defined here, and they have sense as well, if they are found in correct contexts. The word's meaning is of course the intentional history of the word – that is to say the conventional agreement in the culture about what focus the word as a tool can be used to point to. The sense is the actual use of the word in a specific context. I will, however, not go into further details regarding these problems, – I refer to my work on this topic (Schultz, 1988, ch. VI) – but will simply stress the point that *human science in general has intentionality as focus of interest*.

Let us return to the issue of methodology. Our hermeneutical scientists are certainly using other methods than their colleagues in natural science. In short, human scientists use *interpretation of intentions* as a method.

There is a problem, however, if our hermeneutical scientists do not accept the realistic philosophy mentioned earlier. Our anthropologist confronted with the rolling pin may *experience* that this focus of interest is suited for knocking people in their heads, or he may *experience* that it is suited for dough treatment. In this case our observer is *putting two competing meanings into the focus*, and if he believes that in principle any meaning is something he himself constructs, he cannot ask for the *correct* one.

If our observer of the hand–washing focus person believes that any intention in the focus person is the creation of the observer's mind, he cannot evaluate whether his interpretation is correct or not.

It is the claim in this paper that many human scientists are haunted by one of these mind–reducing ways of thinking that, in fact, removes the focus of interest from world realities. Therefore, their methods (and activities in general) acquire a kind of minority–complex–like quality in regard to scientific self–security. This point will be elaborated somewhat more in the following.

Measuring

Let us now imagine that an observer is looking at an anxious child. "What do we mean when we say that a person is anxious?" Eysenck (1953, p. 201) asks, and he gives the following answer to that question:

> We mean that he blushes easily at the slightest provocation, his heart begins to race, his hands may tremble, his mouth goes dry, his digestion is affected, and various other *physical phenomena* of one kind or another will be evoked in him with great ease. These are the *objective facts* to which we may refer... (my italics).

This step in Eysenck's method is a dissection of the "mind form" (anxiety) into it's constituent material parts, in order to get hold of "the objective facts", namely "physical phenomena".

In principle Eysenck is in agreement with the earlier-mentioned second objection to our realistic viewpoint. He claims that the world out there is as nuclear physicists describe it (Eysenck, 1953, p. 222). In the above quotation, however, we notice that he sticks to the third objection. Not only atoms, but also bigger physical phenomena are to be considered "objective facts".

The anxiety, on the other hand, is, in Eysenck's way of thinking, something the observer is interpreting out of the physical facts. It is an interpretation in the sense that it is an observer-mind-construction.

Eysenck argues further, that mind phenomena cannot be *measured*, while physical phenomena can. In that aspect he is right. This is because physical phenomena are dead things that in a *deterministic* way move in accordance with natural laws, and these laws *predict movements*. You can measure the weight of a stone, the gravitation and so forth and predict the way the stone will move down the hillside. Mind phenomena, on the other hand, cannot be measured. You can measure a skier's weight and the gravitation; but you cannot measure his intention of getting down the hillside in the shortest possible time without falling. This intention you have to interpret, and from this interpretation you cannot *predict* which way he will be skiing, because intentions point to *end situations* with *freedom in choosing ways*. There is thus no unambiguous correspondence between movements in time and space and intention; and such a correspondence is necessary for measuring. (For further exploration of this argument see Schultz (1988, ch. XVII)).

Although this "freedom in choosing ways" means that you cannot measure intentions, it certainly does not mean that "the freedom in choosing ways" is an observer quality. It is a focus quality. *It is, in fact, a defining quality about mind*. Although not measurable, it is indeed a focus person quality in an ontological sense. As an observer you have to interpret the intention. But because it is a real quality in the focus you may be wrong or right in your interpretation; there is a correct answer as to what intention our focus person has.

It is, however, very common to think that because you cannot measure intention, it is not "out there" in reality. It is only to be regarded as an observer construction.

Nevertheless, this way of thinking is wrong. Why should the observer's mind be more reliable in identifying measurable physical things than in identifying intentions? The most common answer to that question will be a reference to intersubjective agreement: that observers agree in describing measurements, while they tend to disagree when interpreting mind phenomena.

Let us try to look a little more closely at a measurement. We have a device for counting heartbeats per second. A needle points to a scale on which there are written, from left to right, "too slow", "normal", and "too fast".

The observer has to identify the device, the needle and the written text. According to our earlier definition, the *meanings* of these three phenomena are intentions. In order to carry through a measurement it is necessary to use hermeneutical interpretations of meanings. Of course, all observers agree. That is because we only accept observers with an adequate theoretical level. There are, in fact, people who do not manage to interpret what the device is meant for – who also may be unable to read the written text on the device. (For further details regarding this argument see Radnitzky (1970), Apel (1968) and Schultz (1972,1988).

Surely, measurements are often reliable observations – but they certainly have no monopoly on being the most reliable observations. To be a reliable observer is to have sufficient theory level regarding the focus of interest. That is the same whether the focus is physical movements or intentions. The skilled reader observes word meanings in the paper he reads, and the skilled psychotherapist observes intentional depths in the analysand he is treating, because both observers have apriori the relevant theoretical knowledge to make such observations. Of course, the person who only knows Chinese cannot read a paper written in English, and the lay person cannot observe the same array of intentions as can the skilled therapist. The same is the case in natural science. The skilled astronomer observes that a new star is on the firmament; a lay person is unable to notice that.

In short, there is nothing more secure in observing physical phenomena, with or without measurement observations, than there is in observing intentions. Let us illustrate this a bit more with examples taken from psychology.

To remove intentions in method and focus

Let us imagine that you are an observer who thinks that the world does not contain three dimensions. These dimensions, so you think, (perhaps inspired by Kant), are categorical creations of your own mind.

Now, if you are an experimental psychologist, how would you confirm your theory about these missing dimensions?

You would probably do a trick that psychologists have always done in such situations. You remove the dimensions from your *method* or your *focus of interest,* and thereafter you demonstrate that dimensions are mind creations.

Let us try this. We are observers confronting a box. Our theory wants us to believe that the box does not really have three dimensions, and that we, as observers, are creating them.

Is it possible to remove the dimensions – or just one of them – from our method? Hardly. If we instruct ourselves to disregard the dimensions when we look at the box scientifically, we cannot see anything.

Then let us try to manipulate the focus. Here we get a bright idea. It is possible to draw a box with three dimensions on a piece of paper which only contains two dimensions. Let us do so:

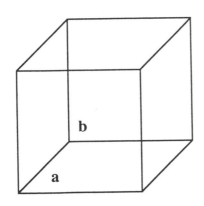

You can show this drawing to countless observers and point to the amazing fact that they all construct the third dimension with their minds. Some observers experience that the point "a" is the closer one, some that "b" is the closer one, and nobody is right or wrong. It depends on the "eyes that see".

Alas, we have, in a little psychological experiment, shown that we human beings, as observers, construct the third dimension, and, ecstatic, we conclude that we also construct the two others.

Indeed, we have shown nothing of the kind. If we compose ourselves and reflect seriously, we can see that all we have shown is that we live in a world that is in three dimensions, and if we manage to cut one of them out in a special arrangement, our minds have difficulties in avoiding seeing things as they use to be. The missing dimension in the focus is really missing, and we all know that. The genesis of our minds has taught us to expect three dimensions in boxes. If we show our observers a real box, all of them will of course see the third dimension *in the right way*.

This trick is, nevertheless, very common in psychological research. We try to get rid of the focus–quality we do not believe to be there in reality, and, having done so, we argue that it is not there.

Eysenck used the trick on the methodological side. As an observer, his focus of interest was an anxious child. Then in his instructions on scientific method, he *forbade* us to observe the anxiety and *demanded* us to stick to "physical phenomena" and make science on them.

In personality psychology we have two examples where the trick is used on the focus side. The one is Heider and Simmel's experiment on "the chase vs. following problem" (Heider & Simmel, 1944). They showed a film sequence to many observers. On the sequence you saw a square and a circle moving around with the circle always in front.

Now, the big question was: was the square chasing the circle or was it following it?

In reality, the square neither chased nor followed anything. To be able to chase and follow things is a mind achievement, and a square certainly does not have a mind. The observers, of course, "interpreted" the movements as either chasing or following, because of the tricky special arrangements. Foci that move in that way usually have minds and intentions, and the genesis of our mind makes it hard to avoid seeing intentions in dead phenomena that in a special arrangement are made to behave as if they had minds. When observers are confronted with real chasing and following in real focus persons, they, in fact, usually see correctly.

The other experiment was made by From (1953). In a setting similar to Heider & Simmel's, he showed a film sequence of a real person. This filmed focus person is performing a long series of *senseless physical movements*. From *allowed* his observers of the film sequence to describe exactly what they experienced. The observers, as it turned out, experienced a lot of intentions in the focus person. The observers did not get any restrictive instructions on the methodological side. They were allowed to interpret intentions in the focus person. They were not asked to do so, but they did so nevertheless. From concluded that, as observers, we are inclined to *put intentions into focus persons*. There were, of course, no right or wrong "interpretations" to be made, because the observers were let down on the focus side in the experiment. Focus persons usually do have intentions, and the genesis of our mind has taught us to see them. When confronted with a focus person who, in a special arranged kind of playacting, performs senseless behaviour not governed by real intentions, our observer mind is hard at work looking for intentions anyway.

From declares his research setting to be a phenomenological setting. On the method side you are, as observer, free to interpret whatever intentions you might experience; but on the focus side things are arranged so that no correct interpretations are possible. Conclusion: The observermind constructs the mind phenomena in the focus person.

Eysenck belongs to a school of psychology often called behaviourism, and From belongs to the phenomenological school. The remarkable thing is, that although these schools are strong opponents in methodology, they agree in rejecting intentions as real phenomena in an ontological way. The behaviourists restrict the observation of focus–intentionality by teaching the observer to reject experienced intentions. They perform the trick on the method level. The phenomenologists encourage the observer to describe at will what he might experience of intentionality in the focus; but they perform the trick on the focus level.

Both schools reject mind, or should we say, *the psyche*, as a focus phenomenon. A sad thing to be a psychologist with no psyche to study. (My doctoral thesis which bears the subtitle: "The Mystery of the Missing Person" refers to this sad situation in our branch of science (Schultz, 1988)).

Popper has an interesting viewpoint that supports the behaviouristic and phenomenological agreement about rejecting mind as a focus of interest. As mentioned earlier, he divides reality intro three worlds; mind is the second world. Popper is clearly a realist. He declares very strongly that all three worlds exist in an ontological sense. But he does not think that we are able to observe mind as focus phenomenon. In other words, he does not think that it is possible to see intentions in focus persons. With our minds we are, as observers, able to see the first world (physical phenomena) and the third world (mind–products), but not the second. The second world is what we use to see the other two.

Popper is clearly mistaken on this point; and he is certainly not supported in his viewpoint by psychological research with its tricky method and focus arrangements. I have made an investigation that shows how wrong he is, so let us turn to that.

To observe intentions when intentions are to be observed

This paper has accused the behaviourists of performing a trick on the method level and the phenomenologists of performing it with the focus.

My investigation was a kind of reversed trick. I used the behaviouristic focus material and the phenomenological method.

The focus material was a film sequence that I borrowed from an investigation made in a human ethological research design (Magnusson, 1980). (Ethologists and behaviourists differ in their view on focus–setting. Ethologists allow their focus material to be as complicated as life can be; behaviourists create experiments where variables can be controlled. Both schools have as a methodological rule the earlier mentioned prohibition against intention–description. Therefore the difference between the two schools is of no importance in our context, and for simplicity's sake we just call the material "behaviouristic").

In the film sequence the observer sees two children playing with a toy. Arrangements have been made to secure that only one child is able to possess the toy at any given moment. The film sequence as behaviouristic focus material is used to record the children's physical movements in the ten seconds that anticipate a shift in toy possession. The observer is forbidden to record intentions; he is instructed to stick to physical movements.

Nevertheless the children on the filmsequence have lots of intentions at work. For this reason I found the film excellent as focus material. Then I used the phenomenological method on it. I showed the film sequence to many observers and instructed them to report the children's behaviour just as it was experienced.

One of my main conclusions, and in fact *the* main conclusion in this context, is that *observers are very good at perceiving intentions correctly. The intersubjective problem is no bigger in observing real intentions than it is in observing real physical phenomena*.

Popper, Eysenck, From and all the other mind–reducing philosophers are simply wrong. Furthermore, it is very natural that they should be wrong. The genesis of our mind through millions of years has given us the ability to identify intentions. For two reasons: One is that the behaviour of our fellowmen is in reality governed by intentions; the other is that it is very important, for survival reasons, that we can see them. A secondary benefit of my investigation is a number of findings that indicate that human observers are much better in observing intentions than in observing physical movements. That means, more precisely, that it is easier for us to see what a fellowman is up to than to register his movements in time and space. We are practiced in the latter ability if we are behaviouristic disciples, but it is not easy for us to disregard intentions.

Why then is it so very widespread to think otherwise? Well, surely the answer lies in the history of science.

What was the finest achievement in early science three to four hundred years ago? It was to discipline the tendency of our observer–minds to see intentions. As mentioned above, it is important for human beings to be able to see intentions, and we have, in fact, a tendency to let this ability run away with itself when looking at focus material without intentions. People looking at a stormy thunder cloud are very apt to experience the cloud's intention – although in reality it has none. "Perhaps the cloud is very angry at me, because of my misbehaviour and rages against me."

In short: Seeing intentions in nature where no intentions are to be found is probably a price we have had to pay on account of the importance of being good at seeing intentions where they are to be found. Therefore the supporting philosophy of early science, positivism, made it a methodological imperative to sharpen and discipline the ability to see dead nature without mind–intentions. A reasonable imperative, indeed, because the dead material has no mind.

But the positivist philosophy ran amuck. It commanded us to continue to discipline our observer–minds when confronted with real focus–minds and to be persistent in our rejection of intentions. What phenomena really do have intentions? The answer is: (higher) life phenomena and their products.

There is thus a natural explanation as to why the positivist philosophy has been so successful in guiding natural science, and so harmful in guiding human science. In the first case, the prohibition of intention–ascription makes it possible to describe the focus phenomena correctly. In the second, the prohibition of intention–ascription insures that the focus phenomena will be described in the wrong way. It is therefore unfortunate that psychologists, following the positivist lead, have been apt to disregard intentions.

Perspectives

In my research I have dealt with the problems considered in this paper in a much more detailed way (Schultz, 1972, 1977, 1979, 1982, 1986a, 1986b, 1987, 1988, 1990, 1991). In this short paper it is not possible to give all points an elaborated argumentation, but five pressing questions can get some sketchy remarks and thereby conclude this presentation.

The questions are: 1) When is an interpretation correct? 2) Are phenomenologists wrong when they demand that we describe foci without using theory? 3) Is it always impossible to predict human behaviour? 4) What is the difference between interpretation and describing? And finally, 5) Has this paper avoided examples that are problematic for the main points?

Re point 1) When is an interpretation correct?

Well, this question is, in fact, not fair, because in science we have never been able to argue our identifications. They are evident, and that is all there is to say.

In natural science this has always been considered a question of the utmost triviality. How does the physicist manage to see a test tube? How does he manage to interpret the sign on his device as the numeral "5"? How does he manage to see that the litmus paper has turned blue?

He just does. Observations have never demanded epistemological considerations in serious science. *In principle* this is the same in human science.

How does the reader of this text manage to interpret the meaning and sense of the words? He just does it. How does he know that he is right? Well, he just knows when he is.

A correct interpretation has the same quality as a correct observation of a physical phenomenon. It is impossible to prove or disprove anything. So has it always been, and it is not fair to demand special reviews on these matters by human scientists. When an anthropologist gets insight into the meaning of a cultural ritual in a foreign culture, this insight will "appear" as a correct observation, and he will experience something like: "Oh, this is the meaning – now I understand!". When a psychotherapist and the focus person suddenly understand why the latter is washing his hands too much, they find themselves in a situation where the interpretation presents itself with the same kind of "obviousness" as the blue litmus paper.

Re point 2) Are phenomenologists wrong when they demand that we describe foci without using theory? They certainly are, although their critique of mainstream psychology runs along lines that to some extend corresponds to the errand of this paper. Let us listen to Giorgi (1983, p. 217):

According to phenomenological theory, one is to bracket all one knows about the phenomenon under consideration (especially scientific formulations) to experience and describe it freshly, and this reexperience and description is to take place in the attitude of the reduction, that is, one is to describe the meaningful presence to the phenomenon but, at least initially, to refrain from saying that it is the way it presents itself to be.

The difference between this phenomenological attitude and the one found in this paper is, in fact, the difference between subscribing to one of the mind–reducing philosophies or being a realist. This paper has claimed, from a realist stand–point, that things experienced are part of the actual reality. Phenomenologists think otherwise. They hold that foci of interest often are experienced in a way other than nature in reality is. I discuss this difference between phenomenology and realism a bit more in my answer to question five. At this point I limit myself to the main objection carried in this paper with the help of a few examples.

Imagine two people observing the same town. The one has lived there all his life and knows the town like the back of his own hand. The other is in the town for the first time in his life.

If we ask the first one to look at one of the streets as if he had no prior knowledge of the actual geographical realities, experience the street with fresh eyes just like the second, and "bracket all his knowledge", we certainly put him into an impossible observer position. The one with the highest theoretical knowledge of the town cannot help to have a pure immediate experience of the focus that *contains his knowledge*.

The same problem arises if we ask the reader of this paper to "bracket his knowledge of the English language" and experience the words here in the same fresh way the Chinese, who only knows Chinese, will experience it.

And what about the skilled anthropologist, who travels with her lay husband in a the very foreign culture she has studied for years. Will she be able to bracket her knowledge of this culture and see it in the fresh way that her husband does? Or what about the skilled therapist confronting some neurotic behaviour? Can he experience this without seeing his knowledge?

The answer to all these questions is no. We experience immediately the focus of interest in a way that always contains our theoretical knowledge. Popper (1972) and Leontiev (1975) are right on that point.

Re point 3) Is it always impossible to predict human behaviour? Well, we have already said that prediction is possible when our focus is a physical phenomenon. It is in principle not possible when the focus is intentionality, because intention involves freedom in choosing ways.

In natural science you always try to predict, and it is always a correct ambition. We know, of course, of situations in natural science where it is impossible to predict with certainty, due to the fact that there are too many uncontrollable variables. A meteorological prediction is the joke example here. In its strictest natural scientifical sense it is a scientific prediction to forecast the weather at five o'clock tomorrow at some geographical place; but it often fails.

In a way, one might think that psychologists are better at predictions. If you have a date with a girl at the time and the place where our unfortunate meteorologist failed to predict the romantic weather setting, the prediction that the girl will show up is probably much more secure. If you statistically count such instances, psychology might very well win the contest of being the more reliable science in prediction ability.

Anyhow, a misunderstanding should be avoided here. The psychologist is not predicting the consequences of natural laws at work. The prediction that the girl will come at the appointed time *makes sense*. Her behaviour is guided by intentionality, which means that she may let you down; and she surely has freedom in choosing ways. Nevertheless, people very often perform in an intentional meaningful way, and that makes prediction of future behaviour very often successful. This apparent "predictability" has, nevertheless, nothing to do with the kind of prediction we use when dealing with dead foci like high pressure in meteorology. The high pressure in a weather context may of course be "freakish"; but that is a metaphor covering an impenetrable richness in lawful variables. The girl, on the other hand, has the freedom of choosing to be freakish as a real focus quality. In psychology, Allport (1937) has given some consideration to this problem.

Re point 4) What is the difference between interpretation and description? In natural science we have a tradition that makes a distinction between description and explanation. Newton described the movements of the moon, and he explained the nature of this movements by pointing to the lawfulness in the movements.

This distinction works very well to a certain point. On closer inspection, it can be shown that descriptions formulated at later times include explanations formulated at earlier times. I mention this only in passing. In many ways it parallels the difference between experiencing on different theoretical levels (the problem dealt with under point 2).

In human science, the traditional distinction is between description and interpretation. This distinction is, however, very problematic. Do you describe what a person is up to, or do you interpret it? The most meaningful sense to be made out of the distinction is to say that an intention–description is intention observed on a low theoretical level, whereas intention–interpretation is intention observed on an advanced theoretical level.

Let us say that a skilled therapist and a lay person are confronted with the same bit of neurotic behaviour in a focus person. The first observer "describes" this as an overprotective, antiaggressive behaviour while the latter "describes" it as a kind, meticulous behaviour. The lay observer will probably call the skilled therapist's description an "interpretation". The natural scientist will probably call both descriptions "interpretations".

If we follow the classical Diltheyan tradition, *intention description is interpretation*, no matter on what theoretical level it is based. That is a good point to follow. It means that human scientists interpret their foci, while natural scientists describe and explain them. This means, simply, that interpretation is the observation of intentions in the focus of interest. It surely does not mean that interpretation is the enrichment of the observed world with observer–mind attributes.

In this way we can see that the controversy between the hermeneutical-psychoanalytical "intention–interpretation" and the phenomenological "describe–intentions–as–you–experience–them–immediately" disappears. The phenomenologically instructed observer cannot help but see intentions in his focus to the depth his theoretical level makes it possible; and the psycho–analytically instructed observer is only allowed to interpret intentions as long as he can observe them. (There is a popular misunderstanding about psychoanalysis that can be corrected here. People often think that such therapist are busy constructing intentions in their focus patients by using books that suggest such interpretations. Popular as this viewpoint is in movies and comics, it should be noted that a very important aspect in training a therapist is to teach him to stick to intentions that are observable).

Re point 5)   Has this paper avoided examples of experiences that are problematic to the main points? Well, to be honest, it has. In the following rows I have listed examples of the type this paper has used on the left. On the right I have listed examples that so far have been neglected.

a sea	a beautiful sea
a house	a home
a girl	a darling
an omelet	a favourite dish
a play	a joyful play
a country	a homeland
an overprotective mother	a repulsive mother

The examples on the left are foci of interest that have nothing to do with the observer. Observers may be able or unable to observe these foci depending on their theoretical level; but in our realistic way of thinking, the foci are in no way created by observers.

On the right hand side, however, we find phenomena that indisputably have something to do with some observer. Is this house a home? Well, maybe – if somebody *lives* there.

Human beings always live in a "Lebenswelt" (Husserl, 1954), and our experiences are in some way nothing but this. Nevertheless, only "in some way".

The examples on the right are the mind–reducing philosophers' favourite examples as arguments against the realism argued for in this paper. The phenomena here certainly point to both an observer and a focus. Take one of these constituting parts away, and the phenomena disappear.

Of course they do. Just as water disappears if you remove either oxygen or hydrogen.

Everything in this world is made of something, and it is in itself a material part of something bigger. And what is valid for everything is valid for water and human beings.

It is a triviality to say that the human being is made of material parts. For a long time in our culture we have had difficulties in comprehending what ought to be just as trivial – that human beings are material parts constituting something bigger than themselves.

The realistic point of view claims that everything that we can experience in this world is to be considered real, including phenomena that have an observer as a constituent material part. The examples to the right belong to this category. The examples to the left do not.

The phenomenologists have truly fought a commendable struggle to get phenomena consisting of observers and something else into the realm of science. But they have gone about it in a wrong way. Listen again to Giorgi (1983, p. 219):

...these "presences" are not a third reality between persons and things;...

Well, yes they are, just as water is a third reality between oxygen and hydrogen. The problem here, is that there is nothing special about mind. It is built of material, and it is in itself a material part of something bigger. If we reduce phenomena that are made of a person and a thing (a home for example) to its material parts (a person and a house), we open the way to reducing everything to its material parts. The next step is to reduce the house into bricks, cement and water, then water into oxygen and hydrogen, and little by little the whole world will vanish, and we end up with solipsism.

Let us, therefore, conclude this paper with some corrections to phenomenology that, nevertheless, include some appreciation of their good cause.

Some phenomena in this world (but by no means all phenomena) consist of an observer and something else. These phenomena are "made of" a person and a focus; they are *relations between* person and focus. Examples are given in the right hand row. When such phenomena are observed, things get a bit complicated.

If the observer of a right–row phenomenon is the same person as the person who is a material part of the phenomenon, the observer–experience could be called an *emotional* or *symbolic experience*.

If the observer of a right–row phenomenon is another person than the person who is a material part of the phenomenon, the observer is experiencing a real focus in which another person is material. Therefore the observer often points to the material person. (Examples: Is this focus a beautiful sea? – Yes, to my mother it is. Is this house a home? – Yes, my good friend Peter belongs there. Is this girl a darling? – Yes to Sam she is, he loves her. etc.).

And now the difficult one: If the observer of a right–row phenomenon is the same person as the person who is a material part of the phenomenon, *but places himself in an observer–position as another*, he can describe his own emotional/symbolic experience by pointing to himself as a material focus part. (Examples: Is this a beautiful sea? – Yes, I feel very allured by it; it symbolizes hidden depths beneath an apparent calm surface. Is this house a home? – Yes, I feel very attached to it, it symbolizes my family lineage. Is this girl a darling? – Yes, I love her very much, she symbolizes eternal erotic and motherly qualities. etc.).

The following can now be concluded: When phenomenologists conceive all focus–knowledge to reflect the observer–mind, they are simply wrong. It is a *mind–quality of the human mind* to be able to disregard the emotional/symbolic part of any observer–experience, and choose observer-independent qualities out there in the world as focus. We might call this kind of knowledge *categorical knowledge*. Observers are, of course, always "inside" their emotional/symbolic knowledge, but they are by no means enslaved by it. They can choose to disregard it. When phenomena that include some observer as a material part are chosen as focus, descriptions of such foci must, of course, always clarify who the involved person is.

When the involved person is engulfed in his emotional/symbolic knowledge, he just lives life fully.

When the involved person is somebody other than the observer, there is one person who lives life fully, and one who observes him.

When the involved person also is the one who observes and when he observes his own emotional/symbolic knowledge in a categorical way, *he is in a position to make phenomenological descriptions*.

My research points to this as the only viable phenomenological position, (Schultz, 1988, ch. V) because only here will it make good sense to talk about how things "seem" to me or how they "present themselves" to me. A psychoanalyst observing his own counter–transference in a therapeutical setting is thus an example of what should be called phenomenology. But, of course, any observer who chooses "his own relation to something" as focus is observing that kind of phenomenon that ought to be the exclusive phenomenological domain. Were this position the one and only way of "seeing things", the psychotherapist could never sort out what were his own intentions and what were the patient's; the anthropologist would never be able to sort out what were the real intentional history of this foreign culture and what was her own "cultural bias". Furthermore, it would become impossible to grasp the nature of the so called "traditional scientific observations".

References

Allport, G.W. (1937): *Pattern and Growth in Personality*, London.
Apel, K–O. (1968): Szientifik, Hermeneutik, Ideologiekritik, *Man and World,* 1, pp. 37–63.
Dilthey, W. (1913): *Der Aufbau der Geschichtlichen Welt in den Geisteswissenschaften*, Frankfurt a.M.
Engelsted, N. (1984): *Springet fra dyr til menneske*, Copenhagen.
Engelsted, N. (1989): *Personlighedens almene grundlag,* I & II, Aarhus.
Eysenck, H.J. (1953): *Uses and Abuses of Psychology*, Harmondsworth.
From, F. (1953): *Om oplevelsen af andres adfærd*, Copenhagen.
Giorgi, A.P. (1983): The Importance of the Phenomenological Attitude for Access to the Psychological Realm, In Giorgi, A.P., Barton, A. & Maes, C. (eds.): *Duquesne Studies in Phenomenological Psychology IV*, Pittsburg.
Habermas, J. (1968): *Erkenntnis und Interesse*, Frankfurt a.M.
Heider, F. & Simmel, M. (1944): An experimental study of apparent behaviour, *American Journal of Psychology,* 57, pp. 243–259.
Husserl, E. (1954): *Die Krisis der Europäischen Wissenschaften und die Tranzendentale Phänomenologie*, Haag.
Karpatschof, B. (1985): *Psykologiens gyldighed*, Copenhagen.
Katzenelson, B. (1989): *Psykens verden, i verden*, Aarhus.
Leontiev, A.N. (1967): *Probleme der Entwicklung des Psychisches*, Berlin.
Leontiev, A.N. (1975): *Tätigkeit, Bewusstsein, Persönlichkeit*, Stuttgart.
Magnusson, M. (1980): Cluster Analysis and Ethological (Component) Coding in an Experimental Study of Object–exchange in Childrens Dyads, Copenhagen, Ms.
Mammen, J. (1983): *Den menneskelige sans*, Copenhagen.
Popper, K.R. (1972): *Objective Knowledge*, Oxford.
Radnitzky, G. (1970): *Contemporary Schools of Metascience,* II, Göteborg.
Schultz, E. (1972): *Psykoanalytisk fortolkning og hermeneutik*, Copenhagen.
Schultz, E. (1977): *Drømmeforståelse og drømmeteorier*, Copenhagen.
Schultz, E. (1979): Psykologi, psykoanalyse og hermeneutik, *Symposion, 3,* pp. 32–51.
Schultz, E. (1982): Om erkendelsen af andres adfærd, *Psyke & Logos,* 1, pp. 55–94.

Schultz, E. (1986a): Søvn og drømme siden Lehmann, In Moustgaard, I.K. & Petersen, A.F. (eds.): *Udviklingslinier i dansk psykologi*, Copenhagen, pp. 220–241.
Schultz, E. (1986b): Intentionalitet, *Psyke & Logos*, 2, pp. 340–355.
Schultz, E. (1987): Seksualitet i almenpsykologisk belysning, *Psyke & Logos*, 1, pp. 135–151.
Schultz, E. (1988): *Personlighedspsykologi på erkendelsesteoretisk grund – lag*, Copenhagen.
Schultz, E. (1990): Det hellige i psykogenetisk belysning, *Psyke & Logos*, 2, pp. 217–236.
Schultz, E. (1991): Drømmetydning og realistisk hermeneutik, *Psyke & Logos*, 1, pp. 157–172.
Spencer, H. (1881): *The Principles of Psychology* 1–2, London.

A PLATFORM FOR MODERN DIDACTICS
IN A POSTMODERN SOCIETY – AND AN EXAMPLE

Mads Hermansen
The Royal Danish School
of Educational Studies

Changed social conditions, characterized, for example, by greater and greater technological refinement and impenetrableness, result in changes in the development of the person. According to Lucien Séve's personality theory, this also results in changed personalities.

The changes in personality can be described, for example, by saying that people find it necessary to live in a continuously greater number of separate modules or compartments with the individual human life split in two, between that which one must learn in order to be able to sell one's working power (a wage earner awareness and qualification), and that which one must learn to be able to live and consume (a leisure time awareness and qualification) – see the topological model of Séve (1975).

This division has significance for the possibility of being able to grasp one's total life situation. The consequence of this increasing splitting–up can be that one actually abandons the wish to assess life in its entirety, and instead seeks only to establish and justify the close and specialized relationship. One area in which this point of view has been emphasized is in the post–modernist debate of recent years.

Post–modernism holds that the age of the great narratives is past, and that the great unifying ideas are dead. This is one of the messages conveyed by Jean Francois Lyotard in his book *La Condition Postmoderne*, Paris 1979. An opposing point of view holds that the splitting–up results in an increased need to seek new methods of creating cohesion, claiming that the unifying relationships still exist but have become more difficult to establish. According to this point of view, there is no talk of these relationships being impossible for reasons of the constantly accelerating division, only that establishing them has become more difficult. Contrary to the post–modernist claim, this viewpoint does not maintain that the great story is dead. Rather it maintains that the great story has never existed as a definitive, true narrative. Like all other attempts at giving a comprehensive picture of human life, it has been ideologically infected and is thus only partly true.

Objects of this inquiry

– to increase the possibility of creating unity and collectivity through educational situations,

– to be ideology–critical and transgressive,

– to create a pedagogical platform for coping with the splitting up of life into compartments of wage–earning and leisure.

Insight – Consciousness

A slight detour via Köhler and Asch, combined with Engelsted's concept of human development, can bring us a step closer to our goals. My discussion will revolve around insight and consciousness as cognitive products (suprastructural psychological products, as Sève would call them), or here simply personality products. The Gestalt psychologist Köhler used the concept insight to characterize the chimpanzee Sultan's ability to see that which cannot be seen, i.e., a linking together of a series of possibilities which are not immediately apparent.

Sultan was capable of "realizing" that in order to be able to get to a banana which was hanging from the ceiling, it was not only necessary for him to climb onto a box, but also to move the box from its present location. In this situation Sultan was able to "see into" the situation, to grasp the meaning of it. He saw the possibilities available to him and he could work with them. One might say that Sultan established a relationship because he could see into it. This seeing into or insight is situation–defined. It is not historical in the sense that it is based upon knowledge of which one is conscious. Leontiev used the concept insight to characterize the last step in natural history, or in other words the highest form of cognition present among animals (and small children up to the age of 3 years).

Here, natural history is set face to face with history. The development of animals, i.e., the "survival of the fittest" discovered by Darwin, is related to natural history. The development of humankind is related to history, but with preconditions in natural history.

One of the important differences between these two is that within natural history the development and transfer of information from generation to generation are bound together by genes. This does not result in intergenerational transfers of learned knowledge, but nor is that the issue in natural history.

The main difference between insight and consciousness is then that insight is closely related to activity within natural history and conscious–

ness is related to activity involving trade and the exchange of benefits. Consciousness is closely related to societal realization as the way in which humans cope with survival.

I draw the consciousness concept from Asch, who in his investigation of *The Will for Thought* (1905) operates with a definition of consciousness as "the feeling for meaning and relations which are not given as content", i.e. not a context–bound but rather an abstracted understanding: A coherent understanding which is raised above or out of the concrete connection.

With the definitions of Köhler and Asch as my argumental basis, I will reserve insight as a concept for that process which is context–bound, and consciousness for that process which is synthesis–forming or generalizing within history, i.e., the story of human activity. Consciousness can not, however, be understood without a medium. The medium of consciousness is language.

This theory can be connected to the following model in which thinking, or cognitive activity, is conceived as taking place on three levels:

1. *The global level.* This is where things are obvious without further reflection. Things are conceived as they are and as they appear in front of us.

2. *The analyzed level.* As the result of a perceived problem one starts to reflect. While reflecting, orientation and coherence are more or less lost.

3. *The synthesis level.* Here one returns to the global level, but now with the ballast of analysis. We might call this the level of reflected globality.

Already here, one can perhaps claim that insight is associated with the global level and maybe the analysis level. But the concept 'insight' can only be selectively applied to the synthesis level, i.e., only in the occasion of the 'little synthesis' – the situation–bound synthesis.

In order to build the little synthesis into a larger one, it must be set in a medium that can encompass past, present and future. This is precisely what language can do. It is through language that consciousness is closely connected with synthesis, or ability to form a theoretical model for comprehension.

But a bit of concept clarification is still required before we can clearly distinguish between the roots of insight and consciousness.

Human activity can be divided into two fields: Social cooperation, which is individual *and* cooperative, on the one side, and societal activity on the other. The essential difference between the two types lies in the relationship of the subject to the product which is the result of the effort.

In social cooperation (also common among higher animals), the product goes more or less directly to the subject's own consumption. Social cooperation is, for example, hunting. Some do the clapping, and some bring down the prey. Even though we talk of a division of labor in a certain sense, all the subjects who participate in the hunt have a common object in what they do. The object is to bring down the prey. Although the clappers walk towards the animal, trying to frighten it away, the animal is still the objective of their actions. The animal is also the motive on the higher level of activity. In this way it can be said that the objective is the hallmark of the action, while the motive is the hallmark of the activity (Leontiev, 1981). The motive is the highest form of cohesive understanding. The activity is planned in light of the motive. Different objectives can lead to the motive's follow-up.

This can be illustrated as follows:

Social activity

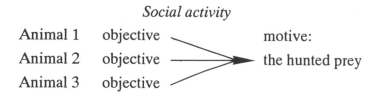

Animal 1   objective   motive:
Animal 2   objective   the hunted prey
Animal 3   objective

One can say that objective and motive are not separated in social cooperation. And naturally neither are they separated in individual activity. Those who make an effort are also those who enjoy the fruits of these efforts.

In societal activity, the product does not go to the subject himself, but to another or others in exchange for something else which is of importance, or that can be used by the subject.

I have earlier used the following example to characterize a societal activity (Hermansen 1987): A man repairs a puncture on his wife's bicycle, while the wife prepares the food. The man's motive – that which he wants to achieve – is to eat the food prepared by his wife. However, she has created the condition that he must mend the puncture (the trade) before he can get the food.

Consequently, the man's objective – what he does – is the mending of the puncture. Conversely, the wife's objective – what she does – is to make the food, while her motive – what she will achieve – is the mending of the puncture. Schematically, it looks like this:

Societal activity

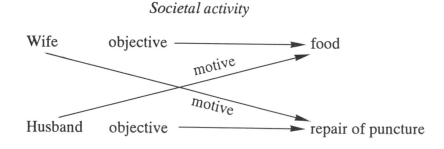

Wife   objective   food

motive

motive

Husband   objective   repair of puncture

In societal activity the one who makes the effort does not always enjoy the product of the activity. Sometimes he enjoys another similar product achieved by trade.[1]

The cognitive result of social cooperation is insight. The cognitive result of societal activity is consciousness. Insight is related to action (work) which is fulfilled when the subject by himself consumes the product (result) of the action (work). Consciousness is related to an action (work) where the product (result) is part of a trade where the product is given away or part of an exchange. The motive is very different. In societal activity the motive is maintained for a longer time. The process from the beginning to the end takes longer when you let the product of your activity enter into some sort of trade–agreement to get other products in return. In this way you may say that consciousness is stretched insight.

Utilization or profit

Trade offers the opportunity for utilization or profit–making because it is not certain that you get as much in return as you gave yourself (we know that from everyday experience in grocery shops, supermarkets, etc.). Thus it is that class differences, as well as consciousness, have their roots in societal activity.

Using Séve's (1975) terminology, insight is the cognitive result of concrete activity. Consciousness is similarly related to societal activity. Its roots lie in the necessity of yield. But paradoxically, the process of consciousness is weakened by the great complexity that exists among related societal activities within the highly specialized and developed capitalistic society. The more development, the more complexity. In model form it looks like this:

Cooperative or individual activity	Societal activity
Can be compared with concrete activity (Séve);	Can be compared with abstract activity (Séve);
The cognitive product tends toward	The cognitive product tends toward
Insight;	Insight or Consciousness;
Result:	↓ Result: ↓
Socialization.	Socialization or Societal realization.

---

1   The distinction between social cooperative activity and societal activity is inspired by Engelsted, see Engelsted (1992). Contrary to Engelsted, I have, however, chosen to view societal activity as basically an activity of exchange.

The concrete activities, especially those that comprise one's upbringing or socialization and are aimed at making one into a competent person able to manage in society, are insight–creating. That is fine as far as it goes, if we assume that the abstract activities are, in turn, consciousness–forming. But this is not always the case, because, paradoxically, even though con–sciousness–forming processes are closely connected to societal activities, the same processes tend towards more and more complexity. Therefore it becomes more and more difficult to both grasp the level at which you enter into societal activities and at the same time achieve a relative synthesis. If you only enter into the activity but fail to grasp the synthesis, the result is merely insight and not consciousness.

A pedagogical problem

This leads to the great problem of transcendence of insight, i.e., getting beyond mere insight. How is this accomplished? One possibility is through *utopian* work.

The advantage of working with Utopia in education is, of course, that it gives you opportunity to work both with the concrete activities (insight) and the possibility of transcendence (consciousness). Real societal realiza–tion is characterized at the same time by the possibility of coping with society and by the ability to criticize the basis of this coping.

At the same time we can attach socialization to the concrete activities and societal realization to the abstract activities. The main task is, of course, to cope with the splitting up of personality by expanding the opportunities for creating synthesis.

This splitting up has brought up needs for new connections between the subject and the products of his abstract activities, still from the point of view that these connections exist but that it has become more difficult to achieve cognitive synthesis regarding them. Under this point of view, the great story is not dead but simply hard to get to.

For all that, we can now describe in model form the pedagogic practice of creating transcendence opportunities between socialization and societal realization. This is important because socialization does not necessarily involve questions and criticism, while societal realization contains que–stions and criticism by definition. In pedagogic practice questions and criticism are considered the roots of consciousness.

The model forms the starting point, and the termination is ideal work or utopian work.

Concrete activity	Abstract activity
tends towards	tends towards
Insight.	Insight or Consciousness.
Result:	Result:
Socialization	Socialization – Societal realization

Ideal work or utopian work
The synthesis or transcendence.

Pedagogy can thus use ideal work or utopian work as its foundation. This may be effected, for example, by actively incorporating ideal utopian elements into the teaching. Examples of this work are future workshops (Jungk & Müllert, 1981) or the imaginary journey (Hermansen, 1988).

But other methods can also be shown. In the following I will give an example of ideal utopian work in practical pedagogy. But first, in order to get an overview of this area of practical pedagogy I will present a model.

The level model

If utopian elements are to be incorporated into the teaching, this can take place at numerous levels, in many ways, and with different objectives. The model depicts the three most important levels, by showing that the developed capacity to solve certain problems can be connected with:

1. An *intrapsychic level,* i.e., the capacity to recognize and adapt facts and emotions in relation to one's own life, and in this way to be actively capable of maximizing vitality in the context of individual activity.

2. An *interpsychic level*, i.e., the capacity to recognize and adapt facts and emotions in relation to one's life together with others (husbands, wives, children, friends, colleagues, etc.), and in this way to actively contribute towards maximizing vitality in the context of cooperative activity.

3. A *societal level,* i.e., competence to be able to recognize and adapt facts and emotions in relation to life as a member of society, and in this way contribute towards maximizing the vitality in the context of societal activity.

The objective for capacity development, as I have formulated it here, also includes a strong normative demand regarding active participation in life. Although there is not a consensus regarding this demand in the pedagogic debate, it is, however, part of the formulation of the objectives of the Danish 'folkeskole' as defined by the Primary Education Act, part 3, where it is stated:

> The school shall prepare the pupils for active participation and co-determination in a democratic society, and for co-responsibility in the solution of common problems. The education by the school and its overall everyday life must therefore be based on spiritual freedom and democracy.

Utopia and pedagogy

To work socio-psychologically with exercises in groupdynamics may have a utopian outcome. The following is an example of a *chain model* used in a class of pupils age 11 to 12 year.

Simon wants to spend an evening over at Peter's.	Asks parents. They say no.	Simon gets sulky and blows his top.	The parents get angry.
Simon is given house arrest for a week.	This makes him angry.	He crawls out of the window, runs over to Peter's and stays there	Simon gets afraid to go home.
Simon doesn't come home until 11.30 p.m.	The parents are now very angry.	Simon gets a good telling off. He is tired	He does not get his home-work done.

The children shall first complete the story, possibly both in a good and a bad version. The group are then given an empty chain model with the following task: "Use this model to describe a conflict from the school or from home."

The group shall now play out its own conflict (which is possibly later presented in assembly), and discuss how this conflict arose and developed (cause-effect), and in conclusion decide how they can come farther (from the conflict situation). Can the conflict be solved? If so, how?

Concerning the chain model, Anne Vibeke Fleischer (1974:203) says the following:

On the basis of the model, in small groups we analyze the cause–effect relationship. One of the actions (e.g., Simon not coming home until 11.30 p.m.), gives rise to an effect (the parents are now very angry). This effect in itself now becomes the cause of a new effect, which in turn becomes the cause..., etc. Here the conflict is carefully studied with regard to the question of why the conflict arises and of how it develops – what can be done in the individual links in order for the conflict to be solved.

This model can be applied from the 4th class and upwards, depending on content. The work has little to do with utopian work if it is used only socio–psychologically as a conflict analysis model. If, however, it is combined with the scenario method, it assumes in the best cases a double function, both as a tool for the solution of concrete problems and of socio-psychological conflicts, and it promotes consciousness of how one can work in an utopian–integrated manner for a future we partially determine by those choices we make here and now. The work takes place predominantly on an interpersonal level, and the contents are of a mainly emotional character. The chain model can also be applied working with community problems, i.e., relationships at a society level.

Consequently, it can be designed as a tool for consciousness work because it is a rehearsal in giving something away while not knowing what you will get in return, but knowing that you have to give away before you can line yourself up in the queue where you do get something back.

This is trade; it is based on consciousness and at the same time it is the basis of consciousness.

References

Engelsted, N. (1992): A Missing Link in Activity Theory, *Activity Theory*, *11/12*, pp. 49–54.

Fleischer, A.V. (1974): Konfliktløsning i klasseværelset (Coping with Conflicts in the Classroom), *Skolepsykologi*, 3.

Hermansen, M. (1987): *Personality teaching. Contradiction or Basis for Learning?*, Aarhus.

Hermansen, M. (1988): *Utopiarbejde* (Utopian Work), Aarhus.

Jungk, R. & N. Müllert (1981): *Zukunftwerkstätte. Wege zur Weiterleitung der Demokratie*, München.

Leontiev, A.N. (1981): *Problems in the Development of Mind*, Moscow.

Lyotard, J.F. (1986): *Le Postmoderne Expliquer aux Enfants*, Paris.

Lyotard, J.F. (1979): *La Condition Postmoderne*, Paris.

Séve, L. (1975): *Marxism and the Theory of Human Personality*, London.

ACTIVITY AND THE DISEMBEDDING
OF HUMAN CAPACITIES
IN MODERNITY

Arne Poulsen
University of Copenhagen

Putting man back on his feet

Human capacities or skills are usually exercised in a social or practical matrix. The disembedding of these capacities from their social or practical matrix is of far-reaching importance, as witnessed by the psychological consequences of the transition from informal education to learning-out-of-context (Scribner & Cole, 1973; Donaldson, 1978; Sinha, 1988, p. 164- 208), from oral language to written language (Olson, 1977; Säljö, 1988), from original work procedures to computerised procedures (Zuboff, 1988), and from traditional to modern forms of life (Ischwaran, 1975; Vernant, 1972; Baumeister, 1987; Logan, 1987; Giddens, 1990).

Many psychological theories, including the socio-historical school, tend to describe the ideal personal development by referring to the reflective attributes that human capacities acquire *after* their disembedding has taken place. In these theories, sometimes referred to as "endstage theories", the endstage of personal development is characterised by logical reasoning, discursive consciousness or metacognition. Highly developed persons are characterised by their use of propositions disembedded from communicative practice, by self-reflection and decentering of intersubjectivity, by their dissociatedness from guileless and prereflective cooperation, and by Kantian morality, with its demand for deliberate inhibition of the natural inclination to act out of sympathy and out of a prereflective morality of care. More often than not, psychological theories not only regard capacities disembedded from the practical and social matrix as the final stage of development, but even as our species character as humans.

The result is that these theories have turned man upside down, by defining the prereflective capacities as substandard and the reflective capacities as "the real thing", instead of characterising the reflective capacities as a resource that may develop under certain social circumstances.

I think that psychology can put men and women back on their feet without losing sight of the enormous importance of the reflective capacities that *some* people acquire under *certain* circumstances. Activity theory (AT) has played its part in this world–wide "intellectualistic fallacy", the upgrading of the reflective at the expense of the prereflective participation in the turbulent give–and–take of the world. Even so, I think that the concept of activity can be useful in the process of reconstructing the axiology of psychology by reformulating the normative questions about "What is up? What is better?" The concept of activity does, however, need some clarifications.

Activity

The advantage of the concept of activity is that it installs the primacy of the person, so the dualism between mind and body is eliminated, and it substitutes the primacy of ongoing activity, during which personal needs may arise, for a concept of a restful person who only becomes active when personal needs make it neccessary. Finally, the concept of shared activity is in accordance with a philosophy of the primacy of intersubjectivity and shared presuppositions, in opposition to the widespread solipsistic point of view, that intersubjectivity must be built on the basis of each person's reflective pondering about the meaning of the other person's behaviour. But the concept of activity is used in at least three different ways:

Sometimes the concept of activity means *any life–activity* of animal life–forms in general. Engelsted (1989, p. 55) has criticised this definition and argued convincingly that the use of the concept of activity at least should be restricted to life–forms with auto–kinesis, because these are the first forms about which it can be maintained that the object–subject relation becomes reversed, whereby a distinction can be made between activity and mere homeostasis (se also Tolman, 1991).

Sometimes the concept designates *the prereflective object–directed work–activity of human beings*. It is at this level that the three–level scheme of activity–act–operation emerges and, correspondingly, motive-goal–instrumental conditions.

In authoritative accounts of AT, the concept of consciousness is invoked so often that there is reason to identify a third use of the concept of activity. Davydov (1989) writes, that man makes his life–activity the object of his will and his consciousness (p. 53) and that man in his individual activity is conscious of himself as a social being:

> Since this individual's own activity becomes an object for his consciousness, when it is reproduced ideally, then he or she can look at, evaluate, and plan his or her activity as if at a distance, with other people's eyes so to say, in consideration of their needs, interests, and points of view (p. 57).

Davydov even invokes a double reflectivity:

> Consciousness is the person's reproduction of the ideal picture of his pur-
> poseful activity and, in this, the ideal representation of other people's atti-
> tudes (p. 60).

It is not very clear what task the word "conscious" performs in statements like these. It can be said to be trivially true, of course, that to know what one is doing, is to be conscious of what one is doing, as opposed to be doing it unawares or by mistake. The word "conscious", however, only came into languages like English and Italian around the beginning of the seventeenth century (Wilkes, 1988). In light of the obviousness of the notion of "conscious" it is interesting to find cultures, including our own culture until recently, that happily dispense with that notion. Aristotle managed to say a lot of sophisticated things about emotions, deliberation and reasoning without using any term that corresponds to "conscious", and he could do that because the lack of the term in the trivial sense was not felt as a need.

"Consciousness" is probably one of the vaguest terms in the humanities. Also Davydov's use of the term lacks precision. On the one hand he uses the term in statements like: "Man is conscious of himself as a social being". Does this mean that someone who is not conscious of himself as a social being is an animal or a zombie? That statement is only true, if "conscious" is used in a trivial sense, in a sense that doesn't imply reflectivity. On the other hand it is obvious that Davydov implies more than the trivial sense when he talks of consciousness as the ability to look at, and evaluate, one's own activity at a distance, with other people's eyes. What he implies is reflection, the non–trivial sense of consciousness. The fact that conscious-ness about own activity is mentioned so often gives reason to identify a concept of *reflective object–directed activity* in AT.

We should ask: When do people actually look at their own activity at a distance, in consideration of other people's points of view? When does a person's activity become an object for his consciousness in any non–trivial sense of that expression? Under special social and practical circumstances only, when cognition has to change from the prereflective to the reflective. It will be argued that certain cultural events, like migration and formal education, require the disembedding and change of personal capacities from the particular to the universal, from the local to the general, from the timely to the timeless, and from the oral to the written.

AT's invoking of the concept of reflection (as well as the cognitivist paradigm's concept of "mental representation") is rooted in the philosoph-ical tradition which views mind as a "Mirror of Nature" (Rorty, 1979). This tradition became full–blown in the beginning of the seventeenth century, at the same time as the word "conscious" came into the language. It is suggestive that the advent of the societal dynamism of modernity (to be defined p. 150) is often dated to the same period.

Prereflective object–directed activity, when combined with non–instrumental support of the development and welfare of other people (children and others you may feel responsible for)[1] probably amounts to far more than half of all human activity from 40,000 years ago till this day. It has always been the activities of people, who did not ask themselves philosophical questions about the social nature of their activity, that produced the bread, the cultural artefacts and the personal capacities that reflection could feed on when neccessary. The capacities neccessary for performing the prereflective and the person–oriented activities were, and are, as human and species–specific as any reflective or metacognitive activity.

To sum up: It is unacceptable 1) that AT uses three different concepts of activity, 2) that it does not distinguish between auto–kinesis and life in general, 3) that it has no place for vital or person–oriented activity, the direct support of the welfare and development of other persons, as opposed to instrumental activity. In addition to that, theorists of AT make an unhappy choice when they emphasize reflection so much. If AT does not describe prereflective activity as the standard, and reflective capacities as something that under particular circumstances may develop on the basis of prereflectivity, it will be difficult to distinguish it from "endstage psychology" where reflective capacities are considered the standard and prereflective activity is described as a substandard variant, the value of which should be measured by its distance from the end–stage. It will be difficult for AT to analyse the social psychology of the transition from prereflection to reflection, and it will be difficult to distinguish its concept of activity from the concept of action that Taylor has called "Cartesian" and "causal".

Taylor's account of Hegel's qualitative theory of prereflective action may enrich AT's concept of prereflective activity without blocking the way for the analysis of the psychological consequences of reflection and its socio–historical preconditions.

The qualitative vs. the causal theories of action

Taylor (1979, 1983) distinguishes between two theories of action, the qualitative theory, stemming from Hegel, and the causal theory, stemming from Descartes and/or the English empiricists (see H. Poulsen, 1991, for an interpretation of the significance of the qualitative theory for AT). In the following account and elaboration of Taylor's presentation of the two theo-

---

1   Non–instrumental work like food–gathering and taking care of children and the sick is a missing link in mainstream AT. See Engelsted, 1992, who distinguishes between instrumental and vital activity, and Sondergaard, 1991, who distinguishes between object–oriented and person–oriented activity. The absence of vital or person–oriented activity makes AT seem somewhat androcentric.

ries I shall refer to two strands of theory, rather than to theories developed by actual historical persons, since these two strands of theory are more relevant to present day concepts of activity than their originators. I shall not distinguish between action and activity, since Taylor's texts do not specify this distinction. Furthermore, it is my impression that the distinction is only neccessary in accounts of the intricateness of the societal nature of activity (se Engeström, 1991, for a slightly different point of view). The qualitative theory of action has nine characteristics, the first eight of which I find useful in AT.

1) In the qualitative theory there is primacy of activity before consciousness. In the causal theory there is primacy of consciousness before activity. The consequence of the qualitative theory is that intelligence is not a tandem operation of first considering prescriptions and then executing them. Intelligence is the skillfulness of the performance, not the rules that precede the performance.

2) In the qualitative theory there is primacy of the person before mind and body. In the causal theory there is primacy of either the mind or the body. The primacy of the person has been defended by Wittgenstein, Ryle (1963), Strawson (1959), and Rorty (1979). In present day philosophy, theories that do not accept the primacy of the person are in a pretty bad way.

3) In Hegel's qualitative theory there is a principle of embodiment: Thought must express itself in a medium. This principle forshadows Vygotsky's ideas about the intricateness of the relation between thinking and speaking, and D.R. Olson's dictum, that "intelligence is skill in a medium" (personal communication, but see Olson, 1977). It also recurs in Sinha's claim that "Knowledge is inscribed, not just in brains and nervous systems, but also in artefacts, institutions, practices, symbols, utterances and languages" (Sinha, 1988). In causal theories with their gap between body and mind, the thinking process is barred from making use of external media.

It seems an overstatement to claim that thinking must become embodied in a medium, but it is true that abstract reasoning attends to information crystallized in external media (and sentence meaning), whereas practical reasoning attends to empirical information (and utterance meaning).

4) In the qualitative theory personal needs arise during ongoing activity. In the causal theory personal needs are the precondition for the onset of activity.

5) In the qualitative theory self–knowledge is mediated by world–knowledge. In radical causal theories it is the other way round. This makes the qualitative theory sociocentric and/or mundocentric, and the causal

theories idiocentric[2]. Among the socio- and mundocentric theories of self-reflection are Brentano (1874), James (1890, p. 339), Baldwin (1899), Cooley (1902), McDougall (1908), Mead (1934, p. 174), Ryle (1949), Geertz (1973) and Gergen (1977). However, the abundance of sociocentrism has not made it a winner. The ideology of idiocentrism and the supposed transparency of the self is part and parcel of modern folk-psychology and western "indigenous psychology" (Heelas & Lock, 1981). As will be argued later, the ideology of idiocentrism may be considered part of the hidden agenda of modernity.

6) In the qualitative theory the mental is the interiorisation of former, embodied activity. This principle is expressed in Vygotsky's statement, that the intra-mental derives from the inter-mental, and in Wertsch' theory about the development of self-regulation (Wertsch, 1979, 1985; Diaz, Neal & Amaya-Williams, 1990).

7) On the qualitative view, action may be totally unreflecting. However, we may eventually become reflectively aware of the means and ends of our activity, and to become reflectively aware ("conscious" in the non-trivial sense) of our activity is sometimes a prerequisite for being able to act in new ways. There is no place for this qualitative shift in the causal theory, where action is seen as neccessarily caused by the conscious will of the mind, and non-conscious action only deserves the name of body-movements.

8) According to the principles 3, 5 and 6, reflectivity or self-perception, rather than a basic condition of our lives, is something that can only be brought off in a medium. To become aware of one-self is to become aware of the medium that one's activity is embodied or expressed in.

9) In Hegel's terminology action or activity is "the Spirit". The development of the Spirit has three stages: Prereflection, with original subject-object unity. Then reflection, with subject-object opposition. This stage corresponds to Kant's stage of personal autonomy, where the person disentangles from his natural inclination in order to act on the basis of conscious principles. And finally the reuniting of subject and object, with total transparency of the self, whatever that is.

There are two simple ways of understanding the third stage. Either it is needed for putting the person back into activity after reflection has taken place, or it is needed because developmental stages always come in threes.

The idea of "the development of the Spirit" is reproduced in the Marxist idea of mankind (or the working classes) becoming the subject of history, and it recurs in the notion (also found in AT) of history as a common progress of human thought towards decontextualised rationality: the universal, the general, the timeless and the written. This idea has been charac-

---

2   The distinction between mundocentrism, sociocentrism and idiocentrism maps Heidegger's distinction between Umwelt, Mitwelt and Eigenwelt.

terised by Toulmin (1990) as "the hidden agenda of modernity", by Wertsch (1990) as "the privileged position of the voice of decontextualised rationality", by Walkerdine (1990) as "the mastery of reason", and by Lukàcs (1971) as "reification".

From eternity's point of view it may be true that there really is a common history of humanity, consisting of the universal Spirit coming to know itself in the developmental endstage of decontextualised rationality. It even may be true that there is a metaphysical Jacob's Ladder, leading to Hegel's Prussian state, to the socialist Utopia, or to the hypermodernity of capitalism. But from many people's more local points of view, the privileged position of the voice of rationality looks more like imperialism, economic expansion, bureaucracy, and cosmopolitan ethnocentrism. To these people the very idea of a "humanity with a common goal" seems nonsensical. The issue is political, of course, but it is entangled with AT's problem about historicity vs. diversity (see Engeström, 1991). I am convinced that we can dispense with the notion of universal development without violating the qualitative theory of action. The notion of universal development of activity or thought seems more related to the causal or Cartesian view of action than to the qualitative view, because it is part of the implicit dogma, that man is destined to rise above his own nature – with women lagging a little behind.

Disembedding

The qualitative theory of action ridded of the notion of the development of the spirit reinstates development where it belongs: on the level of actual persons and groups of persons.

Engeström (1986) has defined personal development as a process of moving from Bateson's Learning II (learning sets) to Learning III (reflective awareness of learning sets). According to this definition, the prereflective acquisition of learning sets is not development, only learning. This is an unneccessarily narrow definition of development, but it pinpoints that particular kind of personal development where the disembedding of previously acquired personal capacities are required.

Donaldson (1978) has given a beautiful description of what formal education requires children to be able to do.

> By the time they come to school, all normal children can show skill as thinkers and language–users to a degree which must compel our respect, so long as they are dealing with "real–life" meaningful situations in which they have purposes and intentions and in which they can recognise and respond to similar purposes and intentions in others. – These human intentions are the matrix in which the child's thinking is embedded. They sustain and direct his thoughts and his speech, just as they sustain and direct the thought and the speech of adults – even intellectually sophisticated adults – most of the time. (p. 121).

Donaldson gives the name "human sense" to the personal skills embedded in a practical and social matrix. When functioning within the bounds of human sense, the person is largely unaware of the functions themselves. He is conscious of the outer world and of his goals in that world, but he does not reflect upon the means that he uses for coping, and he cannot call them into service deliberately when the compelling purpose has gone.

But education requires the child to be able to do just that – to call the powers of his mind into service at will in order to tackle problems which are presented in abrupt isolation by some other person whose purposes are obscure.

This process of disembedding, of moving beyond the bounds of human sense, is a natural potential, but it does not come about spontaneously. It is a natural potential in that most human beings are amazingly open to the challenge of disembedding, once they have learnt to identify the context-markers that say: Concentrate, not on coping, but on your means for coping. But there has to be a challenge for the disembedding to occur, and a time–out from the immediacy of the demands of practical life. On a societal scale, the challenge and the time–out are provided by what will later be characterised as events of taking–off from traditional ways of life and modes of production.

Below is a list of examples of human sense and their disembedded versions. They will be elaborated p. 153.

Human sense	**Disembedded skills**
Cognition–communication:	
Problem–solving in a practical context	Logical reasoning
Communicative skills	Metalinguistic awareness
The medium is transparent[3]	The medium is objectified
Mutual knowledge (the tacit presupposition that "we know that ––")	Iterative reflection (the reflection "I think that she thinks that I think that ––)

---

3   Attention is paid to that which the medium is about. When the medium is objectified, attention is directed to the medium.

Personhood – motivation – morality:

Care–morality	Kantian morality
Personhood by being part	Personhood by autonomy
of a social network	and independence
Social motivation	Separation of intrinsic
	and extrinsic motivation

Perception:

Attention to	Attention to
the perceptual world	the perceptual field
Mundocentric attitude	Idiocentric attitude
Topophilia[4]	Placelessness

It is important to notice that the advent of disembedded skills in history does not mean that disembeddedness acquires a life of its own above the level of individuals. The term "disembedded skills" is to be understood as a short way of saying "personal skills for disembedding from the immediate demands of the practical context of human sense". Attention to *utterance meaning* belongs to the immediate demands of the practical context of communication. Logical reasoning and metalinguistic awareness is the skillful performance of disembedding from this demand in order to pay attention to *sentence meaning*. Kantian morality and Kantian autonomy is the capacity to disembed from the immediate demands of the practical context of care–morality.

Modernity has resulted in an acceleration of the development of disem–bedded capacities. Apart from the problems of defining modernity and disembeddedness, this statement is not very provocative. It is somewhat more controversial to assert that the disembedded capacities are part of the very dynamism of modernity.

Modernity

According to Giddens (1990) "modernity", as a first approximation, can be defined as "modes of social life or organisation which emerged in Europe about the seventeenth century onwards and which subsequently became more or less worldwide in their influence". Unfortunately, Giddens never ventures a second approximation. The reason for this hesitation may be,

---

4   Under conditions of topophilia people feel attached to places and buildings, they are per–
    ceived as existing in their own right. Under conditions of placelessness, places and buil–
    dings are anonymous, they are perceived as existing only by virtue of what they can be
    used for.

that his theory cannot distinguish properly between causes and consequences of modernity.

From the way modernity is described by Giddens and by Eisenstadt (1983, 1987) the following definition can be proposed: Modernity is a societal dynamism caused by capitalism[5], industrialism, surveillance, monopoly of military power, and sovereignty of nation–states.

Capitalism is a system of commodity production, centered upon the relationship between private ownership of capital and propertyless wage labour. *Industrialism* is the use of "inanimate sources of material power in the production of goods, coupled to the central role of machinery in the production process" (Giddens, 1990, p.56). *Surveillance* is the accumulation and control of information about and supervision of subject populations. The *monopoly of military power* within territorially precise borders and with links to industrialism is distinctive to the modern state. "*The sovereignty of nation–states*" refers to the far greater concentration of administrative power, inwardly and outwardly, in nation–states than in their pre–modern precursors, "in which it would be relatively meaningless to speak of "governments" who negotiate with other "governments" in the name of their respective nations" (Giddens, 1990, p. 58).

The *societal dynamism* of modernity consists of events of taking–off from what is usually called traditional modes of production and forms of life. Giddens and Eisenstadt do not attempt to make a complete list of such events, but the following list can be proposed as a working model: Typical events of taking–off are urbanisation, migration, formal education, loosening of boundaries between social classes, labour unions, extension of franchise, development of social services, bureaucracy, secularisation, and extension of new media (money, literacy, etc.). These events may be called cultural steps. The combined impact of such steps is called a transition from Gemeinschaft to Gesellschaft (Tönnies, see Durkheim, 1972, p. 146), from mechanical to organic solidarity (ibid.), from static to dynamic society, or from tradition to modernity (Inkeles & Smith, 1974).

At this point, the sociological accounts of modernity often mention some phenomena said to follow in the wake of modernity. Giddens (1990) calls these phenomena *the separation of time and space, the development of disembedding mechanisms, and the reflective appropriation of knowledge.* The empirical and logical status of these concepts in Giddens' theory remains unclear, possibly because they refer to psychological as well as sociological events, and because Giddens wavers between describing the events as causes of, part of, or consequences of modernity. The concepts certainly make sense, however. Precisely because the concepts can be regarded as referring to psychological events, to actual persons' activities, attitudes and capacities, events that decide what people can contribute to

---

5   Or, theoretically, scientific socialism with plan–economy.

the expansion of the mode of production, it can be determined whether they are causes or consequences of modernity. *They are both.*

In the first place they are consequences, of course, caused by the cultural steps mentioned above: urbanisation, extension of new media, etc. But in the second place they become prerequisites for further modernisation, in the same way as technological knowledge, competent, disciplined labour and need of money are consequences of industrialism and become prerequisites for further industrialisation and further recruitment of labour. As human prerequisites for further modernisation, the personal capacities for time–space separation, disembedding, and reflectivity become part of the forces of production, they become integrated elements of the modes of production of modernity. This makes them change from consequence into cause. Therein lies the dynamism of modernity, and it is this dynamism that psychology loses sight of if the reflective and disembedded capacities are taken for granted as some kind of species character of human beings.

Thus, we end up with a distinction between the causes of modernity (capitalism, industrialism, surveillance, territorial monopoly of military power, and the sovereignty of nation states) and the dynamism of modernity, of which the development of personal disembedded capacities form part. What caused the causes of modernity in the first place, fades into Celtic mists – or peculiarities of the Jewish–Christian tradition.

The regimentation of human sense

Giddens has identified three sources of the dynamism of the transition from tradition to modernity, but he has not specified where they belong. Do they reside in the air or in "society as such" or in individual minds? From the point of view of the qualitative theory of action, the answer is that these dynamisms are something that may happen to activity under conditions of certain cultural events.

The separation of time and space refers to the conditions under which time and space are organised so as to connect presence and absence (Giddens, 190, p.14). For the majority of the population in premodern cultures, time was always linked with space. No one could tell the time of day without reference to other socio–spatial markers: "When" was connected with "where" and with natural occurrences. Each activity had its place and time. Time was connected with space and place "until the uniformity of time measurement by the mechanical clock was matched by uniformity in the social organisation of time. This shift coincided with the expansion of modernity and was not completed until the current century" (op.cit. p. 17).

Giddens does not give much empirical fullness to his concept of time-space distanciation. This can be remedied, however, by connecting the concept with Tuan's (1974) concept of *topophilia* and Relph's (1976) concept of loss of topophilia, i.e., *placelessness*. Topophilia is people's affective connections with their material surroundings, their rootedness to those specific places where they are destined to work and die, their tacit acknowledgement of the non–exchangeability of these places. In premo–dern societies the rootedness often manifested itself in a non–arbitrary relation between the person and her name, persons were named after the place or the house they belonged to, or after their craft[7]. This corresponds to the way human sense usually works: Human sense tends to see the rela–tion between things or persons and their names as non–arbitrary. The opposite of topophilia is placelessness (Relph, 1976). Placelessness refers to more than the sentimental concepts of rootlessness or homelessness, as used in characterisations of "the homelessness of the modern mind" (Berger, Berger & Kelner, 1973). According to Asplund (1983) some topographical spots are anonymous, like a gas–station, the corridors of a block of offices, or a motorway. A motorway is constructed, not for motorists, but for motoring. They are not places in their own right, they are only there for some purpose. Relph (1976) argues that the price of moder–nity is a gradual loss of places to attach to. By way of definition, it can be said that the topophilous perspective is mundocentric, the placeless per–spective idiocentric[8].

The development of disembedding mechanisms refers to the "lifting out" of social relations from local contexts of interaction and their restructuring across indefinite spans of time–space. Giddens intends the word disem–bedding to "capture the shifting alignments of time and space which are of elementary importance for social change in general and for the nature of modernity in particular" (1990, p.22). Giddens appoints two disembedding mechanisms to be of particular importance in the development of modern institutions. The first one consists of *media of interchange* that can be passed around without regard to the specific characteristics of the indivi–duals or groups handling them. These media bracket time and lift transac–tions out of particular milieux of interchange. Giddens mentions the use of money in terms of credit and debt, but the spread of desituated knowledge is of similar importance. The second disembedding mechanism is *expert systems*, i.e., systems of technical accomplishment or professional expertise that organise large areas of the environments in which we live today. We rely on expert systems when we plan our actions, when we drive a car through the night, when we raise our children, and, in the time of AIDS, even when we make love. Giddens does not make it clear why the reliance on expert systems is a disembedding mechanism. I suppose expert systems

---

7   This still happens in niches of modern societies. It is important not to underestimate the extent of premodern niches or sociotypes.

8   Since Leibniz, one of the early philosophers of modernity, the doctrine of "the identity of indiscernibles" (the idea that things are identical with the sum of their attributes) has been prevalent in Western philosophy. See Strawson (1971) for a critique of the doctrine, which, if true, would make the placeless perspective the only possible one.

promote disembedding because reliance on them replaces situations where you have to confide in actual persons you relate to, and because advice from expert systems is used as the reflective basis for reforming social practices.

The reflective appropriation of knowledge: All human beings routinely "keep in touch" with the grounds of what they do. All forms of social life are partly constituted by actors' knowledge of them.

> But only in the era of modernity is the revision of convention radicalised to apply (in principle) to all aspects of human life.-- What is characteristic of modernity is – the presumption of wholesale reflexivity – which of course includes reflection upon the nature of reflection itself (Giddens, 1990, p. 39).

Time–space separation, disembedding and reflectivity can only contribute to the development of the forces of production if the regimentation of human sense succesfully results in the formation of the disembedded skills listed p. 148. The regimentation of human sense on the individual level is a particular instance of personal development. But the ideological function of psychological theories, AT among them, lies in their upgrading of the regimentation of human sense, in their describing the transition from pre-reflective to disembedded skills as the only real kind of development, or, to use Giddens' terminology, in their "presumption of wholesale reflexivity".

Psychological theory and the hidden agenda of modernity: Communication–cognition

The examples of human sense and their disembedded versions, listed p. 148, are clustered under three headings: Cognition–communication, personhood–motivation–morality, and perception.

There are three different attitudes to the question: Is the acquisition of the disembedded skills of communication–cognition an instance of personal development? One attitude is: Yes, and the prereflective skills are only a preparatory step to the development of disembedded skills. This attitude is implicit in end–stage theories like Piaget's. A second attitude is: No, all acquisition of skills only applies to those contexts in which the skills are learned, so the acquisition is only learning, not development as such. Therefore all skills are embedded. A third attitude is: Yes, the acquisition of disembedded skills is one possible kind of development among many, but human sense remains the foundation of human reasoning. The first attitude is idiocentric, wheras the second attitude fails to distinguish between the fact that people's activity is always embedded in a social context and the fact that people in conditions of modernity are often required (and find it increasingly easy) to disembed and detach from the immediacy of the demands of the practical context of human sense. The third attitude is

activity-centered. The activity-centered approach to cognitive development and disembedding may be exemplified this way:

If I show a child below a certain age three apples and two pears, asking:
"Are there more apples or more fruits?" the child will answer: "Apples".
Now the child is one point down for lack of class-inclusion and logical
reasoning. The child is said to be *preoperational*. The next day I am walking in the countryside with a friend past a group of grazing cattle. I ask:
"Are there more heifers or more cows?" My friend, a little proud to be able
to identify the heifers, answers: "It looks as if there are more cows". My
mischieveous reply is: "No, there are more heifers, for the cows are also
heifers". But can I put my friend one point down for lack of class inclusion
and logical reasoning? No, because my trick results in a lot of heated logical reasoning about my offence against a fundamental principle of communication, that speech should be used in its transparent form, so the
attention can be directed towards that which the speech is about. My friend
even concludes by putting *me* one point down for using speech in its objectified form without indicating a context-marker that tells: "Here is a situation where you must step back from speech and objectify it by focusing
your attention on speech itself, not on what the speech is about".

Thus, there are three preconditions for scoring points on a scale of logical (or propositional) thinking: The metalinguistic skill to use speech in its
objectified form, the ability to identify the context-markers indicating
whether speech should be used in its objectified form, and the general
proneness to obey the context-markers. What the experiment with the
preoperational child shows is not that the child lacks a cognitive mechanism, class-inclusion, but that she lacks one, two or three of the preconditions mentioned[9].

The distinction between failure to show class-inclusion and failure to
use speech in its objectified form is in total agreement with the empirical
evidence. When encouraged to demonstrate class-inclusion in transparent
speech (e.g in a dialogue where the two partners attend to that which the
speech is about), relatively young children can speak in accordance to
class-inclusion rules (Markman & Siebert, 1976; Siegel et al. 1978;
McGarrigle et al. in Donaldson, 1978; Rogoff, 1990).

Human sense uses transparent speech. Transparent speech does not sus-
pect that a person might ask a question of which he knows the answer, nor
that he might state something that is evident. In tests of logical reasoning,
human sense, therefore, looks for a communicative intention where there is
only guile. It is this guilelessness of transparent speech that is scored as
lack of logical reasoning. But why is it, that the ideology of modernity has
downgraded transparent speech of human sense to the extent, that it has

---

9   The same applies to experiments showing prelogical thinking in adults in traditional soci-
    eties.

become almost invisible in theories of cognitive development? The main reason is probably that the cultural steps listed p. 150 have resulted in a theoretical graphocentrism that makes us see speech as if it consists of bits of a written text. A second reason is that people who cannot use objectified speech are barred from some of those niches of modernity that give access privileges and power.

Even in linguistic theories of conversation, graphocentrism has made transparent speech invisible. Sperber & Wilson's (1986) theory is an excellent demonstration of the importance of relevance for communication and cognition. But instead of defining relevance as a relation between new information and a shared activity or a shared interest, relevance is defined as a relation between new information and reflective knowledge held by each of the participants. The last definition is true for non–standard situations where the participant is trying to figure out what on earth the other person is trying to say, for which reason she has to objectify the other person's speech. It is not true for standard situations of transparent speech with mutually shared presuppositions, consisting of mutual tacit knowledge. It may well be that non–standard situations of communication flourish in modernity, but they are still non–standard.

The dynamism of modernity encourages the personal development of logical thinking, theoretical concepts, and metalinguistic awareness. But modernity's regimentation of human sense is accompanied by the hidden agenda, that human sense is something that development has to overcome.

Humanism and the hidden agenda of modernity: Personhood–motivation–morality

In European humanistic tradition there is a strong tendency to define the hallmark of being human by such concepts as independence, autonomy, and control of the natural inclination to act in compliance with the connectedness to other people, whereas this connectedness is regarded as belonging to a sub–human or otherwise inferior level. This tradition is understandable in the light of history's mass production of cruelty and suppression, often justified by invoking perverted distortions of the concepts of human sense, connectedness and group–solidarity.

The upgrading of independence and the depreciation of the inclination to feel connected to other people is evident in Kant's philosophy of ethics and in the psychology of ethics following Kantian principles. In Kant's point of view, inclination and duty have as little to do with each other as nature and that in man which rises above nature. Only when a person follows duty and liberates himself from social inclination does he act morally. The categorical imperative implies an injunction to distance oneself from the particular in the situation. If we are faced with a person in distress we must distance ourselves from the particular person's particular sufferings in order to see the person as a representative of humankind and our own act as a display of the social institution that consists of helping people. The ability to control one's own inclination to attachment, compassion and sociability is what Kant calls *the autonomy of the will* (Kant, 1925, p. 56–63). Enlightenment, Kant said, is man's acquisition of autonomy and reflectivity, i.e. his dismissal of his tendency to let himself be guided by others (Kant, 1965, p.1)[10].

This attitude, the dismissal of one's own social responsivity, may be appropriate when we are responsible for political, judicial or bureaucratic decisions. But it is somewhat absurd to demand that we should look upon our own kids and other persons for whom we have a personal responsibility, as mere representatives of humankind, and look reflectively upon our actions of care as mere representatives of a social institution that consists of helping people in general. However, Kohlberg's measurement of the level of moral reasoning does just that. Abstract reasoning is rewarded, involvement in the particulars of the moral dilemmas are punished (Gilligan, 1982). The absolutation of the Kantian imperative is questioned so rarely that it seems reasonable to regard the demand for Kantian morality as part of the ideology of modernity and part of the ideological blindness to vital or person–oriented activity (as opposed to instrumental activity, see p. 144). The Kantian imperative is a warning against high–handedness and exploitation of human beings in modernised forms of life. But as regards activities less modernised, the imperative introduces an unsavoury, if not unethical, reflectivity.

A similar instance of the same agenda is the upgrading of insensitivity to other people's opinions and the depreciation of compliance in experiments displaying the Asch and Milgram effects. The persons in these experiments yield to social pressure, but this yielding is part of what Asplund (1987) has called social responsivity, being an "elementary form of social life". In the psychology of infant development it is an established fact that precisely this social responsiveness or *social referencing* in the infant is a prerequisite for the development of ability to share an interest in something with somebody, and thereby a prerequisite of the ability to act as a person (Trevarthen,1980; Feinman, 1982).

A third instance of the agenda is the blindness towards *social motivation*, a kind of motive in which there is no opposition between intrinsic motivation and extrinsic motivation. Koch (1956) correctly claimed that Western culture is dominated by an instrumentalistic view of motivation, according to which all our acts are seen as means towards an end. This means–end bias has resulted in an exaggeration in psychological theories of the importance of extrinsic motivation. Writing in the fifties, however,

---

10   I have not tried to retouch the androcentric form of such English expressions about "man" because this form nicely conveys the androcentrism of their content.

Koch could not know that the sixties and the seventies were to abound with concepts of intrinsic motivation. In Maslow's theory, extrinsic motivation was called deficit motivation and intrinsic motivation was called growth motivation. In pedagogical psychology it is still a beau ideal that learning should be intrinsically motivated, even though it is admitted that extrinsic motivation often is more effective. This schisma between extrinsic and intrinsic motivation, between naturalism and humanism, has resulted in a blindness towards the positive and development–supporting elements of motivation that have their origin in the person's being part of a social group, motivation to achieve in the eyes of those with whom you have common goals. When exerting themselves to the utmost during monotonous football training drill because of respect for the coach and the team spirit, boys cannot be called extrinsically motivated. Their fervour contradicts that. Nor is their motivation intrinsic. The drill would be point-less without the coach's appraisal, the collectivity, and the matches lying ahead. The same applies to the work of the faculty members of a university. Personally I am not ashamed to admit that I would take less pains in my work, if not for the opinions of my colleagues. Football boys and faculty members alike, their exertions would lose the impetus if there was no social motivation. Who can honestly claim that social motivation is sub–standard?

The dynamism of modernity encourages the development of Kantian autonomy, one of the most exquisite products of human history. But the dark side of this product is the hidden agenda, that autonomy can only be reached by overcoming social responsivity, social motivation, and the pre-reflective morality of care.

The ideological blindness towards the virtues of social responsivity, social motivation, and the morality of care is part of an androcentric world scheme that makes us forget that the rise of modernity depended on the division of labour between men and women, between paid labour and unpaid labour, and between activity that was noticed and activity in obscurity.

Perception and cosmopolitan life

Since Descartes, Western epistemology has been obsessed with the distinction between that which is "out there" and that which is "before our minds" and with the notion that we can only infer that which is out there from that which is before our minds. Descartes' gap between the inferentially known and the immediately known was to be the outset of a genre which includes "Berkeley's phenomenalism, Kant's transcendental idealism (...), James' "world of pure experience", Ayer's notion of minds and physical objects as "logical constructions", and so on" (Rorty, 1982). Ryle (1949) started a revolt against the dominance of the idea that information about the real world can only be inferred from information about what is experienced, by claiming that the two kinds of information are the same, that there is no-thing before our mind apart from that which is "out there". By denying the existence of a special category of first-order knowledge stemming from the mind's awareness of itself, Ryle contradicted modernity's presumption of wholesale reflexivity.

> The radical objection to the theory that minds must know what they are about, because mental happenings are by definition conscious, or metaphorically self-luminous, is that there are no such happenings (Ryle, 1949).

Ryle was probably right in his dismissal of the epistemological priority of that which is before our minds as opposed to that which is out there. Per-haps he was even right in dismissing the category "before our minds" altogether. This should not, however, lead to the conclusion that there is no meaningful distinction between a mundocentric attitude, the perceptual attention to the things themselves, and an idiocentric attitude, the percep-tual attention to the way things present themselves to us. Ryle's main point, that the perception of the real world does not consist of inference from the experience of the world, recurs in Gibson's perceptual realism, where the perceptual *world* does not emerge by way of inferences from the pictorial appearance, the sensation or the perceptual *field*, but is developmentally prior to the perceptual field. In other words, Gibson critisised mainstream theories of perception for giving logical and developmental priority to reflectivity, the inferencing from the perceptual field, instead of looking for the abundance of information in the perceptual world, ready to be picked up by the perceptual systems.

Gibson relegated the concept of sensation and visual field to the status of a psychological curiosity (Gibson, 1952, 1959. For a different point of view, see Boring, 1952). But he overlooked the fact that societal changes during the last, say, 150 years may have changed attention to the visual field from the status of a psychological curiosity to a perceptual attitude that an increasing amount of people have to take on, and have gained the possibility of indulging in, for an increasing amount of time. Somewhat roughly, the following capacities can be clustered:

On the one hand the prereflective perceptual skills that guide us around in the world during our daily activities, making us attend to "that which is out there", the perceptual world, the things and places and events as we see them when we are guided by human sense, with a mundocentric attitude, or sometimes even with topophilia. During prereflective perception there is no Cartesian "doubling of the world". To say that the mundocentric attitude is prereflective, does not imply that the person does not reflect on the goal of her activity, only that she does not reflect on the process of information pick-up.

On the other hand the reflective perceptual skills that allow us to attend to "that which is before our minds", the perceptual field, the information we get when we attend to the way the things present themselves to us, when we distance ourselves from the things and events, when we adopt an idiocentric attitude, or when we look upon things with perceptual skills that are disembedded from practical activity. This perceptual attitude results in a Cartesian doubling of the world.

Mammen (this volume) distinguishes between the perception of historical properties (with perception of the numerical identity of things) and the perception of universal/natural properties (with the perception of qualitative identity). The former kind of perception, according to Mammen, is a perception of "selection–categories", the latter a perception of "sense–categories". Both kinds of perception are fundamental to human perception, but only humans can perceive historical properties, selection–categories and numerical identity.

If Mammen's distinction is valid, reflective perception, according to the argument presented here, is the willed adoption of a perceptual attitude that centers on the universal/natural properties of things, by making an effort to see them as identical with the sum of their attributes (see footnote 8) or as identical with the way they present themselves to the perceiver.

During the last 150 years a number of societal events have neccessitated, and made possible, the refinement of the reflective perceptual attitude: The advent of fast means of transportation that gave people the possibility of attending to the landscape as a perceptual field swiftly passing by, as opposed to the mundocentric attitude, where the perceiver moves about in a static world. Photochemical and magnetophonic recordings of picture and sound. The fin–de–siècle changes in art with the increasing emphasis on the appearance of things. The advent of modern movie technique that neccessitates a sophisticated distinction between the medium and that which the medium is about. The frequent time–out from practical activity. The efforts of scientific positivism to translate historical properties into natural/universal properties. The demand for meta–cognition in modern life. And, finally, the advent of psychology, helping people to acquire an increasingly mediated relation to the world. The idiocentric attitude may be related to the widespread disease of modern life, sometimes called narcissism, that makes people tend to pay more attention to the way they are affected by things and events, than to the actual nature of these things and events.

These cultural possibilities and demands have given adults and children access to new capacities and experiences. But the dark side of the advent of these capacities is the tacit message, that appearance and authenticity are the same. A tacit message, but spelt out and worshipped by postmodernists like Andy Warhol. According to Gitlin (1986, p. 158), the consumer in postmodernity is left with images and "the sheer ejaculatory pleasure in the play of surfaces". Some people bewail this situation, others (e.g, Bau-drillard, 1990) seem to delight in it. Postmodernity, in this sense, is not a successor of modernity, but a delight in the consequences of modernity's upgrading of the idiocentric perspective, combined with a blindness to the practical realism of prereflective, mundocentric perception.

Personal development and acculturative stress

Sometimes cultural changes do not result in personal development, but in acculturative stress. Berry (1980) has defined acculturative stress as the disorganisation or even disintegration of behavior that often accompanies social and cultural change. He cites studies for having shown that immigrants in host countries with culturally plural societies (those pursuing integration policies) have less acculturative stress than immigrants in non-plural societies (those pursuing assimilation policies, where the immigrants are forced to adapt uncompromisingly to the cultural standards of the host country).

The concept of acculturative stress can be used to characterise the dangers of taking part in cultural changes. One important cultural change is the demand for bilingualism in large population groups. True bilingualism (or additive bilingualism) has been shown to be accompanied by increased metalinguistic awareness and logical thinking. But subtractive bilingualism (the situation when the child has to function and learn abstract concepts in the second language while her mother– tongue is excommunicated) inhibits cognitive development (Poulsen, 1992)[11]. The positive element in additive bilingualism is probably the translatability between the two languages with its cross–lingual language base, the ideal point of departure for the personal development of desituated knowledge and formal operational thinking. The cognitive deficiency accompanying subtractive bilingualism and the excommunication of the mother–tongue is the prototype of acculturative stress.

Other kinds of acculturative stress are created by the demands for self-reflection, sometimes resulting in narcissistic behaviour. The demands for logical thinking, sometimes resulting in parrot–talk and pseudo–logical thinking. The demands for objectifying the medium (film and television especially), sometimes resulting in a situation, often claimed to be common among youngsters, where the medium becomes non–transparent, a fetish so to say, resulting in a lack of ability to attend to that which the medium is about. The demands for Kantian morality, which ought not to result in the forfeit of the morality of care. And the demands for attending to the

---

[11]   This situation is sometimes called semilingualism, a somewhat misleading term because it purports that the deficiency is part of the child's language development as such, rather than the cognitive situation underlying it.

appearance of things, resulting in the perverted message of post–modernity, that appearance and authenticity are the same.

Which is more important, psychologically and politically: Personal development or the dangers of acculturative stress and loss of personal integrity? Dewey used the term inauthenticity for acculturative stress in formal education. To him inauthenticity was worse than lack of knowledge. Perhaps he was right. But then, such topics call for empty rhetorics and inauthentic speech, the parrot–talk of the learned.

Conclusion

Modernity is not an epoch, but a societal dynamism that transforms some of the skills of human sense into disembedded skills, thereby changing the consequences of modernity into causes of modernity by rendering possible the expansivity of modes of production. The disembedding and regimentation of human sense is a special case in the overall picture of the potentials of human beings. Modernity, and psychological theory with it, has depicted the regimentation of human sense as if it were the essence of what it is to be human. This hidden agenda of modernity has resulted in a downgrading of human sense and prereflectivity, a downgrading that may turn out to add to the vulnerability of modernity itself.

References

Baldwin, J.M. (1913): *History of Psychology*, vol. 2, London.

Baudrillard, J. (1990): *Revenge of the Crystal*, London.

Baumeister, R.F. (1987): How the self became a problem, *Psychological Review*, 52, pp. 163–167.

Berry, J.W. (1980): In Triandis, H.C. & Brislin, R.W. (eds.): *Handbook of Cross–Cultural Psychology*, vol. 5, Boston.

Boring, E.G. (1952): Visual perception as invariance, *Psychological Review*, 19, pp. 141–148.

Brentano, F. (1874): *Psychologie vom empirischen Standpunkt*, or *Psychology from an Empirical Standpoint*, London.

Cooley, C.H. (1902): *Human Nature and the Social Order*, New York.

Davydov, V. V. (1989): *Udviklende undervisning*, Copenhagen. English edition: Problems of developmental teaching, *Sovjet Psychology*, 1988, XXX.

Diaz, R.M., Neal, C.J. & Amaya–Williams, M. (1990): In L.C. Moll (ed.) *Vygotsky and Education*, Cambridge.

Donaldson, M. (1978): *Children's Minds*, Glasgow.

Eisenstadt, S.N. (1983): *Tradition, Change and Modernity*, Malabar.

Eisenstadt, S.N. (ed.)(1987): *Patterns of Modernity*, London.

Engelsted, N.(1992): A Missing Link in Activity Theory?, *Activity Theory*, 11/12, pp. 49–54.

Engelsted, N. (1989): What is the psyche and how did it get into the world? In N. Engelsted, L. Hem & J. Mammen (eds.): *Seven Danish Contributions*, Aarhus.

Engeström, Y. (1991): Activity theory and individual and social transformation, *Activity Theory*, 7/8, pp. 6–17.

Engeström, Y. (1986): The zone of proximal development as the basic category of education, *The Quarterly Newsletter of Comparative Human Cognition*, 8, pp. 23–42.

Feinman, S. (1982): Social referencing in infancy, *Merrill–Palmer Quarterly*, 28, pp. 445–470.

Geertz, C. (1973): *The Interpretation of Cultures*, New York.

Gergen, K., In T. Mischel (ed.)(1977): *The Self*, Totowa.

Gibson, J.J. (1952): The visual field and the visual world, *Psychological Review*, 59, pp. 149–151.

Gibson, J.J. (1959): In S.Koch *Psychology. A Study of a science*, New York.

Giddens, A. (1990): *The Consequences of Modernity*, Cambridge.

Gitlin, T. (ed.)(1986): *Watching Television*, New York.

Heelas, P. & Lock, A. (eds.)(1981): *Indigenous Psychologies*, Oxford.

Inkeles, A. & Smith, D.H. (1974): *Becoming Modern*, Cambridge, Mass.

Ischwaran, K. (ed.)(1975): *Education and Individual Modernity in Developing Countries*, New York.

James, W. (1950): *The Principles of Psychology*, vol. 1, New York.

Kant, I. (1925): *Grundlegung zur Metaphysik der Sitten*, Leipzig.

Kant, I. (1965): *Ausgewählte kleine Schriften*, Hamburg.

Koch, S. (1956): Behavior as "intrinsically" regulated, In *Nebraska Symposium on Motivation*.

Logan, R.D. (1987): In K. Yardley & T. Honess (eds.): *Self and Identity*, New York.

Lukàcs, G. (1971): *History and Class Consciousness*, Cambridge, Mass.

Mammen, J. (1992): The elements of psychology, *This volume*.

Markman, E.M. & Siebert, J. (1976): Classes and collections, *Cognitive Psychology*, 8, pp. 561–577.

Mead, G.H. (1934): *Mind, Self and Society*, Chicago.

Olson, D. (1977): From utterance to text, *Harvard Educational Review*, 47, pp. 257–281.

Poulsen, A. (1992): Bilingualism, cognitive development, metalinguistic skills and modernity, *Proceedings of the International Conference of Barcelona on Multilingualism in Europe*.

Poulsen, H. (1991): *Conations*, Aarhus.

Relph, E. (1976): *Place and Placelessness*, London.

Rogoff, B. (1990): *Apprenticeship in Thinking*, New York.

Rorty, R. (1979): *Philosophy and the Mirror of Nature*, Princeton.

Rorty, R. (1982): Contemporary philosophy of mind, *Synthese*, 53, pp. 323–348.

Ryle, G. (1963): *The Concept of Mind*, Harmondsworth.

Säljö, R. (ed.)(1988): *The Written World*, Berlin.

Scribner, S. & Cole, M. (1973): Cognitive consequences of formal and informal education, *Science*, 182, pp. 553–559.

Siegel, L.S. et al. (1979): Evidence for the understanding of class inclusion in preschool children, *Child Development*, 49, pp. 688–693.

Sinha, C. (1988): *Language and Representation*, Harvester.

Sondergaard, D. M. (1991): Person related and object related activity (in Danish), *Psyke & Logos*, pp. 305–319.

Strawson, P. F. (1959): *Individuals*, London.

Taylor, C. (1979): *Hegel and Modern Society*, Cambridge, Mass.

Taylor, C. (1983): In Fløjstad, G. (ed.) *Contemporary Philosophy*, vol. 4, The Hague.

Tolman, C. (1991): The critique and development of activity theory in Denmark, *Activity Theory*, 7/8, pp. 56–58.

Trevarthen, C.V., In Olson, D. (ed.)(1980): *The Social Foundations of Language and Thought*, New York.

Toulmin, S. (1990): *Cosmopolis*, New York.

Tuan, Y. (1974): *Topophilia*, Englewood Cliffs, N.J.

Vernant, J.-P. (ed.)(1972): *Psychologie comparative et art*, Paris.

Walkerdine, V. (1988): *The Mastery of Reason*, London.

Wertsch, J.V. (1979): From social interaction to higher psychological processes, *Human Development*, 22, pp. 1–22.

Wertsch, J.V. (1985): *Vygotsky and the Social Formation of Mind*, Cambridge, Mass.

Wertsch, J.V. (1990): In L.C. Moll (ed.): *Vygotsky and Education*, Cambridge.

Wilkes, K. V. (1988): In A. J. Marcel & E. Bisiach (eds.): *Consciousness in Contemporary Science*, Oxford.

Zuboff, S. (1988): *In the Age of the Smart Machine*, Oxford.

CONCEPTUALIZING FUNDAMENTAL SOCIAL PROCESSES.

The path to the comprehension of entrepreneurship?

Ole Elstrup Rasmussen
University of Copenhagen

'Big is beautiful' has for years been the favourite proverb of the successful American economy and still is. But in recent years it has been shown that the huge corporations are in fact losing jobs while the smaller are gaining influence on the labor market and on the economy at an accelerating pace. That goes for public institutions as well. From 1974 to 1984 American economy grew by 24 million jobs, but in the same period the largest businesses lost about 4 million. (Drucker 1985).

> "Ah," everybody will say immediately, "high tech". But things are not quite that simple. ... Only one or two out of every hundred new businesses – a total of ten thousand a year – are remotely "high tech", even in the loosest sense of the term (op. cit. p. 3).

High tech provides the excitement of the headlines, but no single area is the centre of prosperity. Businesses and corporations pop up anywhere. And, argues Drucker, entrepreneurial activities are the reason why.

In Europe the entrepreneurial drive is not as marked as in the USA – with Britain as a possible exception – but knowing the concordance between the American and the European economy and the impact of new trends from abroad, there are reasons to believe that entrepreneurial activities in the coming decade will be emphasized by the government as well as the industry. In Denmark entrepreneurship has been put on the political agenda, one of the reasons being that of the vast unemployment problems, and financial and advisory support has been applied to enterprising persons in the attempt to stimulate the growth of small industry.

The exponential increase in the amount of scientific studies carried out within the field of entrepreneurship is in congruence with the practical interest in the implementation of entrepreneurial activities.

Among those working in the field of entrepreneurship, myself included, it is the general position that the future development of society is heavily depending upon entrepreneurial activity. The scientists and practicians generally agree that entrepreneurship primarily is about *change*, but after that, the agreement comes to an end. It has been discussed what the entrepreneurial activity changes in society – is it products, financial support, ways of trading or forms of organization – and whether the causes of the changes are to be found within the field of individual abilities, or if they are of a social or of a political/economical nature? These differences of opinion, however, have not been settled.

As the concept of change in general and the change of society in particular for years has been a subject of major interest in my own theoretical research, it has been natural for me to examine if my reflections could be implemented within the field of entrepreneurship and by that perhaps help to decrease the opacity of the discipline.

The state of the entrepreneurial discipline

The often, stated idea that there should exist an unique and rare individual talent for entrepreneurial activity goes far back in history. Ever since the French economist Say in the beginning of the 19th century defined the entrepreneur as an agent who unites all means of production and shifts economic resources out of an area of lower into an area of higher productivity and therefore greater yield, it has been discussed whether it was possible to encircle the specific traits of the individual causing this special economic activity. If it was possible to locate the gifted ones, it should be easy to support them and to let them loose on the economical opportunities in order to raise the wealth of the nations.

This belief has brought about a vast amount of scientific studies, but none of them has been able to show any concrete evidence for the assumption that the entrepreneur should be of a special breed. Gartner (1988, p. 47) cites Cole for saying:

> My own personal experience was that for ten years we ran a research centre in entrepreneurial history, for ten years we tried to define the entrepreneur. We never succeeded. Each of us had some notion of it – what he thought was, for his purpose, a useful definition. And I don't think you're going to get farther than that (Cole 1969, p. 17).

Gartner himself concludes after a thorough examination of more recent theories and empirical studies:

> 1. That many (and often vague) definitions of the entrepreneur have been used (in many studies the entrepreneur is never defined); 2. There are few studies that employ the same definition; 3. That lack of basic agreement as to 'who an entrepreneur is' has led to the selection of samples of

'entrepreneurs' that are hardly homogeneous. This lack of homogeneity occurs not only among the various samples listed, but actually *within* single samples. For many of the samples it could be said that variation *within* the sample is more significant, i.e., it could tell us more than variation between sample and the general population; 4. That a startling number of traits and characteristics have been attributed to the entrepreneur, and a 'psychological profile' of the entrepreneur assembled from the studies would portray someone larger than life, full of contradictions and, conversely, someone so full of traits that (s)he would have to be a sort of generic 'Everyman' (op. cit. p. 57).

Having analyzed quite a few studies not examined by Gartner, I must agree with him. Nothing indicates that the road to knowledge of the field of entrepreneurship goes through the search for individual traits.

But what about the economical angle? The field of entrepreneurship is in spite of everything inseparably connected to production and market. The economical theories have, however, been unable to incorporate the field of entrepreneurship in their fundamental assumptions. As Casson puts it:

> The basic problem is that as yet there is no satisfactory account of the economic *function* of the entrepreneur. It is apparent both to the historian and the contemporary observer that entrepreneurs have an important role in the market economy. Yet orthodox theory provides no room for the entrepreneur. For all the economic functions that need to be performed are already performed by someone else (Casson 1982, p. 13).

The problem within economic thinking, if there is one, originates in theories as those of Smith and Ricardo who assumed a state of perfect market equilibrium deriving from the competitive interchange between numerous economical roles such as property owners, workers, investors etc., a market where individual differences were equalized. If changes should occur, they had to be initiated elsewhere. They could not be of an economical nature. Neoclassical theories of economy have not altered anything in respect to the understanding of the part the entrepreneurial activity should play according to these theories. They have, as Casson says, left the initiative to psychology and sociology.

As the Marxist economic thinking has emphasized the aspect of change, entrepreneurship could have been expected to be a major subject within this school of thought. But although Marx vigorously criticized the classical theories – for not being able to explain the emergence of surplus value, among other things – and heavily emphasized the development of the productive forces as a necessity and the main reason for the changes within the political economy, he never succeeded in conceptualizing how these productive forces were developed and changed. He gave an economical reason for the necessity of change namely the intensive competition on the market, but he was never able to substantiate how the development actually took place. Neomarxist theories have, to my knowledge, not even tried to conceptualize how the development of the productive forces takes place.

The field of entrepreneurship does not seem to exist within the economical theories founded on the philosophy of dialectical and historical materialism.

The attempt to solve the problem of entrepreneurship by means of psychological concepts seem to have failed, and the few attempts of conceptualizing the field within an economical frame of reference do not seem to have found an answer to the question asked.

Peterson (1980) agrees that the poverty of theories within economics in respect to entrepreneurship is immense, and points out that the only way to solve the problem is by returning to the old master himself: J.A. Schumpeter, who in the thirties argued that entrepreneurship was neither rooted in common individual traits nor in economic processes in their classical sense, but should be conceived as a special activity, which could be characterized as 'creative destruction'.

Peterson is not the only one who has tried to elaborate further on the theories of Schumpeter in the hope of finding a social solution between the economical processes and the individual abilities. The social activity approaches look most promising, primarily because they do attempt to focus on what actually happens during an entrepreneurial occurrence. The weakness of conceptualizing the field of entrepreneurship in this manner is the partiality of the scientists for the successful and great events. They often use the importance of an occurrence as the decisive factor for categorizing an activity as entrepreneurial. By that they overlook the generality of the phenomenon and make entrepreneurial occurrences into rare events. Consequently they end up with the assertion that the rare events demand rare personal abilities. Furthermore it seems as if the theories here, like those produced within the individual frame of reference, do have a tendency to diversify to a degree that makes it impossible to gain a clear picture of the concept of entrepreneurial activity and of the actual practice involved. The reason for this predicament is evidently an absence of basic concepts. Even the most thoroughly worked out theories like Drucker's (1985) and the most elaborated recommendations like Peters' (1988) lack some fundamental reflections on the conceptual foundation of these theories and recommendations.

Questions to be answered

If the question, "Who is an entrepreneur?" is the wrong question to put, as Gartner claims, then the right one must be: "Why is it the wrong question?". And if the economists haven't been that interested and successful in conceptualizing the field of entrepreneurship, we must ask if there is a reason why? And if the social theories of entrepreneurship do not have basic concepts, we must ask if such ones could be provided?

I think that the answers to these questions – that are necessary for the developing of the field of entrepreneurship into a scientific discipline – are rooted in the reflections on the substance of social activity.

What I hope to accomplish in the following sections is to argue: that the question about the existence of the special faculties of the entrepreneur must be wrong, because the most fundamental abilities that have been ascribed to particular individuals are general human qualities: that the question of why the economics has not been able to contribute to the conceptualization of entrepreneurship is caused by the fact that entrepreneurial activity is of a social and not of an economical nature. And finally that it is possible to produce basic social concepts which demonstrate that entrepreneurial activity is a social activity which does not differ in any essential way from other social activities.

In the attempt to do this I shall first try to rough out the framework of the basic social processes, for later on to be able to return to the question of the entrepreneurial activity.

The social processes

I will initiate the search for the basic social processes by mentioning the problem of *scaling* in the differentiation between individual, social and political/economical processes.

Looking for instance at a landscape from above, we will discover that the density of the population is a significant precondition in the formation of cities, and – looking closer – that heavily populated urban areas are literally incubators for organizations. Pennings (1982) has shown that the number of organizations born in an urban area are positively depending on 'chaos'. The birthrate of organizations increases whenever old structures break down. Humans can obviously not live without being organized.

But it also holds true, that the movement from 'chaos' to organization will be perceived and conceptualized quite differently according to how close we are to the phenomena. We can discuss how humanity gets organized in economic and political terms as well as in social and individual. Therefore it seems that the distance from the phenomena is decisive for those arguments we actually put forward in order to conceptualize the genesis and existence of these phenomena.

This point of distinction brings up the question whether the differences in arguments are due to real strata in human existence or originate from the scaling, i.e., are caused by the observational distance itself? This question is not easily answered. But as far as I can see, it is necessary to distinguish between the political/economical processes and the social processes. Where the social processes are the essence of mankind, the political/economical processes are the way in which the social processes unfold according to the law of competition, supply and demand, cultural trends etc.

How this unfolding actually takes place is not the subject of this paper, but it is, in my opinion, essential to stick to the assumption that the fundamental social regularities are the preconditions of political/economical processes, their vital energy so to speak. Social processes do exist without political/economical processes, but can, however, be determined by these processes.

My point of departure then is the assumption that the social processes are the fundamental ways in which humanity exist and that the political/economical processes are based on these processes although commanded by different laws, e.g., the law of supply and demand. I think that the essential social processes are few in number, but also that these few general social processes *generate* the diversified social world.

I further think that the distinction between social and individual processes has its origin in the scaling only, where the distinction between political/economical and social processes reflects a fundamental difference. This means that the fundamental social and individual processes, in my opinion, belong to the same stratum and that the social and individual processes are congruous. Naturally I shall return to this congruity later.

In the search for the fundamental types of social or individual processes, I believe to have found three – *canalization, correlation* and *combination* – the main purpose of which is resource processing – and a derived fourth, control.

It is of course possible that further social processes could be found, but I actually think that the human basis, from which organized processes spring in the shape of control, are made up of the three social processes mentioned and only these three processes.

Because of the difficulties in catching smoothly ongoing processes it is close to impossible to describe and therefore also to conceptualize these processes. In order to get a closer look we have to freeze and cut up the event into sequences as illustrated in figure 1 for example. We have to transform the process into a *structure*, which consists of *relating functions*.

It is essential to notice that as long as we try to gain knowledge of a phenomenon as a process, we are not able to grasp the functions and the relationships between these functions, i.e., the structure, and when we look at a phenomenon as a structure, the process seems to vanish. It is the same phenomenon we try to conceptualize and each type of knowledge can be true in its own sense, but our ability simultaneously to handle the two ways of analysis is limited.

The reason why I prefer to use the term 'function' instead of person in the *structural analysis* is that a person can unfold several functions simultaneously. A function establishes a simple relationship to another function.

A *person* can establish more relationships at the same time; perform more than one function simultaneously. This complex relating is called to act.

In the *analysis* of processes I want, in a similar manner, to make a distinction between process (matching the simple relationship) and the activity (matching the complex relationship). An *activity* can include more processes at the same time. The distinctions could be systematized as illustrated in the diagram below.

When I therefore talk about person and act, I refer to coexisting functions and relationships i.e., coexisting structures. This means that the person encompasses more functions simultaneously and that the act consequently embraces several relationships at the same time. When I talk about activity I refer to coexisting processes. The acting person(s) are then the structural equivalent to the activity. The acting person(s) are an activity looked upon in a structural manner.

These differentiations might seem a bit pedantic, but too few and too broad concepts do often result in an ambiguity, which can be much more confusing than a larger number of concise concepts!

	Structural analysis	Process analysis
Simple	Relating Functions	Process
Complex	Acting persons	Activity

The canalization process

The first social process is called canalization. As illustrated in figure 1 this process by which something moves from A to B can be described by the functions A & B, the relationship between the two functions and the content, expressed by hatching.

In the social processes it is important to notice that the functions are always represented by individuals. Although we in everyday language with regard to canalization do not distinguish between for example the organization Red Cross sending a shipment of blankets to a refugee camp in Sudan and a kind old woman giving an ice cream to a child, each canalization is always executed by a singular function. There is for instance always a last function in Red Cross that performs the actual handing over of the blankets, even if the blankets eventually have gone through many hands, i.e., other canalizations, before it reaches the end user.

In any case the important point is that a function A transfers *resources* to B (*transference*), where B appropriates resources from A (*appropriation*), and that no resources can be augmented or in other ways changed by canalization alone.

I shall return to the concept of resources later. For now it is sufficient to point out that resources are either *ideas* – knowledge and values – or *objects* to which ideas are attached. An object is not just a material thing but something that includes ideas of the thing. An object is humanized matter so to speak. It is matter that has been included in the human life and thus become an object. It is also essential to notice the concordance, that exists, in this way of thinking, between the processing of object resources and idea resources. There are differences, of course between objects and ideas, but fundamentally material and ideal resources are processed in the same manner.

In spite of the concordance between the processing of objects and ideas, it is still possible to differentiate between canalization of ideas on the one hand and canalization of objects on the other, because of the different *out-comes* of the process. Because of their respective nature no one will, for instance, be any poorer by making ideas available for somebody else, while anybody parting with an object will lose this for good. But the two different types of processes are essentially identical.

Canalization of objects   **Canalization of knowledge**

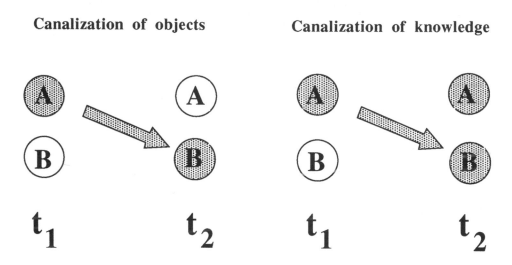

Figure 1. Canalization of resources

Not being poorer by parting with ideas does not, however, imply that they are canalized unrestricted among functions. The competitive position of a corporation, for instance, can hinder an entrepreneur in getting relevant information on lucrative markets. The corporation simply tries to *control* the ideas by preventing its spreading beyond its limits.

I shall return to control and limits in connection with the question about organization and personality. What is important here is to realize that the function somehow can be in control of the transference of resources. Likewise the function can be in control of the appropriation of resources. Even though a teacher takes great pains in transferring ideas to the pupil, it is not certain that the pupil wants to appropriate these ideas.

Naturally canalization is a way in which an individual can increase his or her ideas or possessions free of charge, so to speak, but the more essential significance of the process is that of being the actual creator of human history.[1] The essence of humanity is characterized by the ability to transfer ideas from one generation to another and thus accumulate knowledge.

The correlation process

The second social process has to do with exchange. The most common example of correlation is that of buying and selling, i.e., trading on the market by simple exchange of objects. In this way goods are being redistributed, which is a main purpose of correlation. But this is not the essence of correlation. Correlation is essentially about generalization through equalization.

Figure 2 illustrates that the function A *sends* a resource to B at the same time as B sends a resource to A. B *receives* what A sends and vice versa. But it also shows that this exchange takes place within some sort of frame of reference, represented by the big unhatched arrow.

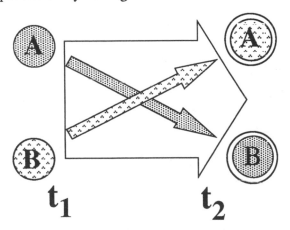

Figure 2. Correlation of resources

---

1 The genesis of canalization – the most overlooked of the social processes – is, as shown by Engelsted (1992), very likely the key to the understanding of the transition from the animal world to the human life form.

Whenever we buy and sell, for instance, we exchange different objects, but during this exchange we do at the same time *equate* these objects in what seems to be a hidden *quality*: The value, represented in figure 2 by the big unhatched arrow. We equate the obvious unequal objects in the category of value. On the market, the category of value can come out of the shadow in the form of money, as money is the way in which the category of value is materialized into an object, i.e., into a resource in its own respect. Money is, so to speak, a way of making the category of value visible.

Value does not, however, need to be of the money sort. It could be value based on a value judgment. If, for example, I have a thing in my possession that would hold meaning or be of some value to someone else, if it were in his possession, and he has something I would want, then a correlation could take place on the basis of experienced value.

In this as in all other correlations the functions do not lose more than they gain. If one of the functions however should experience a loss, part of the object has been canalized rather than correlate, this being an example of a person unfolding two functions in the same act.

Correlation of objects is of great importance for the distribution of goods, but the correlation of ideas is of no lesser significance. What happens in the correlation of ideas is that the knowledge, for example, of an apple is equated with the knowledge of an orange in *defiance* of their *differences* and in accordance with their *identities*, i.e., by abstraction, the result of which is the general category of fruit. By correlation we simply state, that 'apple' equals 'orange' in being 'fruit', which implies that 'apple is fruit' and 'orange is fruit'. This means that the correlation takes place within the very *category*, that the correlation itself generates. The category then being a specific sort of knowledge. It is knowledge from which all differences are strained off.

It is the concept 'is' that actually characterizes this very complicated process. 'Is' means equal to. Apple, for instance, equals orange in the category of fruit, i.e., an apple is an orange in respect to being a fruit. We might say that the equality is mediated by the general category.

As mentioned, categories are produced in spite of the differences between the objects involved in the actual correlation, but if no known differences exist between these objects, the outcome of the process is a special kind of category, which I call a class. In a specific class each object belonging to that class holds the same idea. All apples, for instance, belong to the same class, the class of apples, as long as we cannot distinguish between different kinds of apples. They do of course also belong to the less specific category of fruit.

One of the interesting points about classes, then, is that they can change into categories if our idea of the phenomena belonging to the class changes. If, for instance, we – in the correlation process – discover differences not noticed before, we can divide a class – the class then becoming a category

– into new classes. For me, for instance, a tiger was just a tiger i.e., a class, until someone told me the difference between a Bengalian and a Siberian tiger. From then on 'tiger' became a category.

The difference between category and class is – as we shall see – important for the understanding of some aspects of the control process.

The combination process

The third social process – illustrated in figure 3 – is called combination. What characterizes this process described as structure, is that the function A *connects* a resource with a resource of B, while the function B connects a resource with a resource of A which results in a new resource that subsequently is *internalized* by the functions A and B.

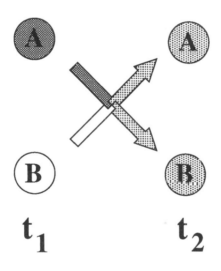

$$t_1 \qquad\qquad t_2$$

Figure 3. Combination of resources

Any cooperative work could be used as an example of combination whether the resources are of idea or object nature. It could for example be the production of a text or that of assembling components into a colour TV on a production line. The result of the combination process can also be a resource which is the first of its kind, a novelty within humanity.

A striking example of the human ability to produce a novelty by combining resources – even without changing the physical quality of the resource involved – was the historical transformation of grain into seed grain and bread grain. Grain was just grain until someone thousands of years ago managed to make a distinction within the grain eventually by putting the grain into differently marked pots or places. By combining some of the grain with one type of pots and the rest with a different type of pots the food gatherers succeeded in producing new resources – grain for consumption and grain for reproduction. In consequence of these combination processes the food gatherers became farmers.

These people did not only humanize the world by making a distinction. They *qualified* the grain and by that themselves. They produced an entirely new concept in the world, that of farming. The nutritious and the reproductive property of the grain did of course exist prior to these combinations, but by making the distinctions, the grain lost its exclusive natural position so to speak. It became inextricably bound up with the human beings.

The seed grain does not exist without the farmer. Farmer and seed grain belong to each other. They *signify* each other in the same manner as a commodity, for instance, signify a buyer and a seller. A commodity is only a commodity as long as it is included in a specific correlation. It is actually the relationship between a buyer and a seller. It is the *boundary* which connects the two opposite extremes – buyer and seller – in a relationship.

Making distinctions is of major importance in the life of human beings. Humans are constantly making new distinctions within the natural world and within the human life itself. A group, for instance, can qualify themselves as 'us' which at once qualifies the others as 'them'. They signify each other where the boundary between us and them could be a prejudice.

The *first* combination like that of transforming grain into seed grain took place at a specific place, at a specific time. But although it was specific persons who actualized the transforming process, it was not because they had special creative abilities given to the chosen few.

The event was a brilliant expression of human ingenuity and had a tremendous impact upon human history, but it does not differ in any essential way from other combinations no matter how obviously insignificant these combinations might be. Acts like that of transforming grain have – because of their importance for humanity – been called entrepreneurial and the acting person in consequence an entrepreneur by some scientists, and the 'special abilities' of these persons have been searched for high and low. But the farmer to be did not act otherwise than anyone else, who participates in a less significant combination process does. The ability to change resources is a general human quality, which – with some justice – could be called entrepreneurial, but the importance of a specific process as seen in the light of history, do not make the important process more entrepreneurial than the less important ones.

When we correlate ideas we produce, as mentioned, new ideas in the form of general categories. This sort of ideas is different from the ideas we obtain from the combination process for instance in the form of a text. The two sorts of ideas differs with regard to the content. The combined ideas contain the specifications of matter and phenomena in the world. The correlated ideas contain the generalizations of matter and phenomena in the world.

By means of combination we try to construe the world and by means of categorization we try to establish order. I shall return to this difference in the section where I will go into more details about resources.

The individual form of social processes

As far as I can see, the individual – executing the functions just described – is constituted by processes which are congruous to the social processes mentioned. The individual, then, is the processes of combination, correlation and canalization.

The three social processes mentioned have been described as interactions between two different individuals, A and B. This, of course, is fundamental. It is, however, very important also to recognize that a single individual can occupy both positions A and B at the same time. That is, the individual can interact *with himself/herself* in the manner of correlation, combination and canalization.

The resources used and produced in this self–interaction, I call *capacity*. Capacity is then the merged knowledge–and–object the individual embraces.

In order to be able to differentiate between functions belonging to the interaction between individuals and functions belonging to self–interaction I name the functions in the self–interaction *self–functions*. The self–functions, then, process capacity.

I do not think it difficult to recognize the correlation and combination processes within the individual frame of reference, as we know that any human being, for instance, can make up categories and produce a text. The individual can also produce new combinations within his/her own capacity and thus be an innovator in his/her own respect. The result of an individual combination process could naturally become of major consequence for humanity and the fortunate one could achieve the title of entrepreneur in some scientific studies, but the self–function is nevertheless executing a general human ability in combining the capacities.

It may, at first, be difficult to see how an individual in the form of a self–function should be able to transfer anything to himself/herself. I think, however, that the individual form of canalization is the social memory. It is an ongoing but unnoticed recognition of the individual capacity by the individual – a feedback loop which implies the continuity of the capacity. It is not self–awareness, consciousness or anything like that but simply the being of one–self as a social individual. The canalization by self–function ensures the identity of the individual. The individual is, so to speak, handing over his/her own history to himself/herself.

Summing up

Canalization, correlation and combination are the three fundamental social processes. Any interaction, be it of either material or ideal kind, is made up of these activity components. Any individual holds these processes and is able to be active as a function within the canalization, combination and correlation process, because the ability to function within the unfolding of social processes simply belongs to the essence of humanity, and none of the aspects of humanity are reserved for its gifted members. That might be the reason why scientific studies have failed in trying to find and isolate a specific entrepreneurial quality within the field of social processes irrespective of their individual or inter-individual form. Even if the combination process should be defined as the entrepreneurial process it will still be impossible to attribute this process to the chosen few because of its constitutional position in the essence of humanity.

Before I move on to the control process I will, for two reasons, elaborate a little further on the concept of resources. First, because I find it particularly necessary to understand the concept of knowledge in order to understand the process of control. Second, because I think that the analysis of the production of knowledge sharpens the understanding of the social processes.

The resources

In order to get a more profound understanding of the resources in general and ideas in the form of knowledge in particular, it is necessary to make a detour to the analysis of how to identify a *source*.

The sources

A source is simply delimited matter. This means that sources exist by their matter being objectively different from other kinds of matter whether we perceive these differences or not. The most simple source is a source which contains only one *aspect*.

This can be illustrated as in figure 4. The hatched circle represents a source which has only one aspect. This aspect A is different from anything else - represented by the unhatched part of the figure - called non-A, because it represents all that is not A.

Logically seen, differences exist by negation, i.e., by the *limit* between something and anything else. If we look at the aspect 'red', red (A) will reflect anything else in the world by negation (the upper arrow) as non-red (non-A). And further by a second negation (the lower arrow) - still sticking to red (A) as the point of reference - red itself will reflect non-red as non-non-red (non- non-A). A is then the same as non-non-A with the first and the second negation as the differences which point at the limit of A.

Whenever a source is perceived, we operate within the difference based on the logical negation which shows us the limit between the specific aspect of the source and anything else. This implies, for example, that the complete determination of the colour of a specific orange will contain the combined differences between the colour of that orange and not only all other shades of colour in the world but also anything else. This means that the colour of the orange is not red, yellow, green or blue, but it also means that the colour is not round, hard or soft etc. It simply differs from anything else.

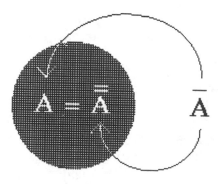

Figure 4. Negation and double negation of a quality A

It is of course very seldom that a source contains just one aspect. Normally a source is determined by a multitude of differences. If we should define a certain source completely by its differences we would have to compare the qualities of the source with each and every other kind of qualities in the world. A procedure like that for arriving at acquaintance with a source is of course so time consuming that it is impossible to handle, but even if we had all the time in the world or gave in and reduced our search for differences to a minimum, we still could not establish *identity*. And as long as we are unable to establish identity, we cannot produce knowledge, because knowledge is based upon these identities. Which means that we cannot transcend the world of sources. Without knowledge we cannot separate and differentiate ourselves from that, which is not ourselves.

Differences then are the precondition of knowledge but not knowledge itself. The cornerstone of knowledge is information as we shall see.

The establishing of information

The problem of identity can be illustrated very simply by looking at two apparently identical spots placed on a wall of a different colour. The reason why we can see the two of them at all is their different placing. What we see are the one and the second spot as different from the background. We actually do not see them as identical, because if we joined them with reference to comparison, we would not see them as two spots any longer but as one spot though of greater size, or if they were superimposed on each other one would simply disappear. The point is therefore that identity cannot be perceived because identity holds no difference. Identity cannot be recognized directly, but has to be recognized indirectly.

The indirect way of reaching identity is by correlation of the differences as in the argument: The first spot is different from the background, and the second is also different from the background, but the differences are not different from each other, because if we superimpose the spots on each other, there exists only one difference that between the spot and the background, therefore they are identical.

When two aspects – here the spots – are different from a third – here the background – but not different from each other, we simply state by correlation that they are identical.

What we actually 'see' in the process is 'nothing', a missing difference, which can only come into existence as something by correlation. This means that nothing – the negated or missing difference – within the correlation is transformed into something. And this something is *information*. Information then, according to this view, is the most simple general category, holding one identity. To hold information is to hold the most simple form of knowledge, the knowledge of identities.

In this way we *identify* the aspects of the sources specified by differences, which means that the sources become resources specified by identities.

What I have tried to explain here is that matter – and social processes for that matter – is based on differences and that the identical differences – the information which is the basis of knowledge are results of correlation processes.

The most important result of this very fundamental correlation is that we by way of information can create a non–objectbound language, i.e., the language which consists of words naming categories, classes and concepts, concepts being the result of combination as I shall describe later.

The In–forming of a resource

The most simple but also the most fundamental combination process is that of *in–forming*. The point of departure of this process is the information reached by correlation. When for instance we have established the identity of red i.e., the information 'red', we can combine this information – being a resource of a function – with an object resource, which means that the information can be ascribed to a resource. We can point at a certain object and call it red, which means that we fill the object with knowledge – the object now being a red object to us, and not a green one, for instance.

Any source can be in–formed, which means that we can ascribe to them information found in the correlation process. By ascribing information to a source we change aspects of the source into *qualities*. A quality then being an in–formed aspect. A source exists by its aspects. An object resource exists by its qualities. An ideal resource exists by its information.

An object resource then is a source which exists *to us*. An object resource is not just delimited matter, it is a humanized source. It is something which exists only because human beings have brought it into the sphere of humanity. It is, as said before, a source filled with knowledge.

The aspects of the sources can be perceived because of their differences. The qualities of the resource are known because of their identities. And it is in the correlation and combination process that the world of differences is humanized. A resource is a humanized source. A resource is a source we talk about, so to speak.

It is important to notice that we by in–forming do not categorize but express a statement. By in–forming we formulate a statement which might be true or false. Of course the object might also be categorized, the result of which is not a statement but an assertion on two or more objects being identical in respect to a specific information. The decision, then, whether a statement is true or false, is a connection between combination and correlation. If, for instance, we have gained the category of red by correlation and then in–form an object as red by combination, we can decide whether the object is red, i.e., decide if the statement is true, by equating the in–formed object with an object already categorized. If the in–formed, i.e., defined object does not differ from the defining object, we claim the statement to be true.

The making of a concept
Another step in the production of knowledge is that of forming *concepts*. As mentioned before we are able to produce information. This information, when created, exists however in a singular manner. It is not put together as a complex unity by the correlation process itself. Not until the combination process is carried out is the information tied up into the complex unity called a concept.

A concept then is a description of a resource by means of the information which this resource contains, symbolized by a word. This means for example, that the concept of gasoline contains the connected information of the qualities of gasoline and the genesis of gasoline, i.e., the actual process crude oil has to run through to become gasoline. In a concept the information is lined up in sequences like: gasoline is hydrocarbon and extracted from crude oil and fluid and inflammable but neither nutritious for human beings nor for animals etc. The concept is thus a simple sequence, which I call *text*. Concepts are of a more complex form of knowledge than the information.

It naturally goes without saying that concepts can be combined into more complex texts which means even more complex knowledge, theories for instance.

Whenever we for example wish to transfer the knowledge which exists in the form of concepts to another person, it is the combination of information, i.e., the text, that we hopefully try to make the other appropriate and not just a quantity of singular information. This means that we not only transfer information but also information about the combination of information. The terms 'and' and 'or', for example, are text information that is fundamental for the existence and with that the canalization of concepts, which could be called ideal resources.

By asserting this I have at the same time pointed out that human beings can establish information of their own social processes. The information 'and' for instance does not exist anywhere else but in the combination itself. 'And' is a fundamental quality of combination. To transfer the information included in that quality we have to be able to create it, therefore we must be able to produce information of the social processes in which we participate and in–form these processes. The processes involved do not, however, differ from any other processes; it is just the object that is different.

It has been claimed that the ability of mankind to make concepts of its own social processes – often called self–reflexivity – is a unique quality of humanity and different from anything else human beings are able to do. I think, however, that it is the social processes which are unique. Self–reflexivity is only different from all other social processes by virtue of the peculiarity of the object.

It is very rare, if ever, that concepts exist in a complete form because usually we are able to find new differences, correlate them into identities, i.e., develop new knowledge in the form of information. Most often our concepts are incomplete, and knowledge is unevenly distributed among people, which means that it is possible for different functions to hold a concept of the same phenomenon without having *identical* concepts of the phenomenon.

Even if two functions may possess a concept of gasoline, the two concepts do not necessarily match. One function can contain concept information that the other one does not include. But – and this is important – they both do hold a concept of gasoline, which means that we can communicate by means of concepts without having exactly the same understanding of these concepts. If I, for instance, ask someone to give me a gallon of gasoline it is not necessary for the canalization that we hold exactly the same concept of gasoline.

A concept can – as the information could – be combined with a source. I call this process *conceptualization*. In the conceptualization process the source becomes an object resource. It becomes a source filled with knowledge i.e., a humanized source. In the conceptualization process we formulate a statement like in the in–forming process. But because of the complexity of the concept it is less likely that the statement can be proven to be true by correlation.

Concepts and categories
A concept is always concrete and specific although it might not be complete. Concepts are knowledge of existence. A category is always abstract and general. Categories are knowledge of order.

The reason why a concept now and then can appear as abstract and general is primarily because of its incompleteness. 'Canalization' as described above, for instance, is an incomplete concept containing only information about functions, relations and the transference and appropriation of resources, and as these emphasized qualities are also general because all canalizations exists by these qualities, it could appear as if the concept of canalization was abstract and general. It is, however, 'canalization' as a category which has these characteristics.

It is of course confusing, that we use the same word for the category of canalization and for the concept of canalization, but it is an inconvenience we have to live with.

Another reason why a concept can appear as general is that the information which in–forms an aspect into a quality is general. But being a quality the information included is specific and concrete.

The canalization process, however, exists in a vast number of variations dependent upon the type of resources, functions and relations. And these various forms of the concept can of course be categorized. We categorize for example some canalization processes as learning processes where some eventually can be classified as master–apprentice–relations while others can be classified as teacher– pupil–relations according to the context in which these canalizations take place. This means that the category contains the information which is general for a specific number of phenomena, objects or events. But if a phenomenon belongs to a class it contains the same information as the other phenomena, belonging to the same class.

It could appear then as if a class was just a generalization of concepts. But this is not always so. The class of teachers, for instance, is not founded on concepts but on a specific qualities of a number of concepts as 'teacher' is just a part of the concept of the teacher/pupil relationship. We can classify a teacher as 'teacher' but we cannot conceptualize the teacher as a teacher because the teacher is only a teacher in a relationship to a pupil. 'Teacher', 'buyer', 'us', 'beautiful' etc., are categories – the categorizing manner in which we keep some order in the humanized world. 'Teacher/

pupil', 'buyer/seller', 'us/them', 'beautiful/ ugly' etc., can be concepts, as well as they can be categories although categories like 'us/ them' most often appears as the distinct classes 'us' and 'them'.

I think, that the problems mentioned by Gartner on the definition of the entrepreneur are founded on the confusion of concepts and categories. Most American studies do not try to conceptualize their source of investigation, they are content with a categorization. But as they treat the categories as if they were concepts they act as if they know their source of investigation, while they, however, only know *of* their source of investigation. They work in a pre–scientific manner since scientific knowledge – in my opinion – is the merged knowledge of existence and order.

The controlling of social processes

The different functions do in a sense steer the resources/capacity by way of their relationship. But neither the functions nor the processes as such are in control of the functions or the processes. The uncontrolled social life simply constitutes a flow of successive and simultaneously existing processes, to which we do not pay much attention in everyday life. The uncontrolled social life could be pictured as units – individual as well as inter–individual – which are incessantly created and destroyed in an everchanging stream, where the ending of one process is the condition of the beginning of the next possible process.

Figure 5 shows the three social processes in a symbolic form.

	Combination	Correlation	Canalization
Mono			
Duo			

Figure 5. Symbols

If we took a snapshot of the social life we would see a vast amount of single social processes in the shape of individual and inter–individual structures as illustrated in figure 6. If we made successive snapshots into a film it would show reiterations but of course also random changes. The persons would participate in much the same activities for longer or shorter periods and interact with one another by the habits that are included in the different historically developed forms of these activities, habits which can be broken by coincidence. In short the film would show social reproduction as it takes place within humanity. It does not need any further explanation because it simply is the way people live as long as they do not pay attention to the manner in which they act.

Figure. 6. Snapshot of social life

There can be a great many reasons why people do pay attention, but the most common is that differences crop up. If, for instance, the outcome of an often repeated process is different from the expectations embedded in the process, people get startled and eventually they begin to wonder. They might try to in–form, conceptualize and categorize the unexpected in order to avoid a repetition or to take advantage of the difference discovered.

Trying to utilize knowledge of past social processes to guide future social processes is what control is about.

As far as I can see, *control* – as illustrated in figure 7 – can be defined as the *sequence* of social processes in which past social processes (t1) are converted into future social processes (t3) by means of present social pro-cesses (t2). This means – in the terminology introduced – that past social processes by canalization, correlation or combination can become social processes of the future. Control is thus social processing of social pro-cesses.

Different social processes are often launched at the same time, inter-twined and linked together into *occurrences*, which also can be controlled. But as an occurrence encompasses more processes, i.e., more relating functions, an occurrence is determined at the level of activity, that is the level of acting persons. I call the controlling of an occurrence *organizing*. A process is controlled, an occurrence is organized. I will however not dwell on the more complex social activities which take place in everyday life. I only want to describe the molecules of human life – to use a metaphor – not its chemistry.

The next question must be, whether distinctly different types of controlling can be discovered?

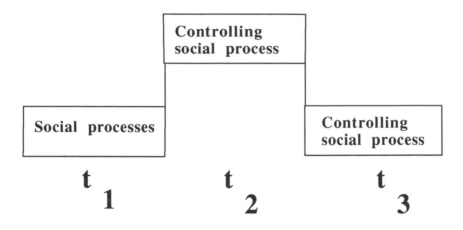

Figure 7. Control

Types of control

As mentioned the *control* is a sequence of social processes made up of the past processes, the present *controlling* processes – which can be either canalization, correlation or combination – and the future *controlled* process – which can also be any of the three social processes. This means that canalization as well as correlation and combination can be in control of future canalizations, correlations and combinations. In the following sections I shall try to elaborate some types of control sequences and illustrate some of the sequences by examples. The precondition of the sequences mentioned in the next section is that past social processes have been *con-ceptualized*.

Rigoristic control

Any conceptualized social process can be canalized and by that be in control of a future process in such a manner that this controlled process is *unfolded* as a duplicate of the past one. A sequence like that where a process is unfolded as a duplication of a past one through canalization could be called *rigoristic control*. The rigoristic control demands that each function in the future process does exactly what it did in the past process. In this type of process there exists no degree of freedom.

But how does this sequence differ from a simple social repetition? To answer that question we have to look a little deeper into the controlling process which actually is a *chain of implications*.

I will use a hunting party consisting of two individuals as an example. The point of departure is that both individuals have a concept of how to hunt pheasants, for example, by way of combination. This means that they know that one of them drives the prey towards the other one who brings down the animal. They also know that Willy the Archer and that Peter the Beater are signified by their habitual functions.

What happens in the controlling process is that one of them transfers the message to the other: "Pheasant hunting?". This request implies an answer, i.e., another transference: "yes!" or "no!". What follows from the "yes!" is a duplicate of the prior pheasant hunt.

The difference between a repetition of a social process and a rigoristically controlled social process – which apparently takes place in a similar manner – is that a repetition is something which happens by chance or by habit while the controlled process is something which happens with a purpose. Any social process includes a *goal*, but a controlled process has a *purpose*, it is *intentional*.

The control prevents the functions from processing resources which do not belong to the process, which means that the process is limited by the controlling process that exists as the context of the ongoing process.

The intentionality is embedded in the controlled process. It is not rooted in a specific quality of the individual but in the fact – according to the view presented here – that the social processes can process other social processes.

There exist three possible forms of rigoristic control since canalization can be in control of either canalization, correlation or combination.

Any requested cooperative work with fixed functions is an example of rigoristically controlled combination. An example of a rigoristically controlled canalization could be a Catholic paying tithe to a specific church each Sunday at the Mass by request of the priest, and that of correlation could be the way in which we buy our daily bread in the baker's shop at a fixed price.

Heuristic and algorithmic control

The possibility of rigoristic control is not always at hand because the circumstances of living contain an element of uncertainty. The knowledge of hunting rabbits or hares, for instance, cannot be applied in a rigoristic manner if the prey is a turkey. To control in a rigoristic manner is only possible within a very restricted frame of reference because of the constraints attached to this form of control like the requirement of the fixed functions in the past process as well as in the future process.

If the restrictions cannot be met we have to shift into another mode of control. The point of departure is still conceptualization and a request/answer implication, but assuming the prerequisite for an unfolding of a prior process does not exist any longer, the individuals involved have to arrive at some sort of agreement on what to do. They could, for instance try to correlate past social processes in order to gain a general category of hunting small animals with the intention of using this category as a context for the future turkey hunt.

In a sequence like that, where the controlling process is correlation, the functions compare different prior social processes with respect to their course of events and by that they gain a common category of processes, which could leads to similar results if implemented. A correlation of this type could be called *negotiation of meaning* because the individuals involved try to gain a common knowledge out of their different concepts of what the past was about.

If the correlation is in control, the concepts of the past processes are generalized in a category, and this category is then the context within which the future process is unfolded. Such a sequence I call *heuristic* control.

The heuristic mode of control means that the controlling process points to the future process in a general manner. We know what we want, which means that we have a *task* to fulfil, but we are not quite sure of how to accomplish this task.

As mentioned before there exists a specific form of categories called classes. Phenomena belonging to the same class are identical and not just similar with reference to a number of identities.

If we, by way of the controlling correlation, are able to classify past processes instead of just categorizing these processes, we can be quite certain that the controlled process will reach its goal. A sequence like that could be called *algorithmic* control. Landa defines an algorithm as a set of rules and specifies its properties as:

> *Specificity* indicating the fact that all actions of the user of an algorithm are unambiguously determined by instructions (rules), and that these instructions are identically understandable and understood by all users.

> *Generality* means applicability of an algorithm to an entire set of problems belonging to a particular class, rather than a single problem. ...

> *Resultivity* indicates that the algorithm is always directed toward achieving the sought–after result, which the user, once he possesses the initial data, always achieves (Landa 1976, p. 108).

An algorithmic control could have a likeness to a rigoristically controlled process. The fundamental difference between rigoristic and algorithmic control is, however, that the algorithmically controlled process is a general and not an exact duplicate of a prior process. It is a process which follows specific rules in fulfilling a classified *task*.

Not all tasks can, as mentioned, be fulfilled within the limits of the algorithm.

> The number of possible paths is usually so great that it is often practically impossible to find a solution by testing all paths *(the algorithmic way. O.E.R.)*. That is why special procedures are sought after and utilized which are based on certain evaluations of paths from the point of view of their ability to lead to a solution more rapidly and economically but with less of a guarantee. Precisely these procedures are called heuristic (op. cit. 115).

Algorithmic and heuristic control are not different in any essential way as the controlling processes are canalization–correlation in both cases. The difference between the two forms of control lies in their respective precision in fulfilling a certain task. In the heuristic control we try to *manage* future processes by way of models. In the algorithmic control we try to *administer* future processes by following rules.

If another person accepts my offer of exchanging stamps, for example, we could control the future exchange by correlating our concepts of stamps. Agreeing that the category of stamps includes small pieces of paper of a certain value we are ready for the exchange within the category mentioned, and all goes well. We try another one, but this time the deal goes wrong. Why? Because the category of exchangeable stamps was not exhaustively described. It was not a class because. Unlike the other person, for instance, had the idea that exchangeable stamps should be from England only and I was offered a Danish one. I had not mentioned anything about this peculiarity of mine because I had never met or heard about anyone exchanging Danish stamps for English ones. It was pure chance that the first stamp offered to me was from England, so the negotiated category was not challenged. Having failed to exchange the second time we are much wiser. We then negotiate until we are certain that all possible paths to a successful exchange are covered.

The first and the second deal was controlled in a heuristic way, the rest in an algorithmic manner. To control in a algorithmic manner we have to traverse all possibilities, and that is difficult.

An example of heuristically controlled combination could be that of starting a pizzeria in Rome; it could be done in many different ways, and the general knowledge of the start of a small business like that could be appropriated from owners of other small businesses in Rome.

In many studies the risk taking, which is connected to the heuristically controlled process because of the uncertainty within categories, has been looked upon as the trademark of entrepreneurial activity. In any case it has been common to categorize enterprising people as entrepreneurs if they, for instance, succeed in building new businesses – like the pizzeria – although the new businesses do not differ in any essential way from those already existing. In my opinion, however, it is not the risk involved in the building of a new business, which makes an activity entrepreneurial, nor the newness of the business, as long as the 'new' one is just another of the same kind.

Stochastic control

When we do not have a welldefined task to fulfil, we can neither guide future processes by means of an algorithmic, nor a heuristic mode of control. When we do not know exactly where to end or how to do it we have generated a *problem*, where a problem[2] is defined as the notion that something could be different. But how does a notion like that appear?

As mentioned earlier heuristic control is control by some sort of order, an order which is reached by ignoring differences. These ignored differences constitute the disorder which order always implies. The disorder existing in an implicit way in the order is the notion that something could be different.

The ignored differences can be signified as an *exception* by correlation, which means that the meaningless exists as some kind of rubbish in the negotiation of meaning in the correlation gains a new significance, the significance of being an exception. We can of course repeat the exception and the exception can become the rule. I am, however, interested in the combination of the exceptions as the context for future processes.

A sequence of social processes where the controlling chain of implication is canalization(request/answer)–correlation–combination could be called stochastic control. When we control by stochastic means, we combine exceptions into a text – a hypothesis – to be followed by the future process not knowing, of course, exactly what will happen in this process. The text then is the known guide–line to the unknown. Stochastic control is like throwing a dice. We do know that we throw a dice, but we do not know which face of the dice that shows. We can, however, expect the result to be between one and six. Stochastic control is some sort of qualified guessing.

---

2   This definition was formulated by one of my students Robert Arne Petersen.

It would, for instance, be a stochastically controlled correlation if we planned to sell pizzas in Saudi Arabia knowing that the locals never eat pizza except when they are on holiday in Rome. Knowing this we could make up the hypothesis that pizzas could be sold in Saudi Arabia. Unfortunately we fail because our pizza has ham on it. We could, of course, have augmented the probability of success, if we had known something about the habits of consumption in Saudi Arabia. This knowledge could also be provided by stochastic control. We know, for instance, by correlation that all embassies holds information of their own cultures. Unfortunately there is no Saudi Arabian embassy where we are, but we have found out that English Embassy as an exception know something of the culture of Germany. This gives us a notion that some embassy might hold information on the habits of Saudi Arabians. Guided by the hypothesis that knowledge of consumption habits could be obtained at one of the other embassies we grab the phone and start asking. From the Israeli embassy – which has a lot of information of Arabian culture – we find out that the pizza can be sold, provided there is no bacon on the pizza – although it has never been tried before, as far as they know – but it must not be imported, and if produced in the country, local raw materials have to be used. Knowing the raw materials and combination process for producing an Italian pizza we can then try by heuristic control to produce a Saudi Arabian ditto. Failing to sell the product, eventually, because of the incompatibility between oregano and Arabian taste buds, we can control the different pizza production by stochastic means in adding local spices to the product.

I think that stochastic control in its various concrete forms constitute the core of entrepreneurial activity. But before I try to elaborate a little further on that subject a short summing up on control and a few words on personality and organization.

Summing up

I do not, in any way, claim to have described the field of control exhaustively. I have only described a few chains of implications that can produce quite different contexts for future processes. These chains of implications can in a general manner – in the notation drawn in figure 5 – be illustrated as in figure 8, using only inter–individual processes.

I have claimed earlier that control should be conceived as a derived fourth social process. I still think that this claim is right, but perhaps this process has a historically developed independent essence in the form of the implication mentioned. Another possibility is that the implication is somehow connected with the political/economic stratum. Further studies can, I hope, reveal the fundamental quality of the chain of implication in the controlling sequence.

Personality

In continuation of the assertion that the individual exists as social processes
it is obvious that the individual can be in control of his/her own 'internal'
processes and by that the external relations to other functions.

The different forms of control – rigoristic, heuristic etc. – in its individual shape appear as I. 'I' being the manner in which the individual controls his/her capacity and self-functions and by that limits of the individual.
When for example a capacity – knowledge, a value or an object – is to be
canalized as a resource to another function *in a controlled manner*, it is the
individual control sequence i.e., I, which is controlling the transference and
the I of the other function, which is controlling the appropriation. The
resulting inter–individual canalization might be controlled by a sequence
involving the individuals in question.

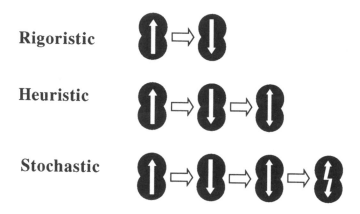

Rigoristic

Heuristic

Stochastic

Figure 8. Types of control

It is the individual forms of control that in their organized form appear as
personality, the personality thus being the individual counterpart to the
organized occurrence. Personality is the controlled way in which the person
acts. The personality is the person in control.

The organized social occurrence is always determined by the personalities involved, but social processes are not necessarily organized. Unorganized social processes effectuated by unorganized individual processes are
processes which evade attention. In everyday life we are not always aware
of what is actually going on. Some processes are automated to such an
extent that differences have to appear before we take any notice.

Organization

Finally a word about the organization. An *organization* is an organized social occurrence in which there is a *separation* between the controlling processes and the processes controlled. The controlling processes are carried out by one or more individuals who do not participate in the social processes being controlled. The limits of the organization – what it can do – are consequently controlled by these individuals, who are in command so to speak. Said in a more straightforward manner: An organization consists of those who lead and those who are led as a unity. In an organization the leaders have appropriated the power of control.

An organization then, is a process which originates from the controlled social process by splitting this process into two interdependent but at the same time independent processes, the process of leading and the process of being led.

I think that the organization constitutes one of the fundamental political/economic processes. It is a process which constitute a level of human existence that is different from the social processes.

We know from experience that organizations can exist by rigoristic, algorithmic and heuristic control, i.e., by mechanic repetition, by bureaucratic administration and by management. The question whether an organization can exist by stochastic control has yet to be answered. And I think that this question will be the most important one within the theory of leadership in the years to come because the rate of change and the amount of information to a great extent will render rigoristic, algorithmic and heuristic control impossible.

Summing up

These were the social processes which can appear as personalities, unorganized and organized social occurrences, which can give rise to organizations. The social life of human beings existing as ongoing interlinking processes – organized as well as unorganized – constitutes the essential forces of mankind, which are the prerequisite for the existence of the political/economic processes, e.g., organizations, supply and demand; processes which sometimes by their own laws are in command of these forces.

As I hope to have shown, no type of activity or act – controlled or uncontrolled – is reserved for certain groups or exceptional personalities. Although the entrepreneurial activity might be a specific way of organizing, the ability to do so is a general and not a specific ability. It is to be found in any field of social activity.

Some scientists have arrived at the conclusion that entrepreneurial activity had to be caused by a specific and very rare ability. The reason why could be that individuals who are led – and that includes quite a lot of people – in their capacity of being led do not have the possibility to exercise their organizing ability, including the stochastic one. But the ability to act in a entrepreneurial way is not rare, it is simply repressed by the organizational way of existence, which keeps some people away from control at all or by the manner in which we organize by rigoristic, heuristic and algorithmic means.

As long as we organize our own activity, the entrepreneurial activity – which I claim to be the stochastically controlled social processes – can be exercised by anyone, and this kind of control probably *will* be exercised whenever rigoristic, heuristic or algorithmic controlled processes fail to reach the goals included in these processes. It can of course happen that people continue to act as usual although they do not reach their goal, for reasons which are not determined by the social processes themselves. Emotional states, for instance, could hinder a person in changing the form of control. The different forms of obstacles for realizing stochastic control, however, is not the subject of this paper.

Entrepreneurship

The economic and political aspect of an entrepreneurial activity is naturally an important issue in the interdisciplinary field of entrepreneurship. But the category of entrepreneurial activity is neither of a political nor of an economical nature. When Say and his successors claim that the field of entrepreneurship can be understood as the shifting of economic resources out of an area of lower into an area of higher productivity and greater yield, I think that they somehow look in the wrong direction. The economical processes of society can be the conditions of entrepreneurial activity – and must be included in the field of entrepreneurship – and the results of the activities could be an increase in and a qualitative change of the wealth of the nation, but the entrepreneurial activities are of a social nature. And that is why the economists, reasonably enough, to a great extent have abstained from trying to find the secret behind entrepreneurial activity within the realm of the political economy. They know, as Marx did, that dynamic changes within the economy are brought about by the development of the economically determined essential forces of humanity, i.e., the productive forces.

The productive forces are most often augmented and reproduced, i.e., repeated on the level of social processes by way of rigoristic, algorithmic and heuristic organized processes, and resources are continuously transformed into commodities. But sometimes this reproduction shows *differences*. And differences can be turned into problems. A difference could, following an example from Drucker (1985), exist between the production and the market of steel.

It is extremely expensive to start a steel mill, therefore the demand of steel has to rise considerably before the steel industry wants to invest in a new one. But when the new mill is running, the output is so large that the supply exceeds the demand. In consequence the price falls, the result of which is that the investment is unprofitable until the demand exceeds the supply again.

Differences like the mentioned ones could, by the steel industry itself, be accepted as an inconvenience, which the industry has to live with. The old solution to the task of augmenting the output of steel could in consequence be repeated in an rigoristic manner; they build a new steel mill when the demand exceeds the supply and accepts the oscillations of the prices. If the steel industry saw the instability of prices as a general obstacle, they might try to manage the situation by keeping the surplus production off the market, i.e., they could try to create an artificial balance between supply and demand. This solution of the task is a heuristic one. It is not just a repetition, but a change within the same categories: The traditional steel mill output and the laws of market.

Differences are just difficulties or obstacles as long as we continue to fulfil the tasks by processes controlled in an rigoristic, algorithmic or heuristic way. But difficulties can grow to an extent which threatens the fulfilment of the goals included in the processes. This means that the differences actually become so significant and general that we cannot ignore them any longer. They are forced upon us as a task to be fulfilled.

To fulfil the task we naturally have to conceptualize the differences involved because we have to know what it is we want to control. By conceptualizing the phenomenon we want to control, we actually analyze this phenomenon by means of prior knowledge as we attribute known identities to the phenomenon. Having repeatedly in-formed i.e., analyzed the phenomenon, we have produced the informational basis from which the synthesizing concepts can be combined. Different paths to the fulfilment of the task can of course be found depending on the conceptualization.

The fulfilling of a task in a heuristic manner has, as mentioned, been called entrepreneurial. But still, a definition of the entrepreneurial activity based upon task fulfilment do not cover, what I think constitutes the essence of the field of entrepreneurship.

I think that the entrepreneurial activity is about the finding and the exploitation of the possibilities which are hidden in differences as exceptions and not just fulfilling tasks forced upon us.

I think that the definition of entrepreneurial activity must grasp the idea of processes which reach for an unforeseen future at the basis of the discovering of differences which can be turned into exceptions.

The field of entrepreneurship will of course – according to the thinking presented here – encompass innovation, but the essence of the entrepreneurial act is the stochastic control, which turns exceptions into possibilities. Turning differences – which for someone is just difficulties or obstacles – into a hypothesis is to give up the rigoristic, the algorithmic and the heuristic way of control without being forced to do so and without the loss of control. This is the entrepreneurial activity.

In the case of steelmilling the difficulties connected with the oscillating prices were seen by someone outside the steel industry and the problem was solved by an innovation called the mini mill which is a completely different production method, cheaper than the traditional steel mill and with a smaller output. The mini mill took the steel industry by surprise since no one, perhaps because of prejudice, had imagined a solution like that to be possible and maybe not even necessary.

A most interesting part of entrepreneurship is the way in which differences are picked up. As unforeseen differences for very good reasons do not crop up on a regular basis we have to organize the appropriation of information in an unruled manner, i.e., by way of stochastic control. We could of course stumble on differences by chance, but to be entrepreneurial, the activity must be organized, i.e., controlled by the personality or the personalities involved. This means that the appropriation is limited and by that goal directed although in an unspecific manner. A group of people, for example, could decide to look for differences within the pattern of consumption of dairy produce. They might discover a difference between the sale of butter in winter and in summer time. The difference does not bother the dairies because the oscillation is counterbalanced by the pattern in cheese consumption. But our investigators make the difference significant and combine the knowledge obtained with the information of the quality of butter into the hypothesis that the consumers do not eat butter in summer because it melts in the heat, and kept in the refrigerator it is too hard to spread on the bread. A hypothesis like that can be confirmed by appropriation of information. During our interviews wee tumble on the information that some of the consumers change to vegetable margarine because this product can be kept in the refrigerator and still be spread on the bread, but they are not very pleased with the stuff.

We now have some information on the relationship between butter and consumers and margarine and consumers. By correlation we find out that the two products are similar in many respects. They belong to the same category, but with exceptions – margarine does not taste as good as butter and butter is harder than margarine coming from the refrigerator. We get the notion that something could be different. We can now put forward two hypotheses – the taste of margarine could be changed, the quality of butter could be changed.

Since no one has put the problem in question on the agenda before, it is unlikely that the problem could be turned into a task, which means that we could organize the future processes by heuristic or algorithmic means. We have to free ourselves from the rules, i.e., organize the social processes in a stochastic manner, and by doing so we might find a solution in combining butter and vegetable margarine.

The solution of the problem is found in a stochastic manner and not merely by coincidence because we already have established a field of reference for example the quality of butter and margarine, but we do not have a preestablished knowledge on the result of the combination of the two.

The result of the combination, spreadable butter, is naturally a resource, but because it has never been seen before we usually call it an innovation. It is a result of an entrepreneurial activity which, as mentioned above, includes stochastically organized processes including controlled canalization and combination.

But how do we get rid of this peculiar product, which is neither fish nor fowl? The resource problem is somehow solved, but what about the consumer problem? During our hunt for information we might have appropriated the knowledge that quite a few of the consumers have left butter altogether in favour of vegetable margarine because it contains sebacic acid of the more healthy kind than do butter. The consumers actually hate the stuff, but who wants to die of a heart attack?

Here lies the final part of the solution. We produce a concept never seen before: The healthy butter, and with that label on the wrapping the innovation sells like hot cakes.

This was an object example of entrepreneurial processing of resources, but social processes themselves can be a result of an entrepreneurial activity. The introduction, for instance, of the master/apprentice relationship in German factories by August Borsig in the middle of the 19th century was – according to Drucker – an entrepreneurial occurrence and one of the most important activities in the last two centuries. The organized transference of ideal resources had a tremendous impact on the efficiency of industrial production (Drucker 1985).

Any entrepreneurial activity will eventually become repeatable, i.e., changed into heuristic and algorithmic organized processes.

As I hope to have shown, the stochastic way of organizing social processes individually as well as collectively could be *the* entrepreneurial activity and thus the core of the field of entrepreneurship. It is a quality of the very essence of the forces of humanity and thus a manner in which all human beings can exist. Our attention is, however, not always directed towards this possibility – maybe because rigoristic, heuristic and algorithmic control seems less complicated – and being under the control of others we might not have the opportunity to unfold this way of organizing social processes.

Although the stochastically controlled processes are claimed to be the core of the entrepreneurial activity, it does not mean that these forms of processes are the only ones which make up the entrepreneurial field. It is very often, for instance, necessary and for many people also desirable to start a small business of their own in order to implement the results of the entrepreneurial activity. Often venture capital and other 'ingredients' are also a necessity for getting an entrepreneurial project off the ground. What defines the field as entrepreneurial is however – in my opinion – the stochastical control of the fundamental social processes.

Entrepreneurship, can it be taught?

A heading like this might seem strange after the assertion that entrepreneurial activity may not only be a general human ability but even an essential one. That an ability is essential, however, does not always mean that it occurs frequently. The opportunity to be in control can, as mentioned, be minimized amongst those led by way of the organization, but another reason why entrepreneurial activity now and then might be a scarce phenomenon in human life could be deeply rooted habits of trying to control by algorithmic and heuristic means. As long as human beings are able to administer and manage their lives within the realm of the existing conditions, it seems as if the attention to the possibility of stochastic control diminishes. It is only when differences, big enough to catch our attention, appear that we try to change our lives. But even obvious differences do not automatically result in entrepreneurial activity.

Unemployment, for instance, which could and should be a challenge to human ingenuity, has apparently become the talk of the day, without any-thing radical being done about it.

Concerning the creation of new jobs, the more powerful concentrations of capital – private as well as semi–public – have obviously lost their momentum. One of the reasons for this shortcoming might be found at the drill ground of business schools and universities. As it is put by Leavitt in a critical article on the teaching of MBAs in the USA, which is worth quoting in length:

> Contingent models are rooted in our prevalent and deep–seated faith in empiricism; the faith that analysis of the external world must *precede* decision. They are essentially reactive models. One decides how to behave following and based upon analysis of the 'situation'. Moreover, correct analysis is expected to produce 'correct' answers. The direction is conver-gent. At the extreme, every student fully equipped with relevant analytic tools, when confronted with the same situation, would behave in the same way. Education for managing thus becomes, conceptually, like education for arithmetic. On their first day, a class of new, not–yet–educated math students might understandably come up with a divergent array of answers

to the same problem. But that had better not happen on their last day. If education for leadership were really to go the same way, the prospects would be terrifying. Can you envision all those 70.000 new MBAs stepping smartly out of our cloistered academic halls, degrees in hand, ready to lead our great institutions by responding identically and robot–like to every situation they encounter? (Leavitt 1989, p. 44).

According to Leavitt that is exactly what is happening at the moment, and he continues:

It is time now to worry less about convergence toward uniformity and standardization, and more about generating innovative divergence (Op. cit. 49)

Another old timer, Argyris (1990), points at the same phenomenon, claiming that especially 'smart people' are so horror–stricken by the thought of putting a foot wrong that they actually make mistakes by sticking to old forms of acting.

Rather than teaching people how to control in an entrepreneurial manner it may be a question of breaking the habit of *always* trying to control in an rigori–stic, algorithmic or heuristic way. To teach to organize by stochastic means is to draw attention to the possibility of doing so, for instance by showing that differen–ces or obstacles, if you like, could be turned into problems to be solved. How the breakdown of the habit of trying to repeat the past eventually could be executed is not the subject of this paper[3].

I will, however, call attention to a research work, which is also a practical course of entrepreneurship – called LFPI – initiated by The Centre for Innovation and Entrepreneurship at the Copenhagen Business School on behalf of the institutions of higher education in Copenhagen (Herlau & Tetzschner 1990).

At this course, bachelors of engineering, business, psychology, chemistry, law, etc., are taught to organize the direction of projects in the up–start–phase by way of stochastic control. The courses show that the entrepreneurial activity can be brought into focus and combined academical qualifications utilized with results so remarkable that more courses are to be implemented in the future as joint ventures between LFPI, county authorities and local industry in Denmark.

References

Argyris, C. (1991): Teaching Smart People How to Learn, *Harvard Business Review* May–June.

Casson, H. (1982): *The Entrepreneur. An Economic Theory*, Oxford.

---

3   Within the rehabilitation sector a case study is described in: Rasmussen (1991).

Cole, A.H. (1969): Definition of entrepreneurship, In J.L. Komives (ed.): *Karl A. Bostrom Seminar in the Study of Enterprise*, Milwaukee.

Drucker. P. (1985): *Innovation and Entrepreneurship*, New York.

Engelsted. N. (1991): A Missing Link in Activity Theory?, *Activity Theory,* 11/12, pp .49–54.

Gartner, W.B. (1989): Who is an Entrepreneur? *Entrepreneurship Theory and Practice*, Summer, pp. 47–68.

Herlau, H. & Tetzschner, H. (1990): *Danske iværksættere – Model 2: Innovation, netværksopbygning og projektledelse*, Copenhagen.

Landa, L.N. (1976): *Instructional Regulation and Control*, New Jersey, Englewood Cliffs.

Leavitt, H.J. (1989): Educating Our MBAs: On Teaching What We Haven't Taught, *California Management Review*, Vol. 31, Number 3.

Pennings, J.M. (1982): Organizational Birth Frequencies: An Empirical Investigation, *Administrative Science Quarterly*, 27, pp. 120–144.

Peters, T. (1988): *Thriving on Chaos*, New York.

Peterson, R. A. (1980): Entrepreneurship and organization, In Nystrom, P.C. & Starbuck, W.H. (eds.): *Handbook of Organizational Design*, New York.

Rasmussen, O.E. (1991): *Startkurserne – et udviklingsprojekt i Revasektoren*, Copenhagen.

SOCIETAL ANOMIA AND
THE PSYCHOLOGICAL TURN OF THE MASS

Benny Karpatschof
University of Copenhagen

This article is meant to transgress the established limits of Activity Theory. The intended transgression is, in fact, on two levels. The very subject of the article belongs to the class of phenomena that – possibly because of their often repulsive, and sometimes terrifying nature – are seldom discussed by activity theoreticians. The theoretical approach to the phenomenon chosen is a provocation on a second level, as I am defending the justification of *psychologism* in the analysis of these particular phenomena.

In fact, my point of departure will be Le Bon, a right wing publicist and pre–runner of social psychology, who is now almost forgotten. The only part of his work still generally remembered is the name of his theory: *The Psychology of the Crowd.*

The hypostaticized spirit of the crowd

Now to avoid overdoing my provocation I shall hasten to admit that I am, in fact, almost totally in disagreement with this notoriously reactionary ideologue. My point is, however, that even if some phenomena are repulsive to us, and even if the theories treating such phenomena are just as repulsive as their subject, we should avoid repressing these phenomena and these theories. We should instead criticize them, that is, analyze what is really the case, and that means finding the rational kernel of the repulsive theory.

So let us for a moment ignore our disgust and look at the central teaching of this *fin de siecle ideologue* when he eagerly theoreticizes about the revolutionary movement that was successfully crushed by the fall of the Commune of Paris.

The postulated entity about which Le Bon made his theory is the *crowd*, fr. *le foule*. His verbose and rather more postulatory than analytic major opus contains the following statement about the semi–human nature of this entity, defining the most conspicuous peculiarity of a crowd in the following way:

> Regardless the characteristics of the individuals of whom it is composed,
> regardless how similar or how different they are in life style, occupation,
> character or intelligence, the very fact that they are transformed to a crowd
> will furnish this crowd with a kind of collective soul, that makes it feel,
> think, act in a way totally different from the way each individual would
> feel, think and act, if he was in a state of isolation[1].

This is, of course, a very primitive kind of discourse. Methodologically we meet a tangle of quasi–empirical phenomena and quasi–theoretical concepts. But let us try to disentangle this mess.

What in fact could be pinpointed as the empirical phenomena are the collective actions carried out by a crowd in a way that can be dramatically remote from the behavioral repertoire of the single individual when isolated from the crowd. On the other hand the theoretical content of the statement is the explanatory entity introduced by Le Bon, the *collective soul*, the spirit of the crowd, that represents some kind of reduction or regression in comparison to the psychological characteristics of the isolated individual.

In fact Le Bon assumes that the conscious qualities of the different individuals, especially the higher intellectual capacities and moral dispositions, tend to neutralize one another, whereas the dark unconscious inclinations will add up to a fatal force of the collective unconsciousness of the crowd:

> In the collective spirit the intellectual aptitude of the individuals, and con-
> sequently their individuality, efface themselves. The heterogeneity is
> absorbed in the homogeneity, and the unconscious qualities are dominat-
> ing[2].

If the reader detects a definite psychoanalytic flavor in this theory it is certainly justified. Le Bon was one of the contributors to the bank of ideas on which Freud was soon to draw. I do not however, find Freud's specific speculation on collective behavior very relevant, whereas one of his expelled disciples, Wilhelm Reich, is worth mentioning on this point.

A scholar who witnessed an even more turbulent period than Le Bon was Canetti (1988), who was so impressed by the crowd behavior he experienced and once even participated in that he dedicated the greater part of his life to the study of this phenomenon. Canetti is much more acceptable than Le Bon in sticking to a descriptive, classificatory – and rather cautious – explanatory analysis. And in contrast to Le Bon his political agenda is a horror of the right wing movement of his time, and not the left wing rebellions. He is, however parallel to Le Bon, in dealing with a certain entity called, the mass (or the crowd and some other distinctive forms of collectives), and he describes this postulated entity in clearly psychological terms.

---

1   Le Bon (1895, p. 15).

2   Ibid., p. 17.

This tradition from Le Bon to Canetti represents what I shall call the *psychologistic* tendency of mass psychology. The research objective is the crowd and the theoretical inclination is psychologistic, that is the collective entity is understood as if it was a human being, although in its concrete behavior a rather sub–human species.

The sociological anomia

I shall now take a jump from this psychologistic approach to the other extreme, the sociological, and to a certain extent even *sociologistic* tradition according to which psychological phenomena are analyzed as products of societal processes. Thus did Durkheim in his classic work *Le Suicide* from 1897 introduce a paradoxical societal state that he characterized as dissolution of norms or *anomia*. In the following quotation he sketches the general condition of social control and the specific crisis of anomia:

> Man's characteristic privilege is that the bond he accepts is not physical but moral; that is, social. He is governed not by a material environment brutally imposed on him, but by a conscience superior to his own, the superiority of which he feels.
>
> But when society is disturbed by some painful crisis or by beneficent but abrupt transitions, it is momentarily incapable of exercising this influence, thence come the sudden rises in the curve of suicide which we have pointed out before.[3]

Now I am not concerned here with the specific phenomenon of suicide, nor with the validity of Durkheim's hypothesis of the anomic suicide, and least of all with his semi–occult concept of the *collective conscience*. But I shall borrow some inspiration from the basic idea of anomia, granted that it is, to my judgment, necessary to change its definition from the idealistic definition of Durkheim to the materialistic understanding of Activity Theory.

Before going into this conceptual matter I will, however, stress the difference between the type of mass psychology met in the tradition of crowd psychology and in the social psychology of Durkheim. Where the former makes the *hypostatization* of a mass psychological entity emerging from the dark depth of individual psyche and forming a new entity of a crowd with a spirit of its own, Durkheim rather sees things the other way round. The societal norms are a precondition for individual life, and when the norms are in crisis so are the individuals.

Durkheim has no need for a mysterious spirit of an autonomous entity composed of hypnotized individuals. On the other hand he has the notion of a collective conscience as a deciding attribute of society. I shall choose to

---

3 Durkheim (1951, p. 252) in his classic work *Le Suicide* from 1897.

interpret this concept, not as another occult kind of spirit, but realistically as an integrating part of society, that is a system of *meanings* in the way Leontiev uses the word.

Serialization and totalization according to Sartre

The last theory I shall mention, is Sartre's *Critique of the Dialectical Reason*[4]. Sartre sketches a taxonomy and a dynamics of social forms. Of special interest are his concepts: *series* and *group*.

By series he understands a collection of people united only by their simultaneous, identical activity, but otherwise separated and individualized. His initial example is a queue lined up at a bus stop. In contrast a group is a cooperating assembly of people united not only by identical goals, but a common cause.

In fact, the group is the prototype of social organization presupposed in Activity Theory, whereas the concept of the series is not met very often.

We see an interesting *chiasm* when comparing the social psychology of crowd psychology and the thinking of the later Sartre. In the former the individualized state is the normal one, whereas the union is seen as a terrifying kind of regression to subhuman and unconscious behavior. Sartre see the series, the individualized type of existence as a kind of alienation, and the union in the group as a transcendence to higher form of human being. The transitional process from series to group is called *totalization* and the regressive turn from group to series is called *de-totalization*[5].

An Activity Theoretical reconstruction of mass psychology

I shall now attempt to make a theoretical synthesis, relating cooperative activity as understood in Activity Theory to the phenomena of seriality and anomia.

In the normal state of social integration the individual will be incorporated into society by the very activity in which he or she participates. The activity, being a process simultaneously progressing on the individual (psychological) and collective (sociological) levels, is, so to speak, the very *coupling* of these two entities, the entity of the person and the entity of society.

This coupling of the person and society naturally involves a coupling of the essential qualities characterizing each of them. That is, the personality of the person and the culture of society:

---

4   See Sartre (1960).

5   Ibid. p. 153f, 398ff, 532ff.

THE ACTIVITY AS COUPLING BETWEEN PERSON AND SOCIETY

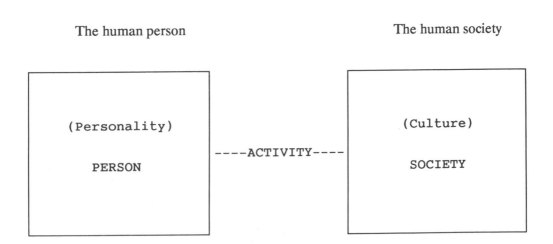

I shall not go into details of personality and culture theory here, but only stress that it is not identity, not even similarity, that characterizes the relation between personality and culture. The relation must, however, presume a certain correspondence. Thus the material culture presupposes certain skills in the personality. The organizational structure can only exist under the condition of certain emotional bonds between individuals, and thus certain stable emotions in the individual personality. To the knowledge system of culture corresponds the personal knowledge of personality, and in the same way the cultural value system can only be maintained in coexistence with the personal value system of the individual.

We can tentatively maintain this relation by hypothesizing a structure of levels of human activity corresponding to the features that can only be communicated and carried out in terms of *meaning*, and the complementary features that can be communicated and carried out as tangible operations:

Accordingly, both entities involved in the coupling by activity can be characterized as having a basic, operational level, and a superstructural, conceptual level:

THE LEVELS OF HUMAN ACTIVITY

The human person   The human society

CONSCIOUSNESS	MEANING LEVEL	MEANING SYSTEM
OPERATIONAL LEVEL	---ACTIVITY--- OPERATIONAL LEVEL	OPERATIONAL SYSTEM

The operational level of activity and of the psychic structure in the individual has a correspondence and a precursor in animals, whereas the meaning level is the specific and characteristic trait of human activity. The category *meaning* is the one that contains all the mediating features which originate in human beings, such as *motive* as the uniting conative idea defining a certain activity.

A further dichotomy arises in the model above if we make a division between the interpersonal (communicative) and object–oriented aspects of activity:

A MODEL OF THE RELATANTS IN HUMAN ACTIVITY

The human person				The human society	
side				side	
inter-personal	object-oriented			inter-personal	object-oriented
personal value system	personal knowledge system	MEANING LEVEL		societal value system	societal knowledge system
emotions	skills	---ACTIVITY--- OPERATIONAL LEVEL		organi-zational system	technical system

In this context it is the interpersonal side that is of paramount importance. I shall therefore briefly sketch the content of the societal and psychological systems attached to this side.

The organizational system is the totality of direct interpersonal relations that constitute the social structure of society; that is, the formation of cooperative groups, of direct hierarchies of superiority and subordination, of family and kinship relations and so on. The social value system is the abstract representation and legitimation of these social relations as virtual commandments governing social life, these commanding rules being constantly interposed on the potentialities of social interactions.

Thus clan and totem group structure among the Australian aboriginals constitutes a value system that defines the relation between individuals who may never have seen or heard of one another. Likewise, in a feudal society, the relationship between two strangers would be strictly defined in their value system and imposed upon their specific interpersonal relations.

For a human person the personality is to a large extent the result of his or her appropriation of the culture of the specific society to which he or she belongs, and the personality is constantly in interplay with the cultural system through activity. Consequently the emotion system of a specific person must correspond to the relations by which he or she is attached to the organizational system, and the personal value system must likewise be in a certain accordance with the social value system. There will even be a system of social control in the cultural system to ascertain whether these correspondences obtain. Now we have to study the organizational and the value system in more detail. Human activity can be organized by principles of either totalization or serialization. And these principles are not necessarily antagonistic. They can, in fact, sometimes supplement one another.

The prototype of the modern, market economic organization of society is the series, but generally we do not have a direct series of serialized individuals, rather a series of groups or even of composite organizations, such as firms. Therefore the interpersonal side of society, and with it the specific organization of the total activity of society, must be characterized by a number of organizational levels. If we take the sector of computer industry, we have a series of international firms that are so big that they need specific departments to control their own organizations, the depths of which may consist of four or five organizational levels. In the reproductive sphere, to use another example, we are rather close to an organization consisting of a series of "family" units that are either:

1. Single individuals (about half of the total population)
2. Couple without children
3. Families with one parent and child(ren)
4. Families with two parents and child(ren)

These social units are again placed in a context that is not totally, but partially serialized, as there are weak and rather transitory social networks contextualizing them.

Whatever the specific social structure of a given society at a certain point in time, a process of serialization can occur, and thus a state of anomia can emerge.

Such a process of serialization and resulting state of anomia is not necessarily occasion for social eschatology. They can, in the extreme case, be the death process of a society whose doom is caused by external or internal conditions leaving no potential for survival. But it can just as well be a process of transformation whereby an outdated societal structure is dissolved and replaced by a new and more relevant one. Whatever the case, serialization and anomia imply a state of crisis, and thus an unusual, but not necessarily abnormal societal state. What is more, in agreement with our model of correspondence, when society is in a state of crisis, the same thing will be the case for the personalities of the individuals involved. In fact, the state of crisis must primarily be attached to activity itself, that is, by its very nature superordinate to both the sociological and the psychological objects.

The dissolution of societal structure in a transitional (or terminal crisis) is therefore always accompanied by a dissolution of the personality structure.

But being a societal creature (living in an organized society) and a conscious being (with a personality) how can this sociological and psychological dissolution take place without the very activity being blocked? Well, mercifully, human individuals are mammals before being persons, and we are born into social relations that to a large extent are based on relations common to all primates. So these fundamental relations remain intact. And, anyway, the social and psychological dissolution is never total, but only partial.

In the analysis to follow I will, however, dramatize somewhat, talking about crisis, dissolution, serialization and anomia, without always specifying the extent or the degree to which these phenomena appear.

I will now examine four historical cases:

1. The great plague as a solvent of feudal society
2. The social revolutions paving the way to capitalism
3. The transition from antiagressiveness to militancy in the Zionist Jews.
4. The dissolution of the communist states

Case 1: **The Great Plague**

The contemporary accounts from the second part of the 14th century witnessed a deep crisis accompanied by social and psychological dissolution. In fact, the most basic fabric of society was in state of disintegration.

The relations of production were suspended by the mass extermination and mass migration imposed by the plague. A similar suspension afflicted the family relations, where the intimate loyalties between spouses or between parents and their children were not only compromised but often totally discarded.

If we now turn to the psychological relatant of activity, we find a corresponding dissolution of the system of emotions and of the personal value system. One expression of this personality dissolution is the apparent loss of normal feelings, a state of indifference to other human beings. In fact, the semi–serialized condition of living during the impact and the aftermath of plague presupposed an abandonment of the previous emotional bonds and value commitments. We have a description of this emotional atrophy in Boccaccio's introduction to *Decameron* where the plague in Florence constitutes the frame:

> One man shunned another [...] kinfolk held aloof, brother was forsaken by brother, oftentimes husband by wife, nay, what is more, and scarcely to be believed, fathers and mothers were found to abandon their own children to their fate, untended, unvisited as if they had been strangers[6].

Another account from Bavaria shows that the anomic state was not only a social disorganization, but also a dissolution of organized behavior in general:

> Men and women [...] wandered around as if mad [letting their cattle stray] because no one had any inclination to concern themselves about the future[7].

That this apparent indifference was actually a symptom of a deep crisis in personality, is proved by the expression of mass hysteria we also find in this period.

The flagellant movement is a characteristic example of this peculiar type of human activity.

Initially authorized by the Pope, but very soon turned against the clergy, this movement was desperate attempt to stop the Wrath of God before humanity was totally devastated:

---

6   Here quoted from Tuchman (1979, p. 97).

7   Ibid.

> Organized groups of 200 to 300 and sometimes more [...] marched from city to city stripped to the waist, scourging themselves with leather whips tipped with iron spikes until they bled [...].

> They were forbidden to bathe, shave, change their clothes, sleep in beds, talk or have intercourse with women without the Master's permission. Evidently this was not upheld, since the flagellants were often charged with orgies in which whipping combined with sex[8].

Although initially authorized by the church the flagellant movement was certainly not of such a placid nature as to be controlled by establishment:

> The movement was essentially anti–clerical, for in challenge to the priesthood, the flagellants were taking upon themselves the role of inter-ceders with God for all humanity[...].

> Growing in arrogance, they became overt in antagonism to the Church. The Masters assumed the right to hear confession and grant absolution or impose penance, which not only denied the priests their fee for these ser-vices but challenged ecclesiastical authority at its core. Priests who inter-vened against them were stoned and the populace was incited to join in the stoning. Opponents were denounced as scorpions and Antichrist. Orga-nized in some cases by apostate priests or fanatic dissidents, the flagellants took possession of churches, disrupted services, ridiculed the Eucharist, looted altars, and claimed the power to cast out evil spirits and raise the dead. The movement that began as an attempt through self–inflicted pain to save the world from destruction, caught the infection of power hunger and aimed at taking over the Church.

> They began to be feared as a source of revolutionary ferment and a threat to the propertied class, lay as well as ecclestical[9].

This description of the flagellants' self–tormenting behavior shows that behind the illusory indifference lay the most violent feelings of desperation and misery. The report also points to the potentially revolutionary forces that can attach to a process of serialization. In this case the tendency to revolt against that part of feudal order existing within the church was not carried through. That had to wait for about a century until the Protestant movements. In fact, the flagellant threat against the establishment was deflected toward a part of society well suited to serve the role of scapegoat without disrupting the basic structure of the formation. That part was the Jews, who already since the time of the crusades had been a favorite target of social frustration. We shall study this phenomenon in the section dedi-cated to the ascent of militant Zionism. Thus the unrest and turmoil during the afflictions of the great plague apparently did not change medieval soci-

---

8   Ibid. p.114.

9   Ibid. p. 115.

ety, which seemed more or less restored in the beginning of the next century.

However, as stated in Perry Anderson's excellent analysis 10 of the transition from feudal to capitalist society, the destruction of social order during the plague strongly facilitated the beginning transition to a new kind of social formation in the subsequent period, the Renaissance. In Anderson's analysis, the calamities of the 14th century of which the plague was only one, although perhaps the most conspicuous, were, in fact, the result of a major expansion of production and population during the preceding century, the epoch of the great Gothic cathedrals. The reigning feudal system was, however, not capable of coping with this expansion. For instance, the use of new and marginal agricultural fields led to a decrease in average yield, thus to aggravating the living standard and health conditions of the peasant population. The plague and the reaction to this mass extinction witness the general crisis of the late medieval times. At the same time it had in itself a causal effect on the ruling feudal order.

Using the terms of Lenin's version of *Historical Materialism*, the beginning of manufacture in late Middle Ages was the *objective conditions* of this transition, and the plague one of the causes of change in the subjective conditions. Personally I do not subscribe to this specific terminology[11]. As I see it, the plague also influenced these so-called objective conditions of social change. The mass extinction resulted in a shortage of man power in the feudal estates, which greatly destabilized the structure of feudal society. The traditional relationship between the squire and his peasant underwent a bifurcation. On the one hand economic and social conditions of the peasants improved under the jurisdiction of the feudal lord. On the other hand many lords tried to tighten up control of their now sparse subordinates by reinforcing the state of serfdom that had existed at an earlier time, and had been abandoned before the plague.

What we now consider to have been a period of cruel and brutal feudalism was to a large extent the effect of a state of crisis, in which the feudal structure was already in the process of transition toward a new societal logic, not yet implemented. That the state of crisis in the society was also experienced as a personal crisis is documented in Huizinga's beautiful book about the dying feudal order[12]. He found numerous descriptions in the contemporary literature of a state of depression, a melancholia, which indicate that it was both a widespread and a celebrated state of mind.

In sharp contrast to this stands the euphoria of the subsequent cultural explosion in the Renaissance. Though even at this stage turmoil – and even

---

10   See Anderson (1975).

11   See the section on Lenin's theory of dialectics in the revolutionary process in Kurasanow (1976, p. 324–220).

12   Huizinga (1972).

to a certain extent anomia – existed, here they were more often combined with growth and creation, as opposed to the dissolution and destruction pervading the late Middle Ages.

Case 2: **The Social Revolutions**

Prior to all the major social revolutions, the Dutch and the English of the 17th century, the French of the 18th and 19th and the Russian of the 20th century, we find, at least locally, conditions of serialization, arising from the structural dissolution of a regime or a social system that had for a long time been badly suited to maintain the necessary societal activity.

The pre–Revolutionary society is thus characterized by a strong, although in some case not apparent societal crisis, the psychological correlate of which is a widespread frustration and a growing discontent. This state of serialized psychological crisis results at some point in a kind of phase transition to an organized and common discontent. This generally occurs within the frame of a social, political or religious movement that attempts to impose its own kind of activity, organizational structure and system of meaning on the whole society.

On the societal level this dissent can be the catalyst to social reformation or revolution. On the personal level it can be the psychological precondition for a transformation of personality in the participating individuals. The crisis and dissolution of the old order make way for the emergence of a new psychological structure.

Let us return to the so–called subjective conditions of a revolutionary state. My main objection to the use of the term "subjective" is its theoretical ambiguity. It is unclear whether the term applies to the societal meaning system or to the personalities of the individuals involved.

In my understanding both systems are involved, but they are interacting in a way that is blurred if the ambiguity persists.

A long standing, bitter dispute between Marxian and non–Marxian historiographers and sociologists has been over to what extent it is the material, objective conditions in society or the ideational, subjective conditions that determine social change. For example, Weber's analysis of the transition from medieval to modern, industrialized society emphasizes the religious and moral features of, what he calls, *The Protestant Ethos*[13]. Whereas Marxians emphasize the material conditions for the movement from feudal to capitalist formation

According to my model the features emphasized by Weber constitutes the societal value system. A Marxian analysis frequently discards these features as mere superstructural epiphenomena of the basic structure of a society, which is constituted by forces of production and productive rela-

---

[13]   See Weber (1920).

tions. In my model this so–called basic structure constitutes the operational part of a society, while the Weberian features belong to the meaning level. The meaning level is just as necessary to the activity as the operational one. Just as human activity requires a technical and organizational system (tools and conscious cooperation), so does it also require that these tools and organizational structures have a meaning. A meaning being a conceptual mediator, just as a tool is an operational one.

Therefore a change in the value system of a society is just as necessary a condition for social transition as is a change in the technology and organization of production.

Case 3: The transition from antiagressiveness to militancy in the Jewish culture.

For any observer witnessing the meandering course of history in this century, the changes in the attitude and behavior of the Zionist Jews must be among the most incomprehensible riddles. How is it that a people who were the very incarnation of (at least physical) antiagressiveness can turn, in an astonishingly short time, into one of the most militant, if not militaristic nations of the world? What are the hidden causes of this swing from scapegoat to occupational power? In this section I shall try to trace the historical background of the traditional attitudes of European Jewry and the remarkable transition from apparent pacifism to the military virtues of contemporary Israel.

The first problem with the Jews is their definition. A most obscure mixture of religious and ethnic qualities has confused both the Jews themselves and their anti–Semitic persecutors in their efforts at definition[14]. To many Marxians, beginning with young Marx himself in *Zur Judenfrage*, the Jews have been so ill–defined in terms of the basic societal structure that a swift and final dissolution of Jewry has been recommended as a remedy to solve the theoretical as well as the practical problems[15].

In fact the fate of the Jews during European history can probably be better understood by a Weberian than by a strict Marxian analysis. In a

---

[14] The authorized definition of Jewishness is simply to be a child of a Jewish mother. We thus have a recursive definition, that would, in fact, need an initial member, the ancestral mother of the Jews. but even if this definition is genealogical rather than religious, Jews recognize the fact of denouncing the Jewish identity, although this is not simply a religious decision, but rather a cultural and ethnic one.

On the other hand the famous Nürnberger laws of Nazism had a more elaborate, but in principle, similar genealogical definition, according to which you were a Jew if 3 out of your 8 great grandparents were Jewish. But in the more bureaucratic practice of the Third Reich the definition was not recursive, but – by using membership of a Jewish congregation as the criterion of the great grandparents – operational in a finite manner.

[15] See MEGA 1: 347–377.

way, the Jews' economic function in the structure of society is as much the result of their religious character as it is its cause. As I see it, the importance of the origin of monotheism in Judaism is key to the understanding of Jewish history. The value system of the Jews presumes that the Jewish people, as the receiver of the revelation of the true and only God, are elected to be witness to and the responsible messengers of the divine plan for humanity.

In earlier polytheistic religions there was a quite simple relation between the strength of a people and the presumed power of its gods. If the strength of the people declined, the gods would be held responsible and could eventually be replaced by more suitable divinities.

This kind of problem solving is not a logical possibility to monotheists. The Jewish theology as well as their philosophy of history has been deeply marked by this restraint. The loyalty to the almighty God has been unconditional: For better and for worse. In prosperity and adversity. In peace and in persecution.

The designation as "a chosen people" – nationally and religiously – can as easily be an election to misery and impotence as it can to happiness and power. Not infrequently, the religious and national leaders of the Jews have explained the suffering of their people by pointing to their sins and ill faith as the reason for God's wrath. But actually the bad fate could just as easily be a part of a divine plan rather than a form of punishment.

As a result of a whole sequence of national catastrophes during the later Judaism, prophets adapted the Jewish meaning system to these calamities. In their interpretation, the Jews were selected to experience a period of punishment and trials as part of the grand plan of God. In the end the ultimate prophet, The Messiah, would arrive to announce the day of Judgment and restore the chosen people from their misery to a life of bliss and glory. There is a certain ambiguity in respect to the specific nature of the Messiah and of the wonderful existence into which he would lead the righteous. In some prophecies Messiah is depicted as a new king–priest like David (of whom he is specifically prophesied to be a descendant). In the more eschatological versions, however, he is a supranational entity sent by God to put an end to this calamitous vale of sorrows, adversities and injustice and to lead the virtuous to a new and heavenly Jerusalem freed of sin and freed of death.

Over the course of the exile in Babel and Persia and the disastrous insurrections against the Roman Empire, the messianic faith of the Jews lost more and more of its nationalistic, political aspirations, and became instead a pious and often mystical belief in a religious salvation – not in this most imperfect (and fortunately transient) mundane existence, but in the hereafter.

The Jewish attitude toward political violence is therefore, already in its religious foundations, very complex indeed. It is not for instance a fixed negative or positive attitude toward national war based on some apriori rule or moral code. The acceptability or unacceptability of violence depends, rather, on whether the violence is in accordance with God's will or not. If it is decided that it is God's plan to follow the Messiah in the war to end all wars, Jew can prove quite militant, as was seen in the final wars and insurrections against Rome. However, if the trials of the Jews are interpreted as a part of a prolonged martyrdom, they have very often proved themselves to be the most antiaggressive and patient of peoples.

A decisive historical condition impacting the transition to militant Zionism is the domination of the antiaggressive attitude from the beginning of the crusades up to the Zionist mass emigrations. European Jews in particular were decisively stamped by the constant succession of persecutions that originated with the crusades, followed by the already mentioned Jew–baitings during the Plague of the later part of the 14th century, by which time pogroms had become an favorite diversion from social frustrations which characterized European history at that time.

Until the 19th century in the western part of Europe, and quite recently in the eastern part, a peculiar ecological relation was established between the gentile (Christian) majority and the Jewish minority.

Because of their stubborn resistance to conversion to the true faith – the only remaining people to show such an obstinacy – the Jews during the Middle Ages were isolated into Ghettoes, forced into a series of civil restrictions and fiscal burdens, and, quite often, subject to pogroms. On the other hand the characteristics of Jewish culture, upheld as they were by a combination of the internal force of religious dedication and the external force of expulsion, proved valuable in the establishment of a certain economic function, not performed by any sector of the Christian majority. This function was banking. Prohibition against charging interest and banking for the Christians, and against almost any other ways of earning a living for the Jews, forced the latter into banking and commerce. An evolution reinforced by the fact that the Jews, at that time, were the only part of a society, beside the clergy, that had maintained literacy. Actually even the Jews had a ban on interest, that after all was the basis for the Christian ban, but reasonably enough, the spiritual leaders of Jewry interpreted this ban to apply exclusively to intra–Jewish relations.

While quite interesting and relevant to the Weberian story about the formation of Capitalism, the economic function of the Jews is not our main concern here. The focus here is the specific attitude and strategy toward violence that has developed during a millennium of persecution.

I see this attitude as a threefold disposition arising in three stages. The basic reaction to the violence inflicted upon the Jews is isolation, a quiet withdrawal into the material or cultural ghetto. Here, the basic strategy is invisibility. It was hoped that by living unnoticed, the Jews would not provoke any violent actions. I will call this fundamental disposition *the strategy of isolation.*

The main objective of isolation was not only to minimize contact with the *Goyim*, as the gentiles are called, but also to adhere to a social and moral code of conduct designed to prevent anti–Semitic feelings, and especially actions. There are actually two related expressions for anti–Semitism in *Yiddish*, the common language of eastern European Jewry. The first is *Risches*, which literally means wickedness, but specifically refers to anti–Semitism. The other is "making risches", which refers to any bad conduct on the part of Jews, which endangers the Jewish community by its potential for inciting anti–Semitic feelings.

The next stage is reached whenever the first strategy fails. When, in spite of their self–imposed invisibility, the Jews were persecuted by some overwhelming enemy, be it the Spanish inquisition, the Polish peasantry or the Cossacks, the obvious alternative strategy was to flee to another ghetto, where the prospects of enjoying a semi–hidden existence were better. The *strategy of escape* is a disposition just as deep–rooted as the disposition to hide. In the period between the Great Wars many Jews always had a suit-case packed and ready. Even though many had lived their whole lives peacefully and, during the ex–ghetto period, were apparently assimilated to the culture of the majority, they still had an emotive disposition requiring that a suitcase stand ready for a quick escape. The strategy of escape was not just a practical disposition but also a way for the Jews to maintain their status in their respective countries as a people living in prolonged exile.

Thus the escape disposition is a constituent part of the meaning system that defines existence in the material or cultural ghetto as an interim period of Jewish history – an interregnum between the glorious past of David and Solomon and the heavenly future to be announced by the coming of Messiah.

The final and ultimate stage in the complex strategy for living in a hostile and life threatening world was the *strategy of Messianic Revival*, or rather the revival of belief in the actual coming of Messiah. With intervals of a few centuries, waves of mass extinction or near genocide hit the European Jews. First came the crusades and the plague. And in the middle of the 17th century there was a mega–pogrom in Eastern Europe[16] in which it is estimated that the same proportion of the world population of Jews was killed as the proportion annihilated during the Nazi holocaust, that is about one third.

In many, if not in most, of the great historic disasters where the very existence of Jewry was evidently in peril the ultimate messianic strategy has been awaked from its slumber. It experienced a revival in both ritual practice and religious expectations.

---

16   The Khmelnytsky massacres that are described in note 18.

Thus during the last desperate insurrection against Rome, at a time when there was only a microscopic prospect of beating the overwhelming power of occupation, the leading rebel, bar Kokhba was anointed[17] as Messiah by the most prominent contemporary spiritual authority, rabbi Akiba. It was an act of sheer wishful thinking, as neither Rome, nor God, accepted this designation as king in either the earthly, or the heavenly Jerusalem.

The scourge of the crusades and the pogroms following the Plague gave rise to a new wave of the messianic movement, namely the Cabbala. This was a form of Jewish mysticism, based on number magic, which involved speculation about the transfer of the letters of the holy bible into arithmetic. Of especial interest was, of course, the calculation of the exact time of arrival of the true Messiah. Due to the disappointing experience with bar Kokhba, Jews were now extremely concerned with the authenticity of any future messianic candidate.

The largest messianic movement of recent times arose after the genocidal pogroms of the Cossacks participating in the Khmelnytsky uprising in the mid 17th century[18]. A young Jew living in the Ottoman empire announced himself as Messiah. Though it may be difficult for contemporary observers to understand the exceptional qualifications of this Sabbatai Zevi[19], immense masses of Jews, not only from Balkan, but from all over Europe, sold their belongings, took up their ready suitcases, and rushed to greet this messianic mirage. The mirage was exposed once this aspiring messiah ran into practical problems in his negotiations with the Sultan about plans for being installed as king in Jerusalem. The disagreement was suddenly solved when Sabbatai, threatened with the refined penal measures of the Ottoman empire, was persuaded to accept conversion to Islam. A type of behavior that not even his most ardent followers found suitable for a true Messiah.

In the century after the pogroms of the Khmelnytsky uprising, many peaceful centuries of refuge in Poland were brought to an end by the partition of this nation. Now the Jews were caught in a trap, the boundaries of which were the surrounding partitioning powers. The frustration of the unhappy Poles gave rise to additional pogroms, in spite of the careful isolation strategy of the Jews. With no escape possible the Jews were primed to receive a new Messiah. The person candidating this time was Jacob

---

17 Messiah means in fact *anointed*.

18 Under the hetman Khmelnytsky, the Cossacks of Ukrainia and Lithuania rebelled in 1648 against the Polish regime, a subordinate part of which happened to be its Jewish tax collectors, who were subjected to the rage, not only of the Cossacks, but also of the impoverished peasantry. The estimation of an extinction rate of one third pertains not just to the Jews in Ukrainia and Lithuania, nor even of the Eastern European Jewry, but to the total number of Jews existing at that time.

19 Sabbatai Zwi was apparently mentally unstable, possibly even of a schizophrenic disposition.

Frank, who appeared in the second part of the 18th century. His charisma was of the same order as Sabbatai's, and his career bore a strong resemblance to his predecessor – including a final sortie by conversion, this time to Catholicism.

After this repeated scandal the appeal of potential candidates running for Messiah–ship was severely diminished. Nonetheless, the messianic strategy remained the ultimate reaction to the threats of annihilation of the last couple of centuries. It became, however, a rather millenealistic movement with a more sublimated messianic content. Thus a popular religious revival arose in the late 17th century in the dismembered, ruined and increasingly anti–Semitic Poland, namely *Chassidism*. This revival bore similarity to the nonconformist Christian movements, as for instance the Anabaptist movement. Chassidism was founded by a character[20] resembling The Holy Francis, and it is still a movement exerting a strong religious and even political influence in USA and Israel.

The next wave of messianism coincided with the general Enlightenment movement in Europe. The specific Jewish version was *Haskalah*, which means "enlightenment" in Hebrew. This liberal movement was patronized by Napoleon, who was the first European ruler to grant civil rights to the Jews, thus bringing to an end the material and cultural confinement in the ghetto. Haskalah, however, was a messianic movement of a new and rather different character. It was not only a reaction to the elimination of the ghetto, but in its content it was assimilative, incorporating general, non–Jewish ideas and values. Haskalah is the first example of a messianic strategy that is only messianic in the generalized sense of being utopian or perhaps millenealistic.

Either because the great ideas of Enlightenment and bourgeois democracy did not become cemented in a prolonged period of authoritarian rule, or because the movement did not include the Jews to any great extent, the rise of socialism was the next messianic movement which conquered the Jewish masses, and, not surprisingly a great number of the important figures in the history of socialism were Jews.

The millenealistic movement of Zionism arose not much later than socialism, but in contrast to socialism it was a return to a more literal messianism. At the beginning of this century the Jewish socialist party Bund and Zionism were the dominant movements among Jews throughout the greater part of the Russian empire. The fact that the latter was to survive the former, was to a large extent the result of the repression of Bund by Lenin's Bolshevik fraction of the general socialist party.

---

20   He is characteristically enough best known by his pet name, Baal Schem Tov, which is Hebrew for *The Master of the Good Name*, referring to the cabbalistic belief in a black and a white magic, where a master knowing the true name (of God) was commanding cosmic forces in the duty of either the good or the bad.

It is not the objective of this paper to analyze the formation of Zionism and its positive and negative affiliation to socialism[21]. In fact, Zionism is a quite heterogeneous phenomenon with conflicting ingredients from such diverse sources as the liberal and secular nationalism of the founder, Herzl, the old religious messianism of Jewish culture, socialism of reformistic as well as revolutionary varieties and, last but not least, the right radical and increasingly fundamentalist religious nationalism that dominates Israel today.

The focus here, however, is not Zionism in general, but only that aspect of it that represents the great shift toward violence in the Jewish value system. I shall restate the paradox that was the point of departure for the present section:

How is it that Jews during one generation, turned from defenselessness to militarism, from a culturally deep-rooted strategy of defense to the strategy of first strike capability?

I see the wave of persecution during the Nazi years as a catastrophe on two levels. On the sociological level it was a cultural catastrophe destroying the cultural system of the European Jews; on the psychological level it was a personal catastrophe for those Jews who survived the Holocaust. Both the fugitives who populated Palestine during the thirties[22] and the survivors from the camps left the inhospitable continent with their former culture and their former personality in ruins. This state of anomia and serialized crisis of personality was the breeding ground for the mass psychological transition from the anti-aggressiveness of the Jewish exile to the militancy, if not militarism of the new Jewish state.

In this article I shall try to document the first part of this mass transition, that is the combined cultural and psychological dissolution and serialization. My historical source is the first volume of the autobiographical trilogy by Elie Wiesel, in which he describes his experiences as a youngster in the death camps of the holocaust.

The following episodes bear witness to the breakdown of family relations and moral principles that occurred. In the first incident Elie's father is running short of inner resources required to withstand the attacks from the *capo* Idek, and we witness the reaction of the young boy who is already much more fit for the life in the camp:

---

21   Frankel (1981).

22   The first waves of emigrations to Palestine came as a result of the pogroms organized by the Czarist state in end of previous and in the beginning of the present century. These state pogroms started with the assassination 1881 against Alexander the 2nd, an action in which a Jewish woman happened to be involved. The massive emigration only began with the Jews flying from Hitler.

Idek's nerves were on edge. He was restraining himself with great difficulty. Suddenly, his frenzy broke out. The victim was my father. 'You lazy old devil!' Idek began to yell. 'Do you call that work?'

And he began to beat him with an iron bar. At first my father crouched under the blows, then he broke in two, like a dry tree struck by lightning, and collapsed.

I had watched the whole scene without moving. I kept quiet. In fact I was thinking of how to get father away so that I would not be hit myself. What is more, any anger I felt at that moment was directed, not against the Capo, but against my father. I was angry with him, for not knowing how to avoid Idek's outbreak. That is what concentration camp life had made of me.[23]

That a drift toward demoralization is a real possibility is proven by the following quotation:

I once saw [a *Pipel* – juvenile assistant to a Capo] beating his father because the latter had not made his bed properly. The old man was crying softly while the boy shouted: 'If you don't stop crying at once I shan't bring you any more bread. Do you understand'.[24]

At the end of the grim odyssey the survivors are deported in cattle wagons away from the advancing red army. As they are offered neither food nor water during this journey the death rate is high. The situation is aggravated by the Germans who amuse themselves by making the prisoners fight among themselves for pieces of bread thrown to them in the cattle wagons:

In the wagon where the bread had fallen, a real battle had broken out. Men threw themselves on top of each other, stamping on each other, tearing at each other. Wild beasts of prey, with animal hatred in their eyes; an extraordinary vitality has seized them, sharpening their teeth and nails.

A crowd of workmen and curious spectators had collected along the train. They had probably never seen a train with such a cargo. Soon, nearly everywhere, pieces of bread were being dropped into the wagons. The audience stared at these skeletons of men, fighting one another to the death for a mouthful.

A piece fell into our wagon. I decided that I would not move. Anyway, I knew that I would never have the strength to fight with a dozen savage men! Not far away I noticed an old man dragging himself along on all fours. He was trying to disengage himself from the struggle. He held one hand to his heart. I thought at first he had received a blow in the chest. Then I understood; he had a bit of bread under his shirt. With a remarkable speed he drew it out and put it to his mouth. His eyes gleamed; a smile, like a grimace, lit up his dead face. And was immediately extinguished. A

---

23   See Wiesel (1972, p. 66)

24   Ibid., p. 75.

shadow had just loomed up near him. The shadow threw itself upon him. Felled to the ground, stunned with blows, the old man cried:

'Meir, Meir, my boy! Don't you recognize me? I'm your father...you're hurting me...you're killing your father! I've got some bread...for you too... for you too...'

He collapsed. His fist was still clenched around a small piece. He tried to carry it to his mouth. But the other one threw himself upon him and snatched it. The old man whispered something, let out a rattle, and died amid the general indifference. His son searched him, took the bread, and began to devour it. He was not able to get very far. Two men had seen and hurled themselves upon him. Others joined in. When they withdrew, next to me were two corpses, side by side, the father and son.[25]

I will now leave Wiesel and the apocalyptic description of human behavior under conditions where the choice between social solidarity and individual survival seemed to be mutually exclusive alternatives.

The next chapter in Jewish history is about the boot strapping process of psychological, social and cultural reconstruction. A reconstruction that happened to replace an abhorrence for violence with a militant, if not militarist attitude toward real and sometimes even imagined foes. But it will be outside the scope of this article to describe this historical process.

One point should, however, be stressed. The very suddenness and radicalism of the change, actually fits into the general pattern of reaction to persecutions of the most acute and genocidal type. As we have already seen, at a certain threshold of violence the normal strategy of invisibility is replaced by escape as the semi–normal mechanism of survival. But when even escape is ineffective as a means of ensuring the existence of the people, drastic cultural changes are necessitated.

This last type of transition is not likely to be a trait specific to the Jewish culture. In fact, most people seem to react in exactly the same way. When even the more extraordinary and rarely used cultural mechanisms are ineffective in dealing with genuinely life–threatening crisis, innovative measures must be found, or the people in question will be doomed.

Case 4: **The dissolution of the communist states**

My final case is the recent dissolution of the former Communist states of Eastern Europe and the Soviet Union. Here the malfunctions of command economics and party bureaucracy resulted in a deep anomia that, while not leading to the necessary economic reforms, has resulted in the removal of the political obstacles. The personality structure, however, is still tuned to a societal system which is no longer in existence.

---

25   Ibid., p. 112–13.

Such societal crises lead to serialisation and a state of personal crisis for those individuals who are mobilizing the psychological processes that eventually can lead to major personality changes resulting in a serialized turn of the mass, followed by a phase transition out of serialization and toward a new formation of societal structure.

But the precise character of this phase transition is not predetermined. More specifically, the euphoric liberal hope of a more or less automatic transition to a combination of market economics and political democracy has not materialized – at least no yet. Instead, demagogic populism, extreme nationalism and even mafia–like criminality arise. The dangerous and unpredictable nature of this process can be witnessed in the epidemic spread of ethnic strife now threatening to fragment larger parts of Eastern Europe into tribal turmoil.

Again we witness a central break down of the meaning structure resulting in a state of anomia and in a serialized mass of individuals who on a personal level are caught in a psychological crisis.

The psychological turn of the mass

My point is that in all the historical cases mentioned, the formation of a new culture began as a mass psychological turn. The sociological mutation was not the cause, but rather the effect, of a serialized, initially uncoordinated assembly of individual turns in personality.

This is, in fact, the rational kernel of the psychologism of mass psychology. When the sociological entity with its cultural frame of reference is dissolved – and that is exactly the case in a state of anomia – we are left with only a disorganized series of individuals in deep psychological crisis.

Thus there will be no help to get from society, no guidelines from the cultural meanings system. Not only is the societal entity out of function, but the cultural frame of reference is irrelevant, if not directly *meaningless*.

It is therefore my point, that the restoring forces cannot come from the now nonexistent (or at least only partially functioning) societal level. Instead they must necessarily originate from the individual, from his or her personality, which has not been totally destroyed, but rather has been suspended during a crisis of transition.

In the new model below I have sketched this transition through 5 phases which are presented as parallel, and closely related, processes occurring on both the psychological and the sociological level.

In the first phase there is an *initial stability* on both levels and a structural correspondence between the initial culture of society and the initial personality of the single individual.

In the second phase, a major social crisis leads to the a *break down* where there is a processual correspondence between societal serialisation and personality dissolution.

The third phase is a *serial interregnum* on both levels. We now have a structural correspondence between the serialized mass on the sociological level and a suspended personality on the psychological level.

The following, fourth phase is the *turn*, characterized by a processual correspondence between a sociological cultural turn in culture and a psychological turn in personality.

Finally in the *reconstruction* phase, we have a structural correspondence between a reconstructed society and a reconstructed personality. In fact the final phase is structurally of the same type as the first; we have a new state of social psychological correspondence and equilibrium, from which the process can proceed with new crises and new turns.

This sketch is of a very general theoretical, if not metatheoretical character. Even in the historical examples the analysis is highly abstract and not intended to explain the specific nature of the peculiar periods and societies.

It is also evident that in spite of the similarities among the examples, there are also major differences. In the case of the Plague we have a crisis with anomia and serialisation, but actually no genuine turn. This is a consequence of the only partial nature of the crisis. What occurred was, in fact, a prolonged dissolution of a very tenacious sociological formation. We thus have all the aspects of the model, but only to a certain degree. And we have no momentary and grand turn, but rather a succession of crises and turns, before the new formation materializes.

In the case of the social revolutions we are focusing only on some of those important crises and turns. Compared to the former example, things are turned upside down, for here we have the dramatic aspect of sudden change resulting in a structural shift, but we lose the perspective of an accumulated state of dissolution and disorganization.

In the third case, that of the turn from antiaggressiveness to militancy of the Jews, the model seems to be rather adequate. But it is granted that it is a very special kind of historical phenomenon, carefully selected to suit the model.

In the final case, the fall of the Communist states, I find the model useful to point out the psychological preconditions for a turn in the societal system.

A MODEL FOR THE PSYCHOLOGICAL MASS TRANSITION

Phase	Societal level	Individual level	Relation
Initial Stability	Initial Society	Initial Personality	Structural Correspondance
Break Down	Serialisation ====>	Personality dissolution	Processuel Correspondance
Serial interregnum	Serialized Masss	Suspended Personality	Structural Correspondance
Turn	Cultural Turn <====	Personality Turn	Processual Correspondance
Reconstruction	Reconstructed Society	Reconstructed Personality	Structural Correspondance

A theoretical reminder

I have presented these thoughts about mass psychology as a double provocation for my colleagues who are just as committed to Activity Theory as I am. The empirical provocation is to focus on some of those historical phenomena that in the Marxian tradition have often been repressed or rationalized as phenomena of a "sick" and decaying social order. The theoretical provocation is a partial support of psychologism, defined as the thesis that it is sometimes correct to see the psychological processes as causes of social change and not vice versa. This psychologism is materially true, whenever the social structure is demobilized as a result of is own disorganization and inability to function. The job of making a new social system then is to be done by serialized individuals who have to rely on their individual resources.

References

Anderson, P. (1975): *Passages from Antiquity to Feudalism*, London.
Canetti, E. (1988): *Masse und Macht*, Frankfurt a. M.
Durkheim, E. (1951): *The Suicide*, Glencoe, Ill.
Frankel, J. (1981): *Prophecy and Politics – Socialism, Nationalism & the Russian Jews*, 1862–1917, Cambridge.
Huizinga, J.H. (1972): *The Waning of the Middle Ages: A study of the forms of life, thought and art in France and the Netherlands in the fourteenth and fifteenth centuries*, Harmondsworth.
Kurasanow, G.A. et al. (eds.)(1976): *Geschichte der marxistischen Dialektik – Die Leninsche Etappe*, Berlin.
Le Bon, G. (1895): *Psychologie des Foules*, Paris.
Lenin, W.I. (1905): *The State and the Revolution*, London (1969).
Marx, K. (1844): *Die Judenfrage, MEGA 1*: 347–377.
Sartre, J.-P. (1960): *Critique de la Raison Dialectique*, Paris.
Sachar, H. M. (1958): *The Course of Modern Jewish History*, London.
Tuchman, B. (1979): *A Distant Mirror – the Calamities of 14th Century*, Harmondsworth.
Weber, M. (1920): *Die protestantische Ethik und der Geist des Kapitalismus* (The Protestant Ethic and the Spirit of Capitalism), Tübingen.
Wiesel, E. (1972): *The Night*, New York.

ON GROWING UP
IN SOCIETY

NOTES ON COMMUNICATION, ACTIVITY THEORY, AND ZONE OF PROXIMAL DEVELOPMENT

Aksel Mortensen
University of Copenhagen

...his (man's) activity is always embedded in communication...
A. N. Leontiev[1]

...mental functioning in the individual originates in social, communicative processes... J. V. Wertsch[2]

The purpose of the following discussion is to present some considerations on the relationship between communication and activity. I will try to show that these phenomena can not be separated and that they can not be unified, and that from birth onward, communication is the origin of activity for every individual. I will attempt to support this claim by drawing examples from ZPD –'the zone of proximal development.'[3]

Let me begin with a quotation from Roman Jakobson's 1968–lecture 'Language in relation to other communication systems' (Jakobson, 1971):

> On the other hand, it becomes ever clearer for psychological, neurological, and above all, linguistic research that language is a vehicle not only for interpersonal, but also for intrapersonal communication. This field, for a long time scarcely explored or even totally ignored, faces us now, especially after such magnificent reconnaissances as those of L.S.Vygotsky and A.N.Sokolov, with an imminent request for investigating the internalization of speech and the varied facets of inner language which anticipates, programs and closes our delivered utterances and in general guides our internal and external behavior, and which shapes the silent retorts of the tacit auditor (p. 697).

---

1 Leontiev, A. N.: *Problems in the Development of the Mind*, Moscow, 1981, 574 pp., p. 413, here quoted from 'Activity: Structure, Genesis, and Units of Analysis', L. A. Radzikhovskii, *Soviet Psychology*, 1984–85/VOL. XXIII, NO. 2, p. 37.

2 J.V.Wertsch: *Voices of the Mind*, Harvard University Press, 1991, p. 13.

3 For further explanations of this Vygotsky–notion look later in this chapter.

Jakobson's request for investigations has been heeded by many researchers in the years since 1968, not least among people working in Activity Theory (AT) circles; *'Voices of the Mind'* (1991) by J. V. Wertsch is worthy of mention as a main source for studies in the field.[4]

In spite of Jakobson's early statement about Vygotsky's 'magnificent reconnaissances' and in spite of the amount of the following research it seems as if we still are searching for a 'break–through' within AT–thinking about the notion of 'communication'.

Davydov in 1990 in Lahti listed 'Unsolved Problems of AT' (1991) and he wrote:

> These last years our specialists are busy discussing the problem of how the notion of activity and the notion of communication are related (ibid, p. 33).

Davydov comes to the following conclusion about the ongoing research in this area:

> That is why the notions of activity and communication must not be op–posed[5], and at the same time we cannot study communication and evaluate its role in people's life without examining their activity which is only shaped by communication (ibid, p. 34).

This bold statement is hard to forget and hard to live with, I feel. If we do not find our footing in our struggle with these concepts, AT can not help us to understand learning and learning difficulties, i.e. to understand what is going on in ZPD.

Also in Lahti 1990 Engeström in his 'opening address' voiced strong opinions concerning the relationship between communication and activity.

> It is somewhat ironic that at the same time as the concept of object–related activity is criticized by some psychologists and philosophers for neglect of sign–mediation, language and communication, some prominent linguists are finding the very same concept of activity increasingly attractive as means of conceptualizing the interface between the sociocultural and lin–guistic realms (Engeström, 1991, p. 9).

---

4   A new Danish contribution to the investigation and understanding of communication, inner speech, egocentric language, and the psychology of description, is written by I. K. Moust-gaard: *Psychological Observation and Description*, Sigma, 1990. Chapter II 4. 'Description and communication' is of special interest here.

5   Likewise V. P. Zinchenko March 21, 1991 wrote in a longer electronic–mail–message the following lines: 'Communication as an opposition to AT in the Lomov's sense is beneath threshold. Research on communication both as direct and indirect in the AT would be more interesting. We expect here very interesting surprise soon. B. D. El'konin has promised me to formulate a new view on communication in the context of culture, activity and religion'.

Engeström supposes that the source of the irony lies partially in Vygotsky's failure to work out the conceptual distinction between activity and action at the time he presented his model[6] and that:

> Leontiev did not elaborate on how the triangular model of action should be developed or extended in order to depict the structure of a collective activity system (ibid).

I think that the article by L.A. Radzikhovskii from 1983 (in Russian, published in English in *'Soviet Psychology'*, 1984–85/Vol. XXIII, No. 2, pp. 35–53) in abridged form gives a good insight into the problem. The title of the article is: 'Activity: Structure, Genesis, and Units of Analysis', and it opens in this way:

> One of the most remarkable events in Soviet psychology in the second half of the '70s was the discussion of the problem of the relationship between communication and activity (....) We considered the following approach to the problem, which we here present in its most general form, the most constructive: Communication and activity are undoubtedly interrelated; but communication (in contrast to perception, memory, etc.) is not usefully regarded as simply one type of activity as it is analyzed in terms of Leontiev's paradigm activity–action–operation, motive–goal–condition. This approach to the problem is useful primarily for advancing the theory of activity: it points sharply to the very essential point, insufficiently developed in the theory of activity, that analysis of social environments and the mechanisms of human activity is both collective and individual.

If we follow Radzikhovskii, explanations are missing:

> In the theory of activity (....) a quite detailed notion of the morphological structure of activity has been developed (activity–action–.....); and the conditions for a transition from one level of activity to another (....), etc., have been demonstrated. This morphological paradigm does not, however, explain very well why activity should change as a consequence of the real or imagined presence of other people; nor does it answer the question of wherein, from the psychological point of view, lies the qualitative difference between "another" person and any other physical object, e.g. questions associated with communication, interaction, etc. In all these cases, if we remain within the theory of activity, we can say only that the motive of activity and its operational–executory aspect are social. But to say this is only to affirm, not to explain;... (ibid pp. 36–37).

Radzikhovskii tells that:

---

6   A. A. Leontiev states in the article 'Ecce Homo' in *Activity Theory*, 11/12, 1992 that he has come to another conviction (than – maybe – Engeström) through close studies of some of Vygotsky's unnoticed works. 'In any case, there can be no doubt that Vygotsky came to the basic formulation of activity theory in 1930' (p. 41) claims A. A. Leontiev and refers to his book *Lev Semenovich Vygotsky*, Moscow, 1990.

Leontiev himself commented: Can we assume that adequate activity is formed in a person under the influence of objects themselves? The untenability of such an assumption is obvious....Relations to the world are always mediated by man's relations to other people; his activity is always embedded in communication. In its initial external form, in the form of joint activity or in the form of speech, or even in only imagined communication, communication is a necessary and specific condition for the development of man in society (ibid p. 37).

Unit of analysis

As the title of the Radzikhovskii article presages, the author – like many contemporary researchers – is searching for a 'Unit of Analysis'.

From a positive statement about: "...E.G.Yudin's idea that there is a difference between activity as an explanatory principle....and activity as a subject of study..." (p. 40) Radzikhovskii proposes 'social (joint) action' as the unit of analysis of activity (p. 41). Placing particular emphasis on the contributions of Bakthin and Vygotsky to this area of research, he quotes the latter:

In analyzing ontogeny Vygotsky stressed the joint nature of the child's first activity (for example, together with the mother) as its most important feature. He wrote that the child 'enters into a relationship with a situation through another person, not directly'(p. 42).

Here the importance of 'sign' is introduced.

Concretely, we are saying that the general structure of ontogenetically primary joint activity...includes at least the following elements: subject (child), object, subject (adult). The object here also has a symbolic function and plays the role of a primary sign. In fact, the child's movement toward, and manipulation of, an object, even when he is pursuing the goal of satisfying a vital need, is also simultaneously a sign for an adult: to help, to intervene, to take part. The findings of child psychology indicate that not only the adult but also the child percieves a situation in this way. In other words, true communication, communication through signs takes place here between the adult and the child...An objective act is built up around the object as an object, and sign communication is built up around the same object as the sign. Communication and the objective act coincide completely here, and can be separated only artificially, by construing them as two different projections of one and the same thing. Of course, then, a sign (in our terminology, an ontogenetically primary sign) is both objective and social at the same time. But this sign does not really have meaning in the traditional, logical, semantic sense. Moreover, we assume that in the course of internalization of a primary joint act, the entire structure of relations existing in it (subject – object (sign) – subject) preserves the union between the objective and the social "coded" in it, and is transformed into the structure of an "internal", uncognized sign, a sign as an element of the base structure of activity. This would explain both the objective and the social nature of the base structure of an individual's activity; it would also

explain the origin of the structure of the individual's activity in joint activity – communication (p. 44).

Now we have 1) a distinction between activity as an explanatory principle
and activity as a subject of study, 2) 'social (joint) action' as the unit of
analysis of activity, and 3) 'communication' as the origin of the structure of
the individual's activity in joint activity.

Radzikhovskii recapitulates in two separate, important phrases on the
last page (51):

> 1) We hypothesize several levels in the structure of activity; these levels
> are not isomorphic to one another, but are linked by relations of genetic
> continuity. The external picture of the individual's activity unfolds on the
> basis of these structures. The deepest basic structure is formed on the basis
> of internalization of ontogenetically primary objective activity and of joint
> activity, which is also, simultaneously, communication.

> 2) Therefore, social (joint) action, i.e., action oriented not only toward an
> object, although an object may be a necessary component in a social ac-
> tion, but also toward the objective action of another human being, is pro-
> posed as a unit of analysis of individual activity....

These two statements serve to emphasize the 3 claims mentioned above:
Distinctive aspects and levels of activity, *Unit of analysis*, and *Communication as the origin*.

Using these three claims as a foundation, I will a) consider activity as a
subject of study (and leave it to others, in this book and elsewhere, to treat
it as an explanatory principle), b) see communication as the origin of the
structure of the child's activity in joint activity (and leave the problem of
finding the relation between the communication–category and the category
of perception, memory etc. to other people), and c) concentrate on
(internalization of primary) 'social (joint) action' as the unit of analysis of
activity.

In my effort to understand communication in the ZPD I will apply the
Radzikhovskii–analysis to that notion – without making him responsible
for the results of the experiment, of course.

Before doing so, I will recommend readers not quite acquainted with the
communication problems in Vygotsky's notion of 'zone of proximal development' to consult Vygotsky, 1978, Wertsch, 1984, Tharp & Gallimore,
1988 and Mortensen, 1990. The communication in the dyad adult – child
has intersubjectivity as the purpose and goal through 'situation–definition'
and 'semiotic mediation' as Wertsch explains it.

Furthermore I will recommend the articles of Stone (1993) and Goncu &
Becker (1992). The two articles are important contributions to the elaboration of Vygotsky's ZPD notion. The former points to the value of the
semiotic notions of prolepsis and implicature in understanding the com-

munication in the ZPD/Scaffolding area. The latter points to the distinction between real world and *pretend world* activities.

Real world activities are those in which a child maintains her day to day living, activities such as dressing, solving an arithmetic problem, or making tortillas. Pretend world activities are directed towards understanding the dynamics of and mastering the real world activities. Pretend world activities are specific kinds of play activity.

> ...in pretend play as in real world activities the child works with, an comes to understand, representations which she initially did not understand. In pretend play the representations not yet understood by the child are produced by the child herself. Thus, for Vygotsky, pretend play constitutes a ZPD regardless of the presence or absence of other people. (Goncu et al., 1992).

In pretend play there is a new possibility:

> The new possibility, is that the process of learning can emerge from the child herself. In Vygotsky's (1978) words, 'play creates a ZPD of the child. In play always behaves beyond his average age, above his daily behavior; in play it is as though he were a head taller than himself (p.102)'. (Goncu, op.cit.)

Communication in ZPD

My younger granddaughter is now living abroad with her family. After she had been away for 6 weeks, we met again. At that time she was nine months old. After a few hours together we were 'communicating' very well. She moved her lips in the same way I moved my lips; she looked at me and, with a smile ready in the event of my response, waved her hand to me, obviously expecting me to wave back.

I consider my 'granddaughter–communication' as a 'social (joint) action' and I consider her part of the action as a part of her 'appropriation–project'[7], her grand effort to cope with life.

The prerequisites for maintaining this project through–out childhood (and later on) are many.

I am convinced that success in communicative processes (in ZPD) is among the most important of these prerequisites, and I base this conviction upon the many experiences I have had with children throughout a long life as a teacher, as a psychologist working many years in the school, and as a father (and grandfather).

Among the children I have met are two boys whose development I believe can best be explained in terms of success and failure in primary communicative processes.

---

7   In German: Projekt der Aneignung.

One was a 12 year old boy from a family where both parents held intellectually demanding jobs. He had problems concerning spelling and syntax. But he also loved to come up with his own different solutions to every task, even when he knew the traditional solution of the task. He succeeded in school, and later in life, partly through hard work and partly because his untraditional problem–solving methods were met from the very beginning with acceptance from both the family and the school – in spite of his peculiar ways of thinking and the many flaws in his writing. I think that his parents were able to create trustful negotiations – verbal and nonverbal – in his ZPD.

The other boy was of the same age and from the same social and economic context. He had – on the surface – similar problems as the first boy. In contrast, he didn't work very well or hard, and when he reached the age of puberty, he began to wander about aimlessly and became depressed. He scored 'zero' in 'block design' (WISC) and average or above on all the other tests. His anamnesis indicated that already from birth he had probably suffered from very specific perceptual problems with colours and forms, followed by connected problems with language and specific concepts presented in the school curriculum. In interviews in connection with the tests, his mother revealed that she had been concerned about him from the time of his birth. My conjecture is that this boy and his family had severe problems establishing successful negotiations in ZPD, and that these carried over into the school experience, where the consequence was the same.

Many years later these two cases seem to me to demonstrate that the respective success and failure of these two boys varied in accordance with their possibilities for 'success in communicative processes' considered as important prerequisites for their development.

Elsewhere I have proposed the notion of 'the idiosyncratic[8] room of the person' (Mortensen, 1990) as 'the ever shifting phenomenological context' (p. 151) and as a phenomenon in everybody's life. The article in which I introduced this notion was concerned with children with learning difficulties; children who didn't answer or gave wrong answers, and the problems we have understanding these situations in schools. What is going on in these cases? As a psychologist I stated that "we don't know..., but we do know that children are doing *something* when they don't answer, we know that in everyday activities, cognitive functions are ongoing, and we know that children with learning difficulties experience problems" (ibid).

The idiosyncratic room of the person can, in accordance with a proposal from Benny Karpatschof (ibid), show up as a good room or as a bad room. We all experience shifts between good rooms and bad rooms, but the balance between them is important. Perhaps one could say that a good room

---

8   *Idiotes* is a Greek word and the original meaning is a private man with no public responsibilities.

contains clear 'meaning' and a consequent 'sense' of trust, while a bad room contains unclear 'meaning' and a consequent 'sense' of fear.

The two boys mentioned above were different in this respect. The first experienced mostly 'good rooms' from the very beginning of life; the other boy experienced mostly 'bad rooms', and nobody could break through the wall to these rooms, not even the psychologist, unfortunately. He could only discover the wall and determine its thickness. No doubt both of the boys had their individual 'appropriation-projects'; the first one kept his project going with success, the other one, in a state of depression, maintained that he didn't believe in it.

Turning now to the question – What goes on in the ZPD in homes and schools? – and bearing in mind both my granddaughter and the two school-boys, we can return to Radzikhovskii (acknowledging that he was not writing about communication in ZPD):

> Moreover, we assume that in the course of internalization of a primary joint act, the entire structure of relations existing in it (subject – object (sign) – subject) preserves the union between the objective and the social "coded" in it, and is transformed into the structure of an "internal", uncognized sign, a sign as an element of the base structure of activity (see Radzikhovskii above).

I believe that during the first years of life, many such 'internalizations of primary joint acts' will occur. The result will be many 'signs as elements of the base structure of activity'. In fact this formulation may be looked upon as an untraditional, alternative way to talk about the creation of 'basic trust' or its opposite. I further believe that it is a better, more concrete way to talk about the problems in ZPD if we acknowledge that "communication and the objective act coincide completely..., and can be separated only artificially, by construing them as two different projections of one and the same thing" (see Radzikhovskii above).

Maybe this is the crucial point. When you try to understand and analyze what constitutes optimal communication in ZPD, when you try to describe in categories the neccesary negotiations aimed at intersubjectivity, then perhaps from the adult point of view, you artificially separate the communication from the 'objective act' taking place; that is, from the 'social (joint) action' wherein the child's part is dependent on experiences with "...internalization of ontogenetically primary objective activity and of joint activity, which is also, simultaneously, communication" (see above). In a way, as the adult partner you can ignore the fact that you are simultaneously object and subject in the ongoing child-activity. As object (and subject) in the situation you are also 'sign'. You are both a 'communicative sign' and an 'informative sign'. When you deal with children predominantly acquainted with 'bad rooms', it is difficult for you to choose your proper role. There is a dangerous tendency to forget that the child "enters into a relationship with a situation through another person, not directly" (see above).

Vygotsky, (1978, p. 30), formulates a parallel theoretical point of view:

> From the very first days of the child's development his activities acquire a meaning of their own in a system of social behavior and, being directed towards a definite purpose, are refracted through the prism of the child's environment. The path from object to child and from child to object passes through another person. This complex human structure is the product of a developmental process deeply rooted in the links between individual and social history.

This quotation is also important for Tharp and Gallimore, 1988 (p. 28). They use the same lines from Vygotsky in their development of a highly elaborated version of ZPD. Furthermore they "derive this general definition of teaching: Teaching consists in assisting performance through the ZPD. Teaching can be said to occur when assistance is offered at points in the ZPD at which performance requires assistance" (p. 31). I see this as a promising definition.

Tharp and Gallimore[9] propose a four-stage model (see figure 1). What in my opinion is really interesting in this model is the line or 'zone' between Stage I and Stage II – and Stage II: 'Assistance provided by the self'.

Four stages of the ZPD

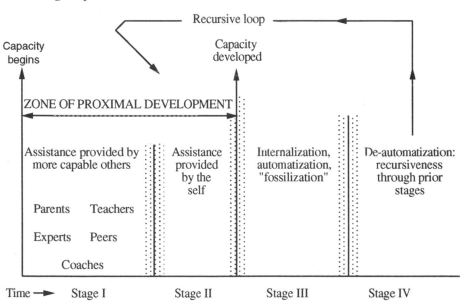

Figure 1: Genesis of performance capacity: progression through the ZPD and beyond.

---

9 Redrawn from Tharp and Gallimore (1988, fig. 2.1, p. 35)

> During Stage I, we see a steadily declining plane of adult responsibility for task performance and a reciprocal increase in the learner's proportion of responsibility. This is Bruner's fundamental 'handover principle' – the child who was a spectator is now a participant (ibid p. 35).

Concerning Stage II the authors write:

> In neo–Vygotskian theory, whether we consider the genesis of a particular performance capacity (microgenesis) or the development of an individual (ontogenesis), the same four stages describe the preponderance of self-control/social-control relationships. During Stage II, the relationships among language, thought, and action in general undergo profound rear-rangements – ontogenetically, in the years from infancy through middle childhood (ibid p. 37).

Tharp and Gallimore provide convincing analyses and advice concerning the demands placed on the adult in teaching situations in ZPD's – demands often, and for many reasons, neglected in pedagogical practices. What is interesting for me here is not this adult-'neglect' but the question about the 'neglect' on the part of the child. How is it possible that so many children do not advance from Stage I to Stage II or fail to complete Stage II in both homes and schools, in spite of what appears to be the most qualified assistance from parents and teachers?

The term 'neglect' cannot properly be applied to the child's part in the exchange. Children, from infancy onto middle childhood and beyond, attack the world and society, they do not neglect it. If it appears that they do, it can only be the result of failure in communication, failure in activity.

Suggestion

Drawing on AT, my suggestion is that when "the relationships among language, thought, and action in general (shall) undergo profound rearrangements – ontogenetically, in the years from infancy through middle childhood" (see above) it is hard or impossible in many cases, in many microgenetic ZPD's, to take into full consideration the fact that you must not "from the adult point of view separate the communication from the 'objective act' taking place', because then the child is left alone in his dependency on experiences with '...internalization of ontogenetically primary objective activity and of joint activity...'".

I feel sure that adult persons – professionals and parents – in their social contact with children often concentrate so hard on *verbal* communication, on the neccesary negotiations toward intersubjectivity, that they separate the communication from the ongoing act or activity, and thereby disregard the children's simultaneous use of action, sign and communication in the existential effort to maintain their individual grand appropriation-projects. Learning-action thereby misses its goal, and learning-activity lacks its motive.

Further considerations on *'primary objective activity'* and *'communication as the origin'* are needed.

References:

Davydov, V. V. (1991): The content and unsolved problems of activity theory, *Activity Theory*, No 7/8, pp. 30–35.

Engeström, Y. (1991): Activity Theory and individual and social transformation, *Activity Theory*, No 7/8, pp. 6–17.

Goncu, A. & Becker, J. (1992): Vygotsky and Early Education, *International Journal of Cognitive Education and Mediated Learning*.

Jakobson, R. (1971): *Selected Writings, II Word and Language*, The Hague, Paris.

Leontiev, A. A. (1992): Ecce Homo, *Activity Theory*, 11/12, pp. 41–45.

Leontiev, A. N. (1981): *Problems of the development of the mind*, Moscow.

Mortensen, A. (1990): Culture and Microcosmos of Individuals: The Idiosyncratic Room of the Person, *The Quarterly Newsletter of Comparative Human Cognition*, volume 12, Number 4. pp. 146–153.

Moustgaard, I. K. (1990): *Psychological Observation and Description*, Søreidgrend.

Radzikhovskii, L. A. (1984–85): Activity: Structure, Genesis, and Units of Analysis, *Soviet Psychology*, Vol. XXIII, no. 2, pp. 35–53.

Stone, C. Addison (1993): What's Missing in the Metaphor of Scaffolding?, In E. A. Forman, N. Minick, & C. A. Stone (eds.), *Contexts for Learning: Sociocultural Dynamics in Children's Development*, Oxford.

Tharp, R. G. & Gallimore, R. (1988): *Rousing minds to life*, Cambridge.

Vygotsky, L. S. (1978): *Mind in Society: The development of higher psychological processes*, Michael Cole, Vera John–Steiner, Sylvia Scribner, and Ellen Souberman, (eds.), Cambridge, Mass.

Wertsch, J. V. (1984): The zone of proximal development: Some conceptual issues, In B. Rogoff & J. Wertsch (eds.): *Children's learning in the "zone of proximal development"*, pp. 7–18, San Francisco.

Wertsch, J. V. (1991): *Voices of the Mind*, Cambridge, Mass.

Zinchenko, V. P. (1991): Contribution to the 'xact–electronic–mail'-discussion on March 21 (on the network initiated by 'Laboratory of Comparative Human Cognition', University of California, San Diego).

WHERE DOES PERSONALITY GO,
WHEN THE CHILD GOES TO SCHOOL?

Kirsten Baltzer
The Royal Danish School
of Educational Studies

Children go to school all over the world. Parents are obliged to make their children go there or to take care that they are otherwise instructed. The ultimate aim of a public school is educating children to maintain the society. Usually this aim is carried on and fulfilled during further education, vocational training and later on in the career.

This paper presents some considerations on the theme: "Personality development during school education." At the outset it takes a look at the role of school in society and the significance of identity and personality. Thereafter it sketches some pedagogical stories. It would have been fine to tell just one story summarizing all the points needed, but such a story could not be found. So a number of stories will be told. You may find some of the stories rather theoretical. Yet the essence of every story is to point out some serious consequences of the teaching and learning taking place in public schools.

The main theme of the following six stories is the ever–present dynamics that exists among cognition, motives and emotions in the personality. The child's experiences in primary and secondary socialization contribute to the development of personality. Conflicting or contradictory experiences and their influence on the dynamics of the personality will be analyzed and discussed in relation to the six stories. The stories tell us about different themes incorporated in the main theme. At the end of the article the main theme is in focus again. But first the role of school in society.

The school as an agency of secondary socialization

The public school is an agency of secondary socialization. In primary socialization the child lives in a "world" defined by the parents. In primary socialization emotional identification is the primary learning process (Hedegaard and Chaiklin, 1990, p. 5–6). In secondary socialization the learning processes are mainly directed by thinking. The different forms of learning often give rise to conflicts in the individual.

In primary socialization the child's learning is motivated by feelings. The satisfaction of the child's emotions and feelings is the principal learning rationale. In secondary socialization, as it takes place in kindergartens and public schools, the child has to develop another learning rationale. The child has to accept that it is necessary to know how to think and act in other "worlds" than a "world" defined by family and significant others. The emotion-rationale is driven to the background, the rational thinking is brought to the fore. Intellectual reasons have to be put forward. The child must learn to accept good reasons even when they hurt its feelings. People experience such conflicts and contradictions every day of their lives. Such conflicts are seen as important as dynamics of development. The child encounters them in both primary and secondary socialization, where they sometimes can be so overwhelming that the child has difficulty coping with them. However, were the conflicts and contradictions systematically removed from the ongoing activities, the child would not have opportunity to learn how to cope with them. The child has to face the reality that one can cope with conflicts, but that every time a conflict is solved, a new will arise. Such are the conditions of life. In the ongoing process of secondary socialization, an already socialized individual enters other objective subworlds of his or her society. Here the child is prepared for taking on the roles of other societal subworlds, for example for vocational training, career making, for citizenhood. The possible sources of conflict are many.

The "roles" taken over from the parents are loaded with emotions. The child cannot escape the parents, and almost every child loves its mother. The mother or the significant others are essential in the formation of the child's identity.

One day this growing identity is brought to school. During primary socialization the child has already internalized certain values and means of action. If the values thus established are out of harmony with the new world – School – conflicts may arise. Though not committed to love its teachers, the child has to spend many years in school, and the teachers and the other pupils are of great importance for the developing identity. Emotional identification does not come to the fore in secondary socialization, but the dynamics between the emotional layers and the cognitive layers in personality are at work. The personal aspects of motives developed in secondary socialization may be better characterized as emotional tint, shadow or color.

Personality and identity

The two different forms of learning influence the formation of personality and identity.

Personality and identity are interrelated formations; the identity is a substructure in the personality. Their developments are intertwined in both primary and secondary socialization.

According to Leontiev (1982, p. 180) personality is a psychic structure of motives. The motives, the individual's personal reasons for engaging in some activity or another, are hierarchically ordered and developed through the activity. The activity has an objective social meaning, but during the activity the individual develops the personal sense of the activity. The objective meaning and the personal sense are only partially identical. The objective meaning of an activity is shared by the members of the society. The personal sense is connected with the individual's affects, emotions and feelings in relation to the activity. It is the personal reason and it is unique for every individual. The personal sense is closely related to the identity.

Identity means both the awareness of who I am and where I belong, and the awareness of belonging to a certain culture or social group. It also means being myself in relation to other people as time goes by. The identity has two sides: an individual side, the feeling of inner unity and continuity; and a collective side, unity with the group or society. The social identity is established in primary and secondary socialization in the dialectic between the individual and society. The total identity is a personal experience of all these aspects. The individual clearly experiences the relation between the personal sense and the identity when she feels, that she has to do something. If this is not the case, she cannot feel that she is really herself.

Personality and identity are developed during the same processes and at the same time. Key concepts in the characteristic of the identity are: Sameness over time, self-concept, self-recognition, coherence, continuity, meaning, significance, influence, confirmation, community, accordance and social attachment (Madsen, 1990, p. 26). All these characteristics can not be confirmed by the intellect alone, they also have to be emotionally confirmed.

Therefore the dynamics between emotions and cognition must always be borne in mind when we talk about identity as well as when we talk about personality. Let us consider some different examples of how personality is established when children go to school.

First story:
Building cultural identity of minority children through social studies education

Chaiklin and Hedegaard conducted an afterschool teaching program with Puerto Rican elementary school children in New York City. The children participated in the program two afternoons a week during one academic year. The program focused on topics in Puerto Rican history and culture.

Chaiklin and Hedegaard used Davydov's and Lompscher's approach of teaching theoretical knowledge and thinking. The conclusion after the experiment was: Formal education, as a process of secondary socialization, can contribute to the development of cultural identity, and, in particular help children to comprehend some of the contradictions and conflicts that they have or are likely to encounter in their lives (Chaiklin and Hedegaard, 1990, p. 15).

There is no doubt: The teaching experiment was good for the children. They got some useful knowledge, and perhaps certain contradictions or conflicts were now easier to deal with. Yet from a theoretical point of view the experiment raises some serious questions.

The children got some useful knowledge about their culture, but they got some other knowledge as well. They learned that Puerto Rican life and history can be a school subject, but only in afterschool teaching. This is a fact of the curriculum of both the public school and the afterschool institution. From this fact the children learn something. It is not directly taught, and therefore we can name this sort of learning: meta–learning or co–learning. The first question is what sort of meta–learning or co–learning takes place in conjunction with afterschool learning? What does the public school teach indirectly, when it teaches students that the history of New York is a proper topic for history lessons, but the history of East Harlem and the experience of Puerto Ricans in New York is not? There is a hidden message in the public school curriculum: The minority's history and culture do not merit status as a school subject.

The motives developed by the Puerto Rican children during the teaching experiment may be very contradictory and filled with conflicts. Their new knowledge and skills may be related to a sort of emotional pain. Perhaps they can understand why they experience pain, but understanding does not take away the pain. Their cultural identity may be more integrated on the intellectual side, yet bear the stamp of double bind on the emotional side. Being part of the public school curriculum gives a topic prestige. In the afterschool program the children are taught that they can be proud of their culture; in the public school they are taught that their culture has low prestige, because it is not part of the curriculum. Therefore the children are placed in a double bind situation. There is no way out of the situation. The children have to learn that the pain is inevitable, and that they must live with it.

Secondly, the goal of the public school is to educate individuals who can take over the burden of continuing and developing the society. During the passage from adolescence into early adulthood we see young people incorporating the societal perspective into the personality. The personality is changed, and the societal motives become dominant. But what will be the character of these motives when the individual is caught in the double bind situation?

Consider again the learning experiment with the Puerto Rican children. It appears that the relation between the teacher and the pupil is, at the same time, an institutional and a social relationship. Through the teaching the student develops new skills and knowledge, and these are emotionally colored – most likely in the colors of conflict and contradiction. These emotions can lead to severe crisis, but can also be a source of further development, especially if the double bind situation is broken down into conscious knowledge and skills that enable the student to act. As mentioned, the afterschool teaching focused on themes from minority history and society and culture. Breaking down the double bind situation might require that these topics as well as the those of majority history, society and culture and the relations between minority and majority become parts of the curriculum.

I am not sure that the teaching experiment is conducive to the development of multicultural personalities who are able to and want to participate in development of a multicultural society.

If the aim is to connect the emotions and the cultural identity, one has to question whether the teaching of theoretical skills and knowledge is sufficient. In the teaching experiment described by Chaiklin and Hedegaard theoretical skills and knowledge are in focus. No doubt these are necessary, but perhaps they are not sufficient. The theoretical skills must be brought in contact with the emotions to achieve a personal sense of cultural identity.

The verbal communication of theoretical skills and knowledge in teaching does not necessarily help to relate this knowledge to the emotional layers of the personality and especially not to the identity. Being a Puerto Rican in East Harlem involves emotional confirmation of one's identity as a member of an ethnic minority in the majority society. My criticism against Chaiklin and Hedegaard concerns this particular feature of the teaching experiment.

The teaching experiment was a purely verbal teaching experiment. Therefore I will make a suggestion which might have mediated between the emotional and the cognitive layers in the personality. To mediate this contact artistic activity may be useful. One might use some of the tools used by the artist, encouraging the students to make sketches, metaphors, drawings, visualizations and the like to materialize the subject matter. The process of materializing makes the still "just guessed" or "faintly seen" aspects of the subject matter communicable. The artistic expressions allow the individual to express feelings, emotions and unconscious knowledge which is on the way to consciousness. The artistic expressions can be dim, blurred or inaccurate and yet convey a message to other people – a message which is important to communicate, but which cannot yet be expressed completely in words or sentences, if it can be expressed verbally at all.

The teaching experiment is not only of relevance for the children of ethnic minorities. The children of the majority culture may also experience cultural differences between the culture of their family or group and the culture mediated by school. Children with different forms of life may share a common language, but the objective meanings mediated by the school and their home can be quite different. They, too, are likely to be confused and have their identity burdened with conflicting emotions. The contradictions are obvious when we look at a minority culture, but they exist in the majority culture as well.

It is part and parcel of the human condition to experience conflicting emotions and conflicts between intellectual knowledge and the knowledge of the feelings. Dealing with these conflicts and contradictions is an important aim of the education in primary and secondary socialization.

Second story:
How can the school cope with conflicts of identity and personality?

In the first example we saw the teaching and learning process from "the outside". The experience of the child in the conflicting or painful situation was not in focus. We saw it from the parents', the teachers' or the societal viewpoint.

But the teaching and the learning occur in different persons. The pupil's experience of the learning process, "the inside" of the learning process, has been described by the concept *"the idiosyncratic room"* (Mortensen, 1990), which may consist of several rooms, some of them good and some bad.

"The idiosyncratic room" is a metaphor. It describes the fact that the individual experiences knowledge and emotions, feelings and affects organized in entities. We call such an entity a scene. The inner scenes are organized with many storage rooms behind. The storage rooms behind the scene are "the idiosyncratic" rooms. When a certain scene is in focus of the mind, some of the necessary props are taken from "the idiosyncratic rooms". An individual can experience strong emotions, bad as well as good feelings, in connection with certain learning situations. In secondary socialization the intellectual motives are at the front of the scene, but emotions play their roles in the wings. Sometimes the play in the wings is more important than the play going on upstage.

We are now following the idea of several "idiosyncratic rooms". Some of the walls surrounding "the idiosyncratic rooms" may be impenetrable, without doors or windows, while others are semipermeable. Under certain conditions some impenetrable walls become semipermeable and vice versa.

Aksel Mortensen (ibid.) refers to investigations he made in his capacity as a school psychologist. He observed that during testing some children had an inner experience of being in a very bad "idiosyncratic room".

Mortensen ascribes these bad experiences to the fact that the children did not understand the meaning of the test, and the tester did not help the children to find the meaning. This situation turned out to be very much like the daily lessons in the school. The children strove day after day to make sense of the subject matter taught, but there was no linkage between what was taught and what was learned. The objective meaning taught did not give the student the opportunity to make this objective meaning partly his own, and thus perhaps the personal sense of the student came to tell him that the subject matter was indeed meaningless.

The cognitive or intellectual aspect of the learning process is important because it gives the child a mean to grasp the world. This is reasonable. But feelings are reasonable too. The feelings tell the child the personal meaning of a situation, a skill or an insight. For the individual child the personal meaning is perhaps more important than the cognitive or intellectual factors of the learning process.

Let me give an example from Eskimo life. It illustrates the role of emotion in learning and also the fact that emotional insight is valuable from an individual as well as societal viewpoint, even when it is painful for the individual.

Early in life Eskimo children have to learn, that they are not allowed to walk onto ice that is not safe. They have to learn it as soon as they are able to walk. This happens during the second year of life, so it is impossible to explain to the child why walking on unsafe ice is prohibited. It is also impossible for the grown-ups to look after the child constantly. Therefore the Eskimos use the shameshock method in the upbringing of their children. The first time the child walks out onto unsafe ice it is not punished or scolded. Instead the members of the Eskimo group form a circle and the child is placed in the center. Now a short sketch is played, showing a child walking out on unsafe ice. The group members in the circle laugh heartily in such a way that the child cannot help understanding that it has done an extremely foolish thing. To be laughed at by all one's significant others is an experience so shocking that the child usually does not tread on unsafe ice again. Undoubtedly the shameshock has saved many Eskimo children's lives as well as many other children's lives.

As mentioned earlier, the small child learns by emotional identification with its significant others. As a part of this learning the small child learns to feel ashamed, the shame preventing the child from exposing itself to danger in a situation it cannot judge for itself. This is one of humankind's evolutionary techniques for protecting its offspring from lethal danger – a very basic sort of learning.

But once it has been integrated in the culture as an acceptable method of teaching, the shameshock may be applied in situations where no lethal danger legitimates the use of the method. Unfortunately, we may be inclined to use this rather harsh method of teaching unconsciously.

This basic sort of teaching and learning also takes place in situations where no child's life is at stake. Teachers and pupils use it, consciously or unconsciously, in the everyday life of school. When children are laughed at by their comrades or their teacher, or are told to be ashamed of themselves, we see situations that parallel the shameshock situation. The teacher and the schoolmates are not as emotionally close to the child as the significant others are (for example, in the Eskimo group), yet successful learning is closely related to positive emotional relations, especially for children. A child who has experienced shameshock in primary socialization in infancy may have found it so awful an experience that he or she wants never to expose him– or herself to it again. So the child will make serious efforts to avoid similar situations.

The shameshock method should only be used when there is no other way to teach and learn. That is the situation when the small Eskimo child walks onto unsafe ice. For Eskimo children, as well as for other children, it is a very painful way of learning, and therefore its use should be avoided.

The fact is, many children are exposed to situations much like the shameshock situation in school. These experiences mold "a very bad idiosyncratic room" in the mind. These observations are intended as a warning to teachers: Shameshock or corresponding unpleasant situations must be avoided. That is not the same as avoiding every conflict, contradiction, uncertainty or difficulty. On the contrary: to be puzzled or confused can be a very fruitful starting point for the teaching and learning activity. However, the student, as well as the teacher, must be emotionally safe in the situation. They must agree that they will not laugh at or deprecate each other in the situation. Otherwise the emotional learning will upstage all other aspects of learning in a very negative way.

Third story:
When are experience and acquisition the same phenomenon?

For many children failing in school is an experience connected with bad feelings. Shameshock, a dreadful experience in itself, only worsens the situation. It is important for teachers to be aware that the emotional learning that takes place in schools and other secondary socialization agencies has an impact on the child as great as that which takes place in primary socialization.

The third story illustrates situations where the cognitive and emotional learning may interplay in a positive way. It is necessary to introduce some key concepts used in the story before telling it. It will be a rather comprehensive introduction.

The story is originally told in Norwegian. In Norwegian the word *'acquire'* means to make something one's own. In the learning activity this means learning some skills or getting knowledge usable in one's own life now or in the future. The implication is that you have a personal reason to learn the matter taught.

The Norwegian educational researcher Stieg Mellin–Olsen (Mellin–Olsen, 1986) investigated several teaching experiments in Norway which led him to develop a set of concepts to be applied in such situations. He calls the concepts the rationales of learning, distinguishing two, the social and the instrumental rationale – *S–rationale* and *I– rationale* – observing that in most situations both may well be present.

The S–rationale is evoked in a pupil by a synthesis of his self–concept, his cognition of school and schooling, and his concept of what is significant knowledge and of possible future value. The key is that the pupil sees what he is being taught as significant for himself, according to his norms. This leaves open the possibility for a subject matter to be interesting, simply because the student finds it so or is curious to know something about it. The teacher can also evoke the student's interest or curiosity about a subject matter. Since the student's norms tend to be largely affected by things like social standing or geographical differences, they tend to be considered a topic of sociology of education.

The I–rationale is related to the way in which the school is viewed as "instrumental" in providing the pupil with a "future". Its most important manifestation is in the way in which the external (examination) system can provide certification (Howson and Mellin–Olsen, 1986, p. 17).

More recently Mellin–Olsen has added a third, *the non–learning rationale*, to the list. This rationale implies that the pupil decides – consciously or unconsciously – that he or she cannot or will not learn a certain matter taught in school.

It is advisable that the teacher examines the pupil's learning rationale in relation to the subject–matter taught. The S–rationale is a necessary foundation for learning, and, if absent, it must be developed. As Mellin–Olsen points out, the rationales exist side by side in every learning situation, but the teacher must ensure that the I–rationale develops (at least partially) into the S–rationale. Clearly, the non–learning rationale should not develop.

This means that the teacher must engage in a dialogue with his students. The teacher must be sensitive to the students' vaguely expressed needs and wishes. Perhaps from the teacher's point of view the students' wishes are not rational. But for the students they are, considering that feelings and emotions have their own sort of rationality.

During such a dialogue the teacher examines the students' rationales for learning, and it is here that the shaping of a new and alternative rationale can perhaps begin. But it is possible that other means should also be considered. The dynamics between emotion and cognition is essential for learning. Therefore, it is not enough to tell the students the reason why they should engage in a certain learning activity. The student must recognize emotionally the importance of a given subject matter. This the teacher must make possible. Here is the real difficulty. The teacher can provide the opportunities, but he or she cannot plan what the student will experience. Different students may need different experiences to develop the same rationale. And the same opportunity may evoke different experiences in different students.

That is why the teacher's job is a difficult one. But when the dialogue succeeds it is a means to creating "the good idiosyncratic room" as a condition for the learning activity. We should not forget that the teacher's own engagement in the subject matter is an important factor in whether the student experiences a subject matter as important. The teacher's and the student's joint efforts to solve a problem or a task, and the teacher's serious engagement in the activity, are of great importance. The teacher may not be a significant other for the student, but she may still be a person worth imitating or identifying with. The teacher becomes a living model in whom the student directly observes the objective meaning and the personal sense.

This may appear to be an unattainable ideal. However, it is an ideal worth striving for. What the teacher cannot prevent are the conflicts or contradictions that can detract from the ideal situation. The conflicts and the contradictions that arise from culturally different socialization agencies may result in conflicting expectations of the content of the subject matters taught in school. For example, many parents find it very positive that all pupils in public school now have to learn mathematics. They have doubts, however, as to the peculiar kind of mathematics their children are taught. Calculation of probability is a subject of school mathematics worldwide. Parents recognize this as a sort of mathematics, but they do not understand it and are unable to help their children doing their homework. Thus, the parents may doubt whether it is necessary to learn calculation of probability. People do not use it when going to the supermarket, cooking in the kitchen or doing handicrafts.

Preliminary conclusion: When the teacher and the students, through their joint activity, succeed in creating a rationale for learning where the S-rationale has a reasonable space, then the first necessary condition for turning experience into acquisition (i.e., acquiring knowledge or skills as "one's own") is met.

Fourth story:
Learning in the Zone of Proximal Development

Now the teacher and the students have a common motivation; they are developing a motive, a good reason for learning. Yet this is only the first condition for turning experience into acquisition. The second condition is that learning takes place in the *Zone of Proximal Development* – zoped – which will be described in the following.

The contents of school subjects are delineated in the curriculum as knowledge, skills, methods, problems, etc., to be mediated through the school.

The student is a competent person who meets the school with expectations about things he or she is going to learn and about their meanings, now as well as with regard to the future. In addition, school will evoke new expectations and motives. The aim of the teaching activity is always double: to create motives and to teach a subject matter.

In *Rousing Minds to Life* R.G. Tharp and R. Gallimore (1988, p. 30) describe learning in the zoped. The experiences of Tharp and Gallimore are derived from experimental teaching in Hawaii: The Kamehameha Elementary Education Program. The concept of zoped implies that the teacher knows the student's actual level of development. The teacher can assess the student's actual level of development by the child's ability to solve problems unassisted. That is an example of what the school psychologist does when testing a child. Yet, what the student can solve unassisted is not the most interesting factor about the student's development. Unassisted performance is only the starting point for the learning of new activities. Essentially, the teacher now considers what the students can accomplish given one or another sort of help. What a student is doing with help today, he or she can do alone tomorrow. Assisted performance is the nexus between development and learning. "The distance between the child's individual capacity and the capacity to perform with assistance is zoped" (Tharp & Gallimore, 1988, p. 30). For every domain of skills, methods, knowledge, etc., it is possible to create a zoped. Zoped is not an individual affair. The activities the students can perform with different forms of help indicate the width of the zoped. In this context the width of the zoped is much more interesting than the actual level of development.

Tharp and Gallimore describe the cognitive or intellectual processes in the learning activity, but not the personal experiences of emotions and feelings, "the inside" of the activity which takes place in "the idiosyncratic room".

Being serious about "the idiosyncratic room" the teacher should seek to meet the student with respect for his competencies. This means that the learning activity must take its departure in the student's competencies and present the new challenges within the zoped. Next the teacher should provide opportunities for the expression of new knowledge and recognitions that have not yet found an exact form.

As mentioned earlier, some of the tools used by the artist may be helpful to this end. The process of materializing can make communicable that which is still "just guessed" or "dimly seen". In addition it gives hints about the feelings evoked by the subject matter.

Finally, when we have done our best to create "a good idiosyncratic room" and personal reasons for the student to engage in the activity, we have yet another issue to consider, namely the sorts of assistance to be offered in the zoped.

Tharp and Gallimore describe four different sorts of assistance to be given in succession, each marking a stage in the zoped:

Stage I: Where performance is assisted by more capable others.

If the student has a very limited understanding of the task, the teacher or a more capable peer may offer directions. Later on the student can be assisted by questions and feedback, for example. Scaffolding is a frequently used metaphor for this sort of learning.

Stage II: Where performance is assisted by the self.

The student now takes over the directions. The child directs or guides the activity by its own speech. As the learning process proceeds the speech turns over into inner speech.

Stage III: Where performance is developed, automatized, and "fossilized".

There is no evidence of self–regulation. Regulation by others or the self is no longer needed. The performance is developed. If the teacher or peers offer assistance, the student finds it irritating; the child does not want to be interrupted. The performance is developed to automatization, yet in a rather fixed manner. The child manages some basic variations of the task, but further variations have to be acquired before perfect mastering of the performance is achieved.

Stage IV: Where de–automatization of performance leads to recursion back through zoped.

If already acquired skills or knowledge are not used for some time they may be partly forgotten. Or new variations may turn up. Then the student uses the forms of assistance described in stages I–III. The student knows of various helping techniques and seeks the ones he finds relevant. The child relearns or develops a higher flexibility in the performance. After recursion, the "new" performance again is "fossilized", eventually at a higher developmental level, or the skill domain has become broader. (Tharp & Gallimore, 1988, p. 33–39).

The description is fitting to children of schoolage, yet it characterizes the development of learning during ontogenesis also.

The paths through zoped are illustrated in figure 1.

Looking at the figure we see that the student in the zoped is a very vulnerable person. The student must rely on the competence of more capable others, and it is essential that the more capable others do not expose the student to something like the shameshock. In such a case giving and receiving of assistance would be impossible. Being "the more capable other" carries with it a high degree of responsibility. The situation is influenced by all the experiences the student and the assistant have had earlier in life. A competitive atmosphere in the classroom may be damaging for learning in the zoped.

Four stages of the ZPD

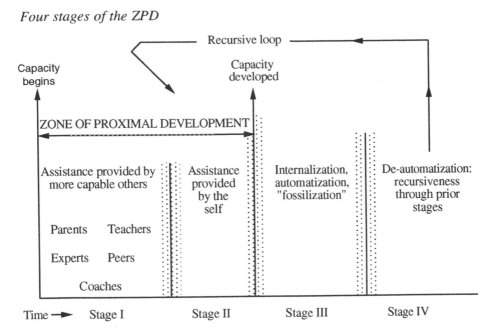

Figure 1: Genesis of performance capacity: progression through the ZPD and beyond.[1]

Social relations are the pivots for this sort of learning, the students' mutual relations and the relations between the students and the teacher. There must be room for success as well as failure. The students must be pleased by their own successes as well as those of their classmates. And they must help each other to avoid or overcome failure. The learning process is always a double process – partly social and partly individual. Social processes are emotionally shaded, and the cognitive learning processes embedded in the social situation therefore take on the color of the emotions evoked.

The child's identity – both the assisted's and the assistant's – is an important factor in this process. The child must have a basic trust in other people and believe in himself. The teacher, the learning activities and the joint social community must confirm to the student that he is capable of learning the subject matters taught in school. As said before: teaching a subject matter implies teaching motives, skills and knowledge at once. Therefore, the whole learning process that takes place in social relations influences the development of identity and personality.

---

1   Redrawn from Tharp and Gallimore (1988, fig. 2.1, p. 35)

When passing from stage III to stage IV the student goes back and forth through situations where assistance is needed and where assistance is disruptive for the learning process. The assistant and the student must agree that it is the student who decides whether assistance is needed or not.

Learning in the zoped relies on the knowing of the student's actual level of development and the width of the zoped. The investigation hereof must always be the teacher's task. Afterwards the teacher defines the tasks for both student and assistant. In the first story I told about teaching of theoretical concepts as a necessary condition in developing multicultural identity in minority children. Certainly teaching AF theoretical concepts is an essential part of curriculum. Yet, as Mellin–Olsen, Tharp and Gallimore suggest, teaching has to take off from the students' already known concepts. Typically these are not theoretical. Further, the development of S–rationale takes place only in the zoped. In educational theory of teaching and learning situations there is, however, no contradiction between learning in the zoped and the learning and teaching of theoretical concepts. For example, Vygotsky points out that scientific concepts and everyday concepts are learned in different ways. Scientific or theoretical concepts are learned as parts of a system. The system of concepts mediated by the learning activity in the school must relate to everyday concepts. Otherwise it will be difficult to create a motive for engagement in the activity. Trying to create that relation in teaching practice in classrooms may seem like attempting the impossible. Nevertheless it is one of the final aims of education.

Fifth story:
Building motives for mathematical learning

I will now describe a teaching experiment from the Danish folkeskole. Teaching and developmental experiments are often practiced in "the folkeskole" (primary and lower secondary school in Denmark). These experiments of development typically approach the child's motivation in a non–theoretical way.

At Vester Mariendalskolen in Aalborg mathematics was taught in 1. and 2. grade (1. and 2. year in primary school) taking concrete activities as a point of departure. Usually the concrete activities were things that were part of everyday life in the classroom or in the school district. The Children managed to express their observations of these activities in words as well as in written signs and drawings. They learned the mathematical language by gradually changing their own everyday language to the "real" mathematical language.

This teaching experiment was initiated as a reaction against the theoretical way in which many mathematics school books introduce mathematics to school beginners. The strength of this work lies in the children's and the teachers' joint engagement, but it lacks the theoretical perspective.

During this experiment the children developed motives for learning mathematics. The aims were fulfilled. Yet the teaching experiment does not make it clear that not every positive motive points toward the ultimate goal of school mathematics. School mathematics education is intended to teach mathematics as both a means of solving everyday problems and as a theory fit for modelling problems of economy, sociology, biology, physics, chemistry, etc. This theoretical aspect was not taken into consideration in the teaching experiment from Aalborg. No matter how motivated the children are, theoretical perspectives have to be considered in both traditional and experimental teaching.

Sixth story:
Ethnomathematics as an inspiration for teaching school mathematics

There is a worldwide interest in ethnomathematics. Ethnomathematics means the mathematics that people use in their daily lives. Ethnomathematics encompasses a multiplicity of activities from buying in the supermarket, cooking and baking, knitting, wickerwork, to building houses.

The current interest in ethnomathematics connects with the fact that the worldwide "New Math" innovation which began in the 1960'es has partly failed, especially in developmental countries that built their school system and curriculum on a European/American model. Here, both the education of math teachers and the teaching of math in school have been huge failures. Therefore many of the educational researchers turned their interest to the mathematics of everyday life in their own culture. And European and American researchers learned a lesson.

In Norway, a group related to Stieg Mellin–Olsen is doing pioneer work in Norwegian ethnomathematics. The following experiment was made by Marit Johnsen Hines and Stieg Mellin–Olsen in cooperation (Hines, 1987). They wished to teach mathematics with the S–rationale as their starting point. They did it like this.

The pupils of 1. grade worked with finger crochet. They chrochetted strings, meanwhile discussing the length of the strings. A girl said that a boy named Åsmund[2] had made a string which could reach from the classroom to the waterpump in the school yard. This had to be examined. Åsmund's string could actually reach from the classroom to the waterpump. In a very short time after that event the children spontaneously used the phrase "an Åsmund–string" to refer to length. For example, they stated the length of distances from home to school in "Åsmundstrings". The class had

---

2 Pronounced like 'Osmond'.

made its own unit of measurement. The class used it for some time before the teacher introduced the formal units of measurement taking outset in the "Åsmund–string". This is a step on the road leading to a theoretical treatment of the concept of measurement.

The example with the "Åsmund–string" illustrates creative thinking in a school class. It is creative thinking because the children create something new, never met before. The children in this class have developed their personality as understood by Davydov: the children have formed something new and they use it shaping their own lives. They change their lives a little bit by ascribing concepts of length to the way from home to school.

The paradigm for Stieg Mellin–Olsen's theory of the mediating of theoretical knowledge is the case in which the attentive teacher finds a starting point for mediating theoretical knowledge in the children's daily activities and everyday knowledge.

Stieg Mellin–Olsen and Marit Johnsen Hines have a problem to solve, however. Their paradigm has the implicit assumption that for all teaching of theoretical knowledge it is possible to find a starting point in the children's everyday knowledge. Can we be absolutely sure that this is possible? They do not discuss this problem.

Towards a synthesis of teaching experiments

I have not told one complete pedagogical story, but rather bits and pieces of one comprised of six separate stories about children's life in school. I would have preferred to tell only one story. But a single story that describes the development of personality in schoolchildren would have to encompass each of the themes presented in these six bits and pieces. I do not know of a story of activity that encompasses all the elements I want to include: the development of personality and identity, "the idiosyncratic room", the development of theoretical thinking and learning in the zoped.

Perhaps that story cannot yet be told, because we have not yet developed a theory that encompasses all the elements. Only such a theory will be able to describe and explain how cognitions and emotions – the objective rationality and the inner personal meaning – or objective meaning and personal sense – interplay in the development of personality and identity.

The child enters school as a competent growing identity. The school's task is to ensure the best conditions for continuing this development. One of these conditions is a good theory of the development of personality. A theoretical gap exists. We need to develop a theory which can fulfill the demands I have set in this article:

– It must encompass the learning activity as well as the personal experience of the learning.

– The development of learning motives must be founded on the S–rationale. Experience must be turned into acquisition.

– The learning activity must develop motives as well as theoretical thinking and thinking mediated by good examples.
– The learning activity must take place in the zoped.
– "The inside" of the learning activities must constitute "a good idiosyncratic" room.
– It must describe how the "just faintly seen or felt" is developed into conscious knowledge.

I have not yet met such a theory. I have seen much fruitful research into some of its important elements, but I have not met them all integrated in one theory. We need such a theory, because it can explain where the personality goes, when the child goes to school.

References

Baltzer, K.: Hvor går personligheden hen, når den går i skole. Unpublished ms.

Chaiklin, S. and M. Hedegaard (1990): Building Cultural Identity of Minority Children Through Social Studies Education, Aarhus, Unpublished ms.

Davydov, V. V. (1989): *Udviklende undervisning på virksomhedsteoriens grundlag*, Copenhagen.

Engelsted, N. (1990): Personlighedens almene grundlag, Aarhus.

Hedegaard, M. (1988): *Skolebørns personlighedsudvikling set gennem orienteringsfagene*, Aarhus.

Hines, M. J. (1987): *Begynneropläringen*, Nordå.

Leontiev, A.N: (1982): *Tätigkeit, Bewusstsein, Persönlichkeit*, Berlin.

Madsen, B. (1988): *Identitetens Thesaurus*, Aarhus.

Mellin–Olsen, S. & Howson, A.G. (1986): Social norms and external evaluation, In B. Christiansen, A.G. Howson & M. Otte (eds.): *Perspectives on Mathematics Education*, Dordrecht.

Mortensen, A. (1990): Culture and Microcosmos of Individuals: The Idiosyncratic Room of the Person, In *The Quarterly Newsletter of Comparative Human Cognition*, volume 12, Number 4, pp. 146–153.

Rasmussen, I. and P. Kjeldsen (1989): *Matematik i 1. klasse*, Aalborg.

Tharp, R. G. & R. Gallimore (1988): *Rousing Minds to Life*, Cambridge.

Vygotsky, L. S. (1967): *Thought and Language*, Cambridge, Mass.

FOUNDATIONS FOR INVESTIGATING THE ROLE OF CULTURE IN DANISH SCHOOL TEACHING

Mariane Hedegaard & Seth Chaiklin
University of Aarhus

Investigating culture

This paper describes some orienting principles for conducting research about teaching for cultural minorities. The presence of cultural minorities in a country is often associated with such societal problems as discrimination, proportionally greater unemployment, language difficulties, and conflicting values that create tensions and conflicts between cultural minority members and the societal majority. A common response by dominant cultural groups is to form a policy that is oriented to integrating cultural minorities with the majority.[1] The specific meaning of "integration" varies from situation to situation, but the public school is often considered a major instrument for addressing the problem of integrating cultural minorities into the dominant forms of life that organize an existing society (Rothermund & Simon, 1986).

The specific teaching practices of schools and their rationale reflect prevailing social policies about how cultural minorities should relate to the dominant society. Cultural minorities, often for historical reasons, are not always academically successful in the public school system organized by members of the majority culture. Existing teaching methods and practices are not always adequate or effective for achieving societally–desired goals for cultural minority children. This situation motivates us to better understand what happens to cultural–minority children when they go to public school.

The school is analyzed as an institution located within a particular country with its specific cultural minorities and a history of interaction between these minorities and the school system. However, we do not want to be limited to a political or ideological interpretation of the schooling of

---

[1] There are, however, also policies that have been based on separation (e.g., blacks in South Africa or the Southern United States) or complete isolation (Jews in Polish ghettos), but we will not consider those here.

cultural minority children as a problem of societal integration or intellectual development. We also want to consider the potential contribution of schooling to the development of children's personality as a whole, including a capability to function inside and outside the school setting with a positive emotional and social relation to other people.

First we discuss some theoretical principles that orient our work on the problem of how to develop culturally–sensitive school teaching. Second, we describe some empirical work in which we have made a teaching program for a cultural minority. Third, we describe some characteristics of the Danish school tradition. Finally, we describe our current research plans that respond to issues raised in the first three sections.

A theoretical framework for studying schooling of cultural minorities

Integrating minority children into a new culture

From a political point of view, the school can be seen as an instrument for supporting a social policy. For example, one approach for acculturating minority children is to try to assimilate them as much as possible to the culture of their host country. The dominant school policy in Denmark is to help immigrant children become Danes, which implies support to acquire the Danish language as fast as possible and behave like Danish children (Hjarnø, 1988; Kromayer & Weltzer, 1990). This has not been a very successful policy, neither in Denmark, nor in other countries (Lynch, 1986). Another approach for acculturation is the American melting pot model or "fusion model" where all cultures in principle are seen as equal, and out of their meeting a new tradition will develop (Gordon, 1964). A third possibility for acculturating minority children into a dominant society is an approach that tries to develop respect for and knowledge of the minority cultures as well as of the majority culture (Gibson, 1976, pp. 9–11).

These approaches are grounded more in political ideology than in scientific analysis. Therefore, it is necessary to develop an approach that incorporates the ideology as one part of an empirically–oriented analysis.

These general political goals are often supported or accompanied by subgoals such as equalization of educational opportunities for culturally different students, helping all students to value and accept cultural differences, and the development of specific cultural abilities. The label *multi–cultural education* is sometimes used to describe different programs of teaching that try to achieve one or more of these subgoals (Gibson, 1976; Lynch, 1986). Underneath the general political goals and specific subgoals are the following concrete and practical questions: (a) how should children from minority cultures become acquainted with the dominant culture of their country, (b) how much should they be supported in keeping their original language, cultural traditions, and values, and (c) how much should the school adapt its existing teaching content and methods?

In conducting our studies, we take a cultural–approach in which we try to learn from existing analyses of the schooling of cultural minorities as well as our own empirical investigation of the particular conditions of cultural minorities in Denmark.

Cultural groups and the concept of culture

To identify a cultural group is to characterize specific cultural practices that delimit social groups who are carriers of these practices. At first glance, it might seem easy to define cultural minority groups. For example, we could take all people who live in country A while having a passport from country B. The problem is that this bureaucratic definition does not always reflect a homogeneous, temporally–stable group of people. For example, Selmer (1991) investigated Turkish people in Denmark, where one might expect clear contrasts to the majority culture. She discovered different characteristics within this group, and changes in ways of living over time which became difficult to differentiate from Danish ways of living. This situation warns us not to construct a concept of "cultural minority" that serves to constrain people within prescribed norms of belief and behavior. Instead, it may be necessary to characterize cultural minority groups in more dynamic or developmental terms.

Culture can be seen as an analytical concept, grounded in an empirical phenomenon. Regardless of the scientific definitions, people have a way of living their everyday lives and some ideology to interpret their experiences and formulate goals. These ideologies are often developed and supported within a group of people through common and sometimes communal practices (e.g., church–going, festivals, awards). Researchers use the concept of "culture" to refer to this collection of daily practices and ideologies. The description of these practices and ideologies is problematic. A researcher's descriptions of a culture are often rooted in contrasts to her own cultural experience. The cultural description emerges through the differences between the researcher and the group of people being researched (Hastrup, 1988).

This view of culture, even if it is grounded in some empirical phenomena, also has some additional, analytic differentiation that the researcher has added according to a particular research interest or purpose. Each classification of cultural groups or minorities has its problems. We do not see any way to avoid these problems other than to attempt to be conscious about how we define minorities groups and evaluate those definitions when we can.

Academic success

A common way to examine the experience of minorities in school is to assess whether they have been successful according to the standards (e.g., grades, standardized tests) used to evaluate the majority groups (Scribner & Cole, 1981).

A minority relation is not sufficient to determine whether children will have difficulties in being academically successful. Ogbu's (1987) comparative analysis of school success among different minority groups described the following pattern: When a minority group is an indigenous people or has some sort of colonized relation to the host country (e.g., Blacks in the USA) then members of these groups, on average, have more difficulties in being academically successful in the host country's school system.   If members of a minority group are voluntary immigrants to the host country, then they tend to become academically successful, even more so than the dominant group in some cases.

An important implication of this pattern is that it is counter–evidence to a simple hypothesis that minority cultures necessarily have problems in majority–culture schools because they are minorities. Both indigenous and immigrant cultures may have differences from the dominant culture: language, child–rearing practices, cultural practices (holiday celebrations, relations between children and adults). It does not appear likely that academic difficulties can be explained in terms of these differences alone. From the research literature we have identified three different classes of explanation that can be offered for success or failure of minority children in a school setting.

Parental attitudes and actions. Ogbu's analysis supported the idea that there is a critical interaction between a minority parent's perspective on the school system and the objective possibilities to use the education obtained therein. Voluntary immigrants often saw the educational opportunities to be better (i.e., easily accessible, free) compared to where they came from; they believed that education would make a difference (because they had not been in the new country long enough to evaluate the actual tendencies); they expected difficulties in school because of language; and believed that they could always use their education back in their original country if it was not possible to find employment in the new country.

From this analysis, we conclude that in order to understand the experience of a minority culture in a dominant culture's schools, it is necessary to consider the interaction between the minority's perceptions and expectations from the schools with the objective societal conditions within which the minority functions. Ogbu's analysis makes clear that we cannot simply make two lists of characteristics, one for the majority culture and one for the minority culture, and compare similarities and differences. What is more important is to understand the pattern of conditions and how they interact with each other. Specifically this includes a need to examine (a) a minority's perceptions of what they want their children to get from the school, (b) the objective amount and kinds of experience the minority has had with the official school system, (c) the objective (or perceived) possibilities for using the education that is obtained, and (d) the structure of the social support that comes from the immigrant community.

Mismatch between content of school knowledge and out–of–school knowledge. Critical analyses have argued that schooling is neither oriented to the objectives of minority groups (Ogbu, 1987) nor to the kinds of knowledge these minority groups actually possess (Moll & Greenberg, 1990). Moll and his colleagues have investigated the knowledge held among adults in Mexican–immigrant communities in the Southwestern United States. They have showed that there are rich and varied "funds of knowledge" in these communities, but this knowledge is not usually included as part of the school teaching that their children receive. Similarly, the language studies of Labov (1972) have shown that black young people have a rich, non– academic language that does not find an opportunity for expression in school classrooms.

Differential values of aspects of learning. Scribner and Cole (1981) analyzed the function of literacy for Vai, Muslim, and English communities in Liberia. Their analyses showed that these groups have different literacy objectives, reflecting the function it serves for them. The people in this research were adult males, who were acquiring specialized kinds of literacy. Vai literacy was primarily used for letter writing about social affairs, while Arabic literacy was connected to Koran reading and memorizing for a religious purpose. English is the language of instruction in the public schools as well as the official language in commerce and government affairs. Scribner and Cole found that these three types of literacy did not have the same effect on cognitive abilities. The Vai and the Arabic literates scored lower on tasks related to logical reasoning compared to the English schooled literates, but the Vai literates scored higher on semantic integration task, while the Arabic literates scored higher on a memory task. This shows that the objective of literacy influenced these adult's cognitive functioning.

Cultural identity

The question of teaching for cultural minorities should encompass more than political integration and academic goals. The ideological foundation of schools in most Western countries is that the school should support the well–rounded development of a child's personality. An important part of personality development is the acquisition of knowledge about one's own culture, both in its own terms and in relation to the dominant culture in the society in which one lives. We use the term "cultural identity" to refer to this process. Conscious cultural identity arises when a child surpasses the homogeneous culture of the first socialization in the family, and when the child can acknowledge the existence of other ways of living– other kinds of cultures.

Formal educational activities can help minority children integrate cultural differences in their life experience. Our hypothesis is that education can contribute to the development of cultural identity by helping children in a process of knowledge and skill acquisition related to understanding their culture and its relation to another culture, usually a majority. In other words, schooling, as a secondary socialization, should try to support an integration and continuity with the minority child's primary socialization.

How to make teaching for cultural minorities

In the preceding section we presented theoretical arguments about important factors to consider in formulating teaching for cultural minorities. In this section we briefly describe some practical work we have undertaken in this area. This work was inspired primarily by a general pedagogical perspective that we then tried to integrate with a cultural perspective. A longer–range goal is to integrate the pedagogical ideas described here with the theoretical considerations described above.

Teaching theoretical thinking and learning to reflect upon society

We give a brief example of the teaching methods used in our work. The example comes from a teaching project with Puerto Rican children in New York City (Hedegaard, Chaiklin, & Pedraza, 1992).

Puerto Ricans are the second largest minority group in New York City, comprising about one million of the city's eight million inhabitants. The city's school curriculum has not enabled Puerto Rican children to learn about their own history and culture, or to understand their culture in relation to the forms they encounter in school. Social disadvantages and discrimination have characterized their experience in New York.

In teaching the Puerto Rican children we formulated the main problem as a lack of positive Puerto Rican identity. Negative feelings about being Puerto Rican gave negative experiences and attitudes for going to school. Consequently, in trying to build the cultural identity of Puerto Rican children, we wanted to help them develop a means for understanding their culture in relation to a dominant culture. Through the teaching program we tried to give the children knowledge about their own past and the positive aspects of their community by developing their capacities for literacy, mathematics and computers.

The teaching project was a form of action research known as a developmental teaching experiment (Hedegaard, 1987; Markova, 1982). The approach of teaching theoretical knowledge and thinking to elementary school children comes from Davydov (1982) and Lompscher (1985) (See

Aidarova (1982) for an extended example). Its further development by Hedegaard (1988, 1990) in the double move approach to teaching was the concrete basis for the teaching experiment in the Casita after–school program.

The objective of the double move approach is to let children, through own activity, acquire a motivation and capacity for theoretical reflection and knowledge about their surrounding world. Development of this theoretical knowledge requires that teachers have a profound knowledge of the concepts and general laws of the subject. This knowledge is used when planning the lessons so that they advance from the general to the concrete. The general laws must precede knowledge of the concrete reality in all its complexity. To teach the general laws the teacher chooses concrete examples that demonstrate the general concepts and laws in the most transparent form. At the end of the teaching, the criterion of success is that the children can use these laws on the reality in all its complexity.

Whereas the teachers planning must advance from the general to the concrete, the children's learning must develop from preconceived action and everyday concepts to the symbolization of the knowledge they obtain through active exploration of the central problem of the subject area and its subproblems. The teacher must secure that the children's initial activity is oriented toward concrete exploration. Such activities can include exploratory analyses of objects and pictures, museum visits and analyses of films. The next step is to get the children to symbolize the conceptual relations they perceive through their activity of exploration and analyses. This symbolization can be done through drawings and modeling the relations.

The teaching experiment with Puerto Rican children was conducted as an after–school teaching program, two afternoons a week during the 1989–90 academic year. The site of the teaching was a community house in the heart of a large Puerto Rican community in New York City. The community house provided daycare for the children while their parents were still at work. The teaching program was a voluntary activity offered to the children instead of the normal activities (which was usually playing games and/or doing homework).

The basic logic that organized our teaching project can be described in the following condensed form. There were four main, interrelated teaching objectives: (a) teaching substantive content about Puerto Rican culture and history, (b) developing the children's capacities for developing theoretical models that can be used as tools for analyzing the substantive content in relation to their lived world, (c) forming interest in and motivation for investigating the content of the teaching, and (d) developing knowledge of specific procedures (i.e., social science methods) for testing and elaborating the models.

Realizing these four objectives in the teaching, helped the children to acquire knowledge that contributed to the development of their cultural identity. In particular, we provided the children with a tool for analyzing their societal conditions so that they could explicitly relate their own cultural traditions and history with the more dominant one within which they live.

The individual teaching sessions were organized by the general objective of working with relations in the content analysis. Over the course of the teaching experiment, we worked with three main themes: (a) living conditions in Puerto Rico around the turn of the 20th century, (b) living conditions in New York City, and (c) living conditions in the children's East Harlem community. This content gave the possibility to integrate the children's different social worlds: the community of their parents with the larger community of New York City which they encounter in their school experiences.

First, each theme was related to the general problem formulation that organized the teaching plan for the year: the historical development of the Puerto Rican community in New York City, with a particular focus on the change in living conditions from Puerto Rico at the start of the century to the present–day New York City community where the children lived.

Second, to explore this problem area, a theoretical model was used as a germ cell to depict the basic conceptual relations (family life – living conditions – resources – community) that differentiate and characterize the two societies we worked with.

Third, class dialogue and concrete tasks that required active exploration of problems, conflicts and contrasts were used to help the children learn to formulate the different relations in this model and use these relations in their explorative tasks. More generally, these tasks should develop the children's capacities for constructing models which can be used as tools for analyzing the diversity in their lived world. The models serve as abstractions which can be used to study concrete phenomena.

Fourth, the selection of tasks was aimed at integrating children's acquisition of specific knowledge about history and social science with an ability to perform tasks to investigate these content areas.

Societal schooling objectives

Before considering the school as an institution for the social integration of minorities, we think it is important, as researchers, to understand the school's objectives in relation to the dominant majority. The basic frame for school teaching should and will be oriented to the goals of the majority culture. These objectives also provide a reference frame for interpreting a country's integration policy as well as the desires for schooling expressed by cultural–minority parents.

Societal objectives for schooling in Denmark

In a homogeneous society the relation between the goals of teaching and the societal function of school education is relatively easy for community groups to agree upon, so the general debate in Denmark reflects the interests of most of the population.

Reflecting a long–standing social–democratic tradition, Denmark has had a liberal objective for its schooling and liberal principles for the function of the educational system. This orientation reflects a general trend in Western democratic countries where:

> Education has been considered a part of the democratic conception of people's rights in a democratic society, at least until the mid–1970s. "Education for Life" and "Equality through Education" have been slogans which referred to a common solidarity, inherent in the society's perception of itself. Teaching was aimed at the breadth of the pupils and not at the elite (Bjerg et al., 1991, p. 6).

Within this general orientation, there are some distinctive characteristics of the Danish educational system. Bjerg et al., (1992) described these characteristics in four principles. Here is our free translation of those principles:

1. Democratizing tendencies: Untracked schools where students of all ability levels learn together; parent representation, with student and other concerned parties having influence.

2. Free choices for the single pupil to specialize in the last year of school.

3. Orientation to a general education that combines the sciences and humanities.

4. Teachers are free to select teaching methods within curriculum guide–lines.

These principles, all supported by law, are the basis for the Danish school system's ability to adapt to local community and student interests within the general national frame.

Recent developments in Denmark have created some social forces that are likely to affect the practices of the school. First, educational policies expounded by a Liberal/Conservative government over the past ten years have tended to promote principles that are opposite to the four existing principles described above, namely:

1. Privatizing and deregulating tendencies, with a stronger, hierarchially–organized leadership structure.

2. Number of choices in public schools becomes limited, and oriented to occupational and earning potentials.

3. Limiting of the humanities to idealized presentations, and fragmented presentation of subject matter.

4. Freedom of teaching method becomes subordinated to quality control.

Second, Denmark's membership in the European Common Market/European Community means there will be pressures to accept a standardization of educational practices across the member nations. The liberal principles of the Danish school are not readily found in other member countries, especially in the larger members, so that one can be concerned about the possibility for their continuation. In this situation, the Danes can be seen as a cultural minority.

Third, starting in the late 1960s there was a migration to Denmark of people from outside a Western European tradition, in particular from parts of Turkey, Pakistan, and Yugoslavia. Danish schools have made efforts to provide education for these children, but it is generally believed that there are problems with achieving the goals normally set by the schools.

These three developments create pressures on the principles described in Bjerg et al. (1992). We agree with Bjerg et al. that these principles are a worthy basis for developing educational practices and we would like to develop teaching for cultural minorities that build on these principles rather than undermine them.

For example, an untracked school is based upon commonly accepted goals for teaching in a homogeneous culture. Should an untracked school survive in a complex, heterogeneous society then the teaching may have to adapt to the objectives and needs of the specific communities who send their children to school. This adaptation is a continuation of the general principle of parent representation and student influence rather than a change in the basic principles of the school.

Similarly, the idea of a general education depends on having some common objectives that the community agrees upon. Lompscher (1985) described three general content areas—nature, culture and communication—which he considers to be crucial to modern life. These areas serve as ideals toward which students should develop their competence for understanding questions and solving problems. These general concepts provide an organizing bridge between the specific content and activities that occur in the daily school teaching and the more general, political analysis about the goals and expectations of how schooling will contribute to societal development. One could argue about whether these three ideals should be accepted or others included, but the important point in this context is to ask how these ideals can be interpreted when cultural minorities will participate in their realization. It is not a question of whether people are capable of achieving particular goals, but rather what goals are desired to be achieved.

We expect that it can be possible to formulate general goals of education that are sensitive to the needs of different communities in Denmark.

Future research based on problem analysis

Through theoretical and experimental study, this paper has identified several points that are important to consider in future research about teaching minority children. These are:

1. Parental conceptions about the importance of education is central for understanding a minority group's success or failure in school.

2. A minority group's objectives with education or literacy can affect what knowledge is valued and developed.

3. Integration of the school world with the lived world through its significant persons may be worthwhile to explore. As Moll & Greenberg's (1990) study suggests, the "funds of knowledge" of the minority group could be represented in the teaching program as an information source. How can we get support from persons outside school, who are significant for the children, given that this is demanded by the Danish school law, and empirically shown to be conducive to better school experience?

4. Schools can work with a concept of cultural identity through teaching the history of the minority group and by drawing upon this group's way of living in the local community.

5. There is a problem in doing teaching that is sensitive to different cultural groups in the same class. How can we teach using the children's historical background and community experience when there is more than one minority culture present in the class? Is it possible for a teacher to integrate the cultural history of different groups in relation to the country in which they currently live?

Ultimately we want to develop teaching advice and teaching programs within the Danish school system that are cognizant of cultural minorities. At the same time, we want to support the idea of a democratic untracked school system, with diversity in teaching methods, that aims at integrating humanities and natural science competence.

These issues and problems cannot be addressed and solved in general but need analyses that are specific to a cultural group in a particular location. Our focus is on Turkish children who are in Danish classrooms. As we have tried to show above, it is important to understand the conceptions of the people involved in this situation. Our plan is to study the problems that these children meet in their school experience, as well as the objectives and conflicts that surround them in the interactions between parents, teachers, and decisionmakers. We are now making an anthropological study based on interviews and participant observation, to describe the problems, expectations, objectives and conflicts experienced by the following groups of people who might be concerned about the experience of Turkish children in the Danish schools: (a) the Turkish communities (represented by immigrant organizations), (b) Turkish parents, (c) the Danish school system as represented by headmasters and ministry officials, (d) Danish teachers, and (e) what problems and conflicts can we observe ourselves for the children in school.

References

Aidarova, L. (1982): *Child development and education* (L. Lezhneva, Trans.), Moscow.

Bjerg, J., Callewaert, S., Elle, B., Mylov, P., & Nissen, T. (1991): Educational theory and the Danish educational system, paper presented at the meeting of the Nordisk Forening om Pædagogisk Forskning, Copenhagen.

Bjerg, J., Elle, B., Callewaert, S., Mylov, P., & Nissen, T. (1992): Pædagogisk teori og udvikling af det danske uddannelsessystem (Pedagogical theory and development of the Danish educational system). Unpublished ms, Roskilde.

Davydov, V. V. (1982): Ausbildung der Lerntätigkeit (Development of learning activity), In V. V. Davydov, J. Lompscher & A. K. Markova (eds.): *Ausbildung der Lerntätigkeit bei Schülern* (pp. 14–27), Berlin.

Gibson, M. A. (1976): Approaches to multicultural education in the United States: Some concepts and assumptions, *Anthropology and Education Quarterly, 7 (4)*, pp. 7–18.

Gordon, M. M. (1964): *Assimilation in American life: The role of race, religion, and national origins*, New York.

Hastrup, K. (1988): Kultur som analytisk begreb (Culture as an analytic concept), In H. Hauge & H. Horstbøll (eds.): *Kulturbegrebets kulturhistorie* (pp. 120–139), Aarhus.

Hedegaard, M. (1987): Methodology in evaluative research on teaching and learning, In F. J. van Zuuren, F. J. Wertz & B. Mook (eds.): *Advances in qualitative psychology: Themes and variations* (pp. 53–78), Lisse.

Hedegaard, M. (1988): Teaching and development of school–children's theoretical relation to the world, *Multidisciplinary Newsletter for Activity Theory*, 1(1/2), pp. 36–42.

Hedegaard, M. (1990): The zone of proximal development as basis for instruction. In L. C. Moll (ed.): *Vygotsky and education: Instructional implications and applications of sociohistorical psychology* (pp. 349–371), Cambridge.

Hedegaard, M., Chaiklin, S. & Pedraza, P. (1992): *Building cultural identity of minority children through social studies education*, Ms submitted for publication.

Hjarnø, J. (1988): *Socialt arbejde blandt flygtninge og indvandrere* (Social work with refugees and immigrants), Copenhagen.

Kromayer, H., & Weltzer, H. (1990): *Fremmedsprogede børn i daginstitutioner: Udvikling af integrationsmodeller* (Foreign–speaking children in day–care institutions: Development of integration models), Aarhus.

Labov, W. (1972): *Language in the inner city: Studies in the black English vernacular*, Philadelphia.

Lompscher, J. (1985): *Persönlichkeitsentwicklung in der Lerntätigkeit* (The development of personality in learning activity), Berlin.

Lynch, J. (1986): *Multicultural education: Principles and practices*, London.

Markova, A. K. (1982): Das ausbildende Experiment in der psychologischen Erforschung der Lerntätigkeit (The formative experiment in the psychological investigation of learning activity), In V. V. Davydov, J. Lompscher & A. K. Markova (Eds.): *Ausbildung der Lerntätigkeit bei Schülern*, pp. 74–83, Berlin.

Moll, L. C. & Greenberg, J. B. (1990): Creating zones of possibilities: Combining social contexts for instruction, In L. C. Moll (ed.): *Vygotsky and education: Instructional implications and applications of sociohistorical psychology*, pp. 319–348, Cambridge.

Ogbu, J. U. (1987): Variability in minority responses to schooling: Non–immigrants vs. immigrants, In G. Spindler & L. Spindler (eds.): *Interpretative ethnography of education: At home and abroad*, pp. 255–278, Hillsdale.

Rothermund, D. & Simon, J. (Eds.) (1986): *Education and the integration of ethnic minorities*, London.

Scribner, S. & Cole, M. (1981): *The psychology of literacy*, Cambridge, Mass.

Selmer, B. (1991): *Hvor anderledes er de fremmede? Indvandrerkultur i Danmark* (How different are the foreign? Immigrant culture in Denmark), Aarhus.

PEDAGOGICAL INTERVENTION AND YOUTH DEVELOPMENT

Theory and practice in a pedagogical youth–evaluation project[1]

Sven Mørch
University of Copenhagen

Søren Frost
BUPL[2]

The problem of visibility in pedagogical work

Social work, including working with youth, has its own "logic". Individual and social problems make themselves apparent. They are "visible", and the immediate expectation is that they should be solved. Youth– and social workers are expected to solve problems. For this reason they *take action,* they intervene – and often feel frustrated when problems *are not* solved.

The modest results in most social work have led to a quest for improved techniques in social work and an interest in developing methods for gene– rating and evaluating results. Documentation and evaluation of intervention have become a must.

This development has established a need for research in practice.

Surprisingly, one of the obstacles one encounters in research and development of empirical knowledge in practice, is the visibility of social problems. If social problems are visible and perhaps "obvious" problems,

---

[1]   This paper presents the theoretical and practical model for development of pedagogical youth–intervention as this has progressed in planning "The Youth Project". The Youth Project is an evaluation project for improving and implementing pedagogical activities and the organization of activity of youth–work among professional youth–workers. The Youth Project is organized by the Danish National Union of Pre–school Teachers and Youth Clubworkers, BUPL.

[2]   ʿThe Danish National Union of Pre–School Teachers and Youth Club–workers.

they will be seen as practical, real–life problems, and responded to at the same practical level as they are experienced. Problems are seen, not as challenges to the understanding, but as things to be solved. "Problem-solving" itself becomes the challenge, and intervention the practical activity. But for research in practice this creates a problem. If we want to develop experiences about intervention, intervention has to be seen as an *answer to problems*. And to choose or develop the right answer to a problem demands a broad problem–understanding. If problem–understanding and problem–solving are not closely knit, systematic and empirical knowledge will be missing. It will be hard to demonstrate results as real problem–solving.

When, however, practical intervention as immediate "problem–solving" creates results it could be seen as the effect of intervention that has been guided by *practical experience*. But often practical experiences do not exist, are unsystematic or only exist as experiences of what normally has been done as institutional or standardized routines. Practical experiences often seem to tell how things should be done, even if the activities have never been evaluated for their results, and the adequacies of the results have never been questioned.

So, results are often absent, and possible changes would not be intelligible as interventional results or as real problem–solving.

If it is not possible to trace the connection from problems to results systematically, experience of intervention is not possible. Problem–solving becomes problem–shooting.

For research in practice, it is necessary to overcome arbitrary activity-planning and intervention. Social problems have to be analysed, and the first step in this analysis is to understand that social problems do not only exist as problems of social systems or individuals. Social problems are developed problems, and the analysis of problem–development is a prerequisite for intervention or problem–solving.

When social problems are perceived as problems that have developed, their development will usually be seen as having an underlying cause[3]. But causation presents a specific problem in social work: In a living and complex world, causes themselves are often complex, hidden, not–understandable, etc., and only open to assumptions and guesses. In contrast to scientific research, where causation or causality is the issue for investigation, in social work and research in practice, the issue is personal or social change, and causation is only hypothetical or assumed.

How the choice of "causes", the identification of elements and relations in the problem–development process, is made is often confused with per-

---

3   In this paper cause is understood as "underlying cause" and we use the concept causation to refer to this broad understanding of problems as having underlying causes. The terms causal or causality wil be reserved to a more confined context, when assumptions of causality are discussed.

sonal, ideological or commonsense arguments. If, however, the guidelines in this process of identifying causes are social or psychological theories, then theories are "selected" from a repertoire of theories that are very often of a general or abstract nature.[4] Often they will not be theories about the specific phenomenon, but arbitrary theories for interpreting the phenomenon.

The understanding of the problems depends of course on the choice of theory, but this choice is not the issue of understanding. A specific difficulty in this way of developing problem–understanding in social or pedagogical work is that theoretical knowledge is often low or even neglected, or seen as opposed to practical work.

The necessity of having a theoretical basis for problem–understanding makes the use of theory implicit. Theories are not discussed, they are taken for granted by practical consensus. Practical work then does not develop experience regarding problem–understanding, at most it gives support to the practical usefulness of existing assumptions.

The problems of causality in social problem analysis

In understanding social problems most mainstream thinking works according to the assumption that phenomenon Y should be seen as caused by X. If we want to understand "misbehaving" youngsters we should look for underlying causes, probably childhood experiences, etc.

This way of thinking creates problems in social work. Even if we have good reasons to believe in the existence of a correlation between childhood experiences and "misbehaving", we are left without interventional possibilities. We are not able to change childhood experiences – at most their current significance.

This way of thinking also limits our understanding of human phenomena and the development of "misbehaving". The merging of mainstream thinking about phenomena as having causes, and the existence of correlating evidence, support practical thinking about individual phenomena as having causes[5]. This is not only impracticable but also incorrect. Human development is not "caused" in this sense of the term.

Even if we are able to show a correlation between X: childhood–experiences, and Y: misbehaving, this correlation refers only to the measured phenomena. If phenomena are considered as developed phenomena, the situation looks quite different. The development of the phenomena and the individual situation have another "logic".

---

4   The discussion of this problem of arbitrarity might be seen in Mørch (1990) and Jensen (1992).

5   Thinking in problems as having causes is often followed by thinking in "elements" or the individuals as isolatet units. This aspect will not be developed in this article.

The individual only *develops misbehavior* because he lives in a world of opportunities. It is the individual who – due to his activities – so to speak "uses" his childhood experiences in developing misbehavior. He "mediates" between X and Y.[6] While doing this he is constantly changing his preconditions or history and his own abilities in developing new ways of acting.

To explain misbehaviour as caused by childhood experiences is a selective way of understanding that ignores the role of human activity and its capacity for changing the situation. Correlational studies are, of course, important, and have broad political implications, but they should not be seen as arguments for causality in human life.

This position may be illustrated by a practical example, the behaviour of Susan and Poul[7] (fig. 1).

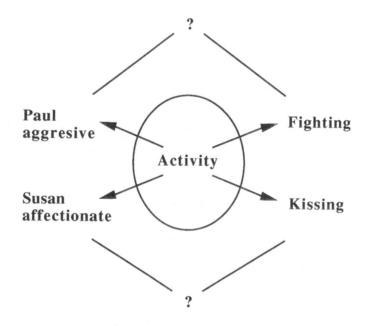

Figure 1

The problem we observe is that Poul and Susan are having a fight. In mainstream, causal thinking we would "find" some reasons for this beha–

---

6   The use of the concept "mediate" is quite common in qualitative research–thinking. As I will show later, a broader understanding of activity makes it more reasonable to use the word actualize.

7   Aspects of this argumentation could be seen in Shotter (1987) and Døpping (1991).

vior: Poul is known to be an aggressive youngster[8]. Now the problem might be explained as a result of Poul's aggressiveness. On the other hand, if we had experienced Poul and Susan kissing each other, we probably would feel content to explain it as being caused by Susan, whom we know as a very affectionate girl.

This could be illustrated as follows: Obviously, Susan and Poul's fighting or kissing are central parts of their activity.

But activity does not only mediate between conditions. It actively both selects conditions and "creates" results and may even change the initial conditions at the same time.

Even if it might seem reasonable to talk about the fighting as caused by Poul's aggressiveness, this explanation disregards the most obvious other perspective: Namely, that behaviors are not caused, but created.

If we generalize from these two perspectives we will find that whatever "problems" or activities we try to understand, we have to focus on them as activities and reconsider the use of the simple x–y thinking.

Activity creates the connections between conditions by *actualizing* conditions in the situation. This seems to be valid for both social and individual conditions.

A theory of human actualization

To overcome some of the problems of mainstream causal thinking we should regard human activity as the central concept in the understanding of social phenomena. In analysing human phenomena and individual development we have to look at activity as the use of social and individual conditions in the individual life, as the "actualization" of conditions.

Activity actualization is shown in the following model (fig. 2): The main point of this model is to emphasize that human activity actualizes conditions. Societal conditions are historically organized possibilities and restraints of social life. Individual conditions are individual prerequisites as these are developed and exist as individual capacities or modes of individuality.

Conditions at each level as well as between the levels are often contradictory, thus forcing the individual to act. In this way the individual not only has to mediate conditions, but to master problems.

Actualization is not only reproduction or use of conditions, it is mastering of conditions in social development. Actualization in this way reproduces and changes conditions.

---

8   This type of explanation is most widespread in social science. It could be called to explain by pointing to action–dispositions. Attitude and prejudice explanations would serve as the case in point.

At the individual level, actualization means changing one self, and at the societal level changing of social and societal life.

Conditions (both social and "personal") should not be viewed merely as the resources or "milieu" of the individual. Rather, they are the basis of individual and social development and *"the tools" of activity*. Also, they are the basis of practical and discursive consciousness. To the individual they have meaning and give reasons for activity.[9]

In this model we stress *activity as actualization*. This seems very important in order to avoid a reductionistic trend in activity theory,which

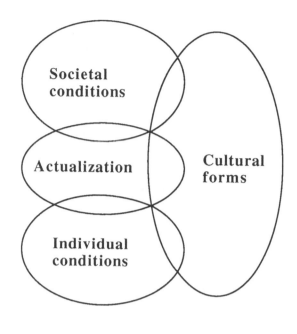

Figure 2

only analyses individual problems and development as acts of the individual.

Activity is not just doing something or "mediating" different possibilities, but actualization. Human activity actively uses and organizes conditions according to the actual challenges. Social conditions of course have a fundamental importance in "creating" social issues and individual conditions in creating personal problems[10], but both societal conditions and individual conditions have to be analysed as prerequisites and results in an ongoing process.

In need of a theory in practice and applied research

Youth work as well as other social work is in need of a "theory" of its subject. To plan and intervene in youth life presupposes knowledge of youth

---

9 For this discussion of meaning and reason in activity see Markart (1986), Holzkamp (1983), Giddens (1987).

10 Here we use C. Wright Mills' way of pointing to problems as existing at different levels and with different consequences.

and youth development. It is necessary to have categories[11] and concepts for analysing youth problems and for reflecting youth problem solutions. Pedagogical activities among youth should be based on an understanding of youth and youth problems and focused on the problems of youth as these appear in ordinary life: The problem of youth and development should be understood within a theory of human actualization.

"Youth–work" has to analyse youth and to intervene in youth life according to the perspective of youth development as the actualization of developmental conditions. For this reason we need knowledge of the basic developmental conditions of youth and knowledge of – or means of analysing – how these are organized contextually. Youth life is actualization of both societal youth conditions and individual "childhood"–preconditions.

Pedagogical work with youth has as its objective the promotion of youth development insofar as it is made possible in the society. It should carry developmental perspectives for youth in its pedagogical activities, and these should be connected to the current problems of youngsters. This means that youth work should function in accordance with short- and long–term goals. In obtaining the goals or successes of youth development, pedagogical methods of intervention should work within a contextually based structure of activities, which actualize aspects of youth development.

The following model (fig. 3) outlines, how pedagogical planning and intervention could be related to a categorial and contextual understanding of youth. The model is a model for planning intervention. When problems are recognized they should be reflected inside a contextual youth–theory of youth–actualization, and goals or successes of development should be pointed out. The model illustrates that pedagogical work or intervention should be seen and organized in relation to it's expected results or successes. In this way activities and results become closely coordinated. The model illustrates a principle for the planning of activities as preparation for results. For the involved youngsters and youth–workers *the model esta-blishes the connection between problems, success, intervention–activities and results*. At the same time it outlines the possibility of getting experience from intervention by *creating a connection between a success and its basic activities* and making this connection open for evaluation.

The overall need for planning and intervention in youth is based on a concept of youth which point to "necessitated" youth development as part of societal individualization.

---

11 Categories schould be understood as historical developed and organized conditions of development. The category of youth point to the development of conditions of youth-development.

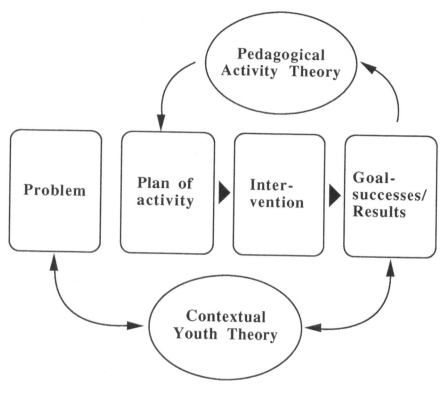

Figure 3

When this realization of the developmental necessity is part of youth work and planned activities, it calls, on the one hand, for knowledge about developmental conditions, organized as they are as possibilities and restrictions – that is, for a contextual theory, – and on the other hand, for knowledge of the existing ways of reaching success – a theory of pedagogical activity for youth.

Elements of a contextual youth Theory

1. Youth is organized

Youth, both as a general phenomenon and as a basis of the development of the individual youngster, is "arranged". The arrangement is a historical result of the specific way the developmental conditions for individual youth are organized and contextualized in society. Developmental conditions are the "offers" or the demands by which young individuals are confronted in different contexts, e.g., school, clubs, etc. Developmental conditions are changing constantly, both socially and historically. For different groups of youngsters they appear or exist at different times and in different forms. Conditions of youth are organized societally, and they express societal possibilities or demands for development of youngsters in different social contexts. As conditions of societal individualization, they organize and distribute the possibilities youngsters have for "societalisation" (the development of capacities for activity in society) and for individualization (the development of abilities for social/individual functioning and personality development) in one and the same process. In our societies this in itself is often antagonistic. Societal conditions often contradict individual interests. Societal or social possibilities are not the same for all, so the individual youngster must develop societal individualization for his own life as this exists for him. This process places heavy demands on the individual youngster for understanding – and accepting – both the society, himself, and the way he should relate to society.

The questions about the quality of developmental conditions and their distribution are the "political issues" of youth. Conditions are not the same for all. Girls and lower–class youth still experience this difference. Nonetheless western societies have seen a basic generalization of developmental conditions for youth in recent years. Today "all" youngsters are confronted with some demands for development of youth and simultaneous with the inherent contradictions these pose for individual development.[12]

2. Youth is an individual actualization of societal conditions

To speak of an individual as being "young", he or she must both be confronted with and use the conditions of development and youth. This is not a passive process. Because of the contradictions built into the conditions of youth, the individual is forced to "respond" or relate to these contradictions. The individual must reproduce the conditions of youth as his own and in this process "solve" or act with and within the contradictions according to his own situation. Not until the individual person acts and takes part in maintaining and changing the youth conditions, has youth become a reality in his individual life.

Youngsters can be at risk for not meeting or being confronted with adequate conditions of youth–development, or they can refrain from or fail to act upon the conditions which, in principle, they are presented with. In so doing, they develop a specific sort of "non–youth" problems of youth, that is, problems arising from a general opposition to existing developmental possibilities. Misplaced demands on youth in school, rejection of or failure to use the available school conditions by the individual, are illustrations of this type of problem. Also, youngsters can have difficulties in using or reproducing societal conditions as conditions in their own life. On the one

---

12 See Mørch, S. (1990).

hand, they may "blindly" try to follow and live up to conditions in different contexts. Thus they may have problems mastering and handling their own lives when the contradictions of the developmental conditions "hit" them, so to speak. On the other hand, they may – for individual or social reasons – have problems in "solving" or responding to the contradictory conditions that form their own developmental base. These may be seen as "genuine" youth–problems. This point becomes clearer when we consider youth as an individual phenomenon.

3. Youth as an individual phenomenon

Conditions of youth development must be seen as societally contextualized possibilities and restraints. As such, these are the basis of the individual youngster's development and formation of his life. On the basis of the conditions of youth the individual youngster not only uses or reproduces societal conditions as conditions in his own life, but also reorganizes his individual past and creates individual aims and directions for his future life. In using the conditions of youth, the youngster emancipates himself or "grows out of" his dependent relationship to parents and family. In youth development, parents or "family" should, of course, not be rejected, but they should be given a new and changed meaning and influence in the youngsters' life. The individual uses the societal or social conditions as "steps" to grown–up life.

Difficulties in this process of individualization can result in particular types of problems. Perhaps the youngster does not find the conditions fit for use. Perhaps he or she does not master well enough the conditions that lead to emancipation from the parents. When the process fails in this way, problems such as rejection of or fixation to the parents may arise.

Or, perhaps the youngster does not use his conditions in a way that enables him to take steps forward. The problem then may arise that the youngster simply replaces parental dependency with group or peer dependency, thus inhibiting his further development.

The following model (fig. 4), points to activities as actualization of organized conditions for youth development. As we show in the next pages, the organization of conditions as possibilities and restrictions of youth development makes youth development a "problem of youth". The individual youngster must act according to "conditions of qualification" and "social relations". As the model illustrates, youth activities should be seen as "strategies of the youth problem". Youth activities are based on youth conditions, but the individual youngster also employs existing norms and ideologies and uses the potentialities of his past and the perspectives of his future in his development from child to adult.

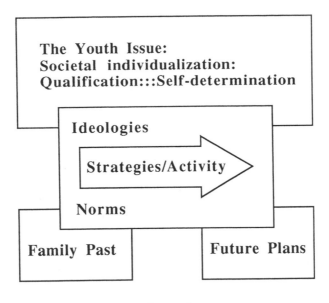

Figure 4

A contextual youth–theory

Now we can outline a youth concept and a contextual youth theory. Just as youth is being "organized", "actualized" and "individualized" in reality, so must these aspects form the basis of a theory of youth. However, general sociological or psychological theories do not point to clearly defined goals for youth development. Developmental goals of youth are neither social integration nor identity–formation as such, but rather successful utilization of contextually organized developmental conditions. Youths have to actualize and individualize their conditions. No clear prescriptions for youth activities are part of this theory. It is not a normative theory in the sense that all youngsters should be alike or adjusted. Nonetheless, the theory is normative in the sense that central contexts and means are seen as necessary for the process of individual development. The variety of individual solutions indicates the range of individualization in modern society. This does not mean that it is not possible to use or develop other, alternative means of individualization. But it is important to stress that a general youth concept should not be based upon some particular forms of creative differentiation which are only valid for a small group in society. A youth concept and theory must point to central conditions, possibilities and restrictions, as these are organized within the society and capable of being actualized in individualization. As such, the concept is part of a historical and social reality.

The first task is to demonstrate how the conditions of youth are organized, actualized and individualized. It is necessary to make clear that this demonstration is in no way intended to be complete. It is a task that could be further developed as a systematic experience in practical youth–work.

However, some basic trends have been analysed, namely the development of the categories of youth, as they can be concluded from historical youth research.[13] The development of the youth category as a psychosocial reality is based on the recognition of the need for and organization of conditions for competence (qualification) and social functioning (self-determination).

On the one hand the basic conditions of youth were established in accordance with the development of current and necessary "structures of qualification" within the society. This process largely took place within the area of educational organization and the school system.[14] Historically, the first phase in the development of youth conditions was the development of an exclusive upper–class school–system that only admitted a select few and in this way created an exclusive upper class youth. The second phase was a more open school system which, by the use of "sorting–out" mechanisms and an emphasis on the acquirement of abstract knowledge, gave youth–conditions and youth to the specifically talented (individually and socially) "young" persons. The third phase, which exists today, is a school system which in principle distributes conditions of qualification to all youngsters according to individual ability in development of competence for mastering of grown–up life in a changing and demanding society.

The conditions of youth development are, on the other hand, organized according to society's requirements for individualized societal functioning. Historically, youth conditions also had, as their basic purpose, the emancipation of youngsters from the family and from childish behavior patterns.[15] These conditions were intended to create a basic framework for the appropriation of acceptably grown–up behaviour. This process, too, was originally placed within the school system and its pedagogical curriculum. In the start of this century the processes changed, and the school system was supplemented by organized after–school activities, such as scouting and sport, and, later, youth centers, etc. Today, most children have access to a whole range of after–school activities comprising new pedagogical forms, means and contents. The conditions for development of individualized societal functioning have changed. Where one once was dependent on grown–ups and positioned authorities, one later experienced a period of "self–dependency" or development of a strong *individualized* or egocentric

---

13   This analysis has been developed in Mørch, S. (1985).

14   For the analysis of the school–system as part of social integration see Lungstrøm, C. (1984).

15   See Mørch, S. (1985).

function. Today societal and social conditions ought to further individua-lized *societal* functioning. In this context, "self–determination" emphasizes the ability of individual persons to influence societal conditions that specifically impact the course of both their own and the lives of others.

Now it is possible to sketch a model of qualified self–determination (figure 5):

	Dependent	Independent	Self-determination
Differentiated Qualification	Undeveloped Youth (Psychological problems)	Oppositional Youth (MC-groups)	Premature Grown-ups (Young prostitutes, Street-kids)
Abstract Qualification	Passive Youth (Followers)	Individualistic Youth	Activist Youth (House occupyers)
Qualified Differention	Opportunistic Youth	Egocentric Youth (Yuppies)	Optimum Youth

Qualified
self-determination

Figure 5

The point of this model is to show the two dimensions "qualification" and "self–determination" as basic dimensions of youth development. The vector or "resultant", created by the two basic dimensions, shows central deve-lopment of youth: A qualified self–determination in a historical and soci-etal form.

The "place" or "cell" that the youngster occupies in the model, points to his possibilities and restrictions of youth–development according to "use of youth condition". In this way, the model not only "explains" youth–prob-lems, it also indicates appropriate interventions for creating conditions and actualization among youth. Intervention should help youngsters to respond to and reproduce developmental conditions in their own lives.

Even though conditions of qualified self–determination are and should be present in all contexts of youth, different contexts set focus on different dimensions of youth development. For example leisure time contexts focus specifically on the dimension of self–determination. This is quite natural considering that the "problem of self–determination" primarily has been connected with emancipation from family life. The contexts of youth–clubs have developed their pedagogical activities with specific reference to "self–determination", but, of course, in relation to, or built upon the overall perspective of qualified self–determination.

Social reorganization

To illustrate the development of self–determination, one could point to the process which we call "social reorganization". By social reorganization we conceptualize the changing use of social relations.

The development of social relations among individual youngsters is organized in steps of actualization and individualization on a background of changing conditions. From social relations in the family, to a reorganization in "peer–groups", to a reorganization in "interest–groups", to reorganization in "educational groups", etc.

The following model (figure 6) illustrates this step–by–step development. The model neither presents nor is based upon any "psychological theory". It shows steps of social reorganization as practical activity caused by necessary reorganization in the contextual developmental process.

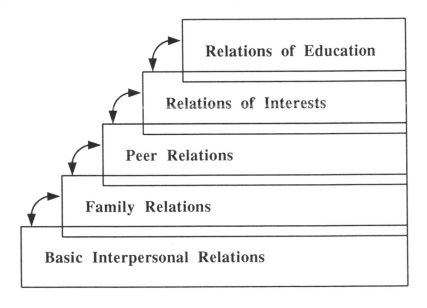

Figure 6

The point of the model is to illustrate that every step develops from and with the conditions of youth, and for this reason the steps change with history and societal change. The model reflects the current Danish social reality.

Every step is based on contextual conditions, and the actualization and reproduction of the conditions create new forms and processes of individualization – personal development – by reorganization of the previous forms of sociality.

This means that the activity of the different steps is formed both by the individuals' active utilization of the conditions "at this step", and because it reorganizes the forms of the previous steps. The previous steps are not dissolved, but reorganized and influential in the new social organization. As an example, we can look at step 2 where there is often a difference between the activities of girls and boys. This, of course, can be caused by still–existing differences in conditions for boys and girls "at the step" – the first years of school – but also by the fact that social activities are used to reorganize previous steps. It is still a fact that conditions, actualization and individualization in the family are different for boys and girls. The girls are made "socially responsible" in the family, they are more "closely involved in family life". The close sociability and dependency among girls could be seen as a way to overcome or emancipate from this specific background. Also, it can be pointed out that later "educational relations" change previous forms and contents of "peer–relations", but do not dissolve social relations as peer relations. All "steps" exist at the same time, but they are reorganized according to the current positioning.

A last perspective on the model should be drawn. The model represents development. It shows a progressive organization and actualization of youth conditions. In this way it makes youth–development perceptible as an object for intervention.

Dimensions of pedagogical intervention.
A theory of practice

Pedagogical practice is always determined by two factors: On the one hand, it is a contextual activity. For this reason pedagogical practice is made possible and limited by the resources of the context. Pedagogical practice is a resource–conditioned activity. On the other hand, youth workers are also influenced and limited by their own theoretical understanding or theory regarding the phenomena and problems they are involved with. Often the theories are results of education and job conditions. These two sets of conditions or limitations can be seen as dimensions in social work and intervention. They determine the structure and focus of practical and theoretical work conditions. At the same time the awareness of these dimensions can be more or less developed. To some persons they have never been developed and conceptualized, but are only *present* in ordinary life. To others, they seem very obvious and well reflected.

In daily work it is often these two dimensions that come under discussion when new interventions are to be planned. They can be described as in fig. 7.

The vector or "resultant" describes the results of planning. It varies according to the relative importance of theoretical understanding and practical concerns in the institution. The resultant is, so to speak, the result of the interests in the work–group. It shows the practical compromise which might be developed in the group concerning job–engagement.

As long as we consider youth problems in ordinary terms, the model shows the result or the compromise between goals for youth development that can be formulated in the group, and the intervention that is practicable. Let us try instead to use the model of youth, combined with the general understanding of youth, as a model for the organization of intervention in, for example, youth clubs. And let us make the resultant the primary focus of interest. We now recognize a surprising change of focus. The resultant now expresses the aim of the pedagogical work, that is, the development of interest of the youngster.

Now it is possible to define the youngster's interest in development independently of

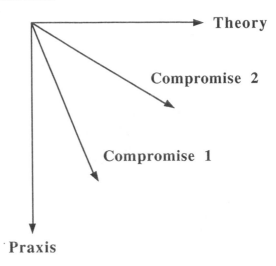

Figure 7

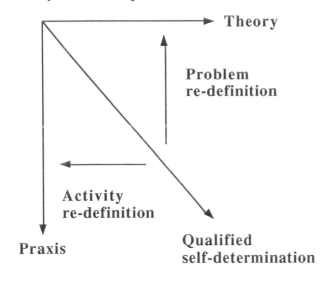

Figure 8

the daily pedagogical practice. It is centered on realizing and individualizing the developmental conditions of youth, on developing qualified self–determination (figure 8):

The model has now been turned upside down. It moves the analysis of practice and theory away from being founded in practical/insti–tutional or theoretical/abstract considerations. Now the model demonstrates that the pedagogical intervention is directed towards the promotion of the practical or institutional conditions that will encourage the development of the youngsters. And, at the same time, the model will focus on the theoretical aspects that might be part of the youngster's actualization and individualization of the conditions of youth. By this change of focus, pedagogical work and pedagogical discussions find their rational basis and are maintained as a foundation for practice.

Elaborating pedagogical intervention

The youth club project takes its starting point in the existing the Danish youth clubsystem. Historically the youth clubs in Denmark have a prophylactic aim. In accordance with our youth–model it means that we first and foremost are trying to establish contact with, and are actual meeting, the youngsters who, to different degrees, are showing limited use of the possibilities in youth. The youngsters in the youth clubs could be seen mostly as belonging to one of the "cells" in figure 5, which represent "non–optimum youth". The prophylactic work of the youth club is not concerned with pacifying or "storing" the youngsters so that they do not disturb the citizens' Sunday walks, or the profits of the insurance companies. We are trying to create possibilities for development in the direction of the "resultant".

In the youth club, social workers or pedagogues are confronted with youth of different types. Among these are youngsters who, to a relatively high degree, have used the possibilities in youth and show "qualified self–determination". But this kind of youth is a small minority in Danish youth clubs. This kind of youth is able to use a broader register of activities offered by private and public organizations.

Most youngsters in youth clubs will be in one of the other "cells". Thus not all cells will be represented. Street prostitutes, "street kids," and so on, will not show up. Nor do we meet the passive youth, because the youth club is a free offer which the youngsters themselves have to be actively seeking. The passive youth doesn't dare to show up.

The youth model enables us to understand the youngsters' attempts, individually and in groups, to take advantage of the possibilities in youth, and it enables us to understand their successes and failures in doing so. Using the categories, we are able to outline a model for practical pedagogical intervention for the group of youngsters who show up in the youth club.

In the following we will argue that it is possible to set up relevant criteria for content and quality in a pedagogical club-practice, which can lead the youngsters to an optimum use of youth conditions. Pedagogical practice engages youngsters in the initiating and performing of activities. By focusing on what we call "challenging activity", it is possible to avoid landing in either the ditch of the authoritarian pedagogy or the ditch of laissez-faire.

A "challenging activity" is an activity which in its outer form is not different from ordinary and traditional club activities (moto-cross, music, skateboarding, metalworks, etc.), but in its inner form it is qualitatively different, as it finds its content basis in the analysis of the level of the social reorganization of the youth group and its place in a "cell" (figure 5). What makes it a "challenging activity" is its relation to the current activities of individuals or groups. It is an activity that actualizes new steps of individual or group development.

From the point of view of the individual

In his attempt to carry out the conditions of youth, the individual youngster acquires specific qualities according to the given conditions or action-base. This does not take place as a simple reflection of the purely outer action-conditions, but inside the sphere of personal meaning that the youngster ascribes to his life on the level of development (fig. 6) on which his activity is taking place. The youngster's activity must be understood as motivated, and the concrete activity as an attempt to carry out the *leading motives*.[16]

The leading motives form the meaning of life for the youngster and constitute in that way the youngster's experience of his world as "the best of worlds".

Respect – but not necessarily accept

Our pedagogical starting point is that we must *respect* the youngsters' modes of expression. We understand these modes of expression as their attempts to carry out, in the best way, their individually given conditions of youth. Here we relate to Klaus Holzkamp's famous a priori: "No man will act consciously against his own interests" (Holzkamp 1986, p. 26). On the other hand, we must not always (or should definitely not) *accept* an activity

---

16   Our level model, figure 5, should also be understood as an attempt to understand the leading motives in youth in a new and more differentiated and elaborated way. Implicitly it is also a critique of the traditional understanding of the youngsters' leading motives as an expression of "world-oriented activity", as we see it for instance in D. B. Elkonin and V. V. Davidov. Youth changes over history and the leading motives change accordingly. New forms of leading motives will develop, which means new forms of personal meanings of life according, to the organization of youth conditions.

other hand, we must not always (or should definitely not) *accept* an activity if it restricts the use of developmental youth conditions. The prophylactic character of the youth club makes it a context for youth development. It organizes possibilities for youngsters to develop personality, understood as optimum use of the conditions of youth directed towards qualified self–determination.

In the forming of a model for pedagogical practice we have taken into account Leontiev's understanding of the relation between motive and goal and the development or "birth" of new motives.

Leontiev (1983, p. 218) points out that, inside a certain frame of activities, which carry out a system of motives, there will develop acts that are progressively more *rich*, and these acts will "grow out of the frame of activities they carry out". In this way the possibility of the birth of new motives arises: "The result is that the motives will change to goals, a change in their hierarchy, and new motives, new forms of activity will be born."

Intervention I

We can now form a practice–model for the initiation of the development of qualified self–determination in youth. While this model can be applied to the individual youth, it is most commonly applied to groups of youngsters (the theory of social reorganization) such as "peer–groups" or professional and technical interest groups (mopeds, music, etc.).

In the first step we have to understand the concrete conditions which this particular group of youngsters is facing. We have to analyse what level of social reorganization the group belongs to in order to analyse the leading motives which are embedded in the youngsters' activities. The youngsters' motives and their ways of "objectifying" these motives in the form of idols, interests, values, perspectives, etc., are mediated by the peer–group. Also, they reflect how the group is able to use the conditions in a motivated way. In fact, often it is the pictures and modes of expression presented through mass–media that dominate the concrete "objectifying" of the youngster's motives.

The club–pedagogue or the social worker faces the task of *analyzing*:

1. The youngsters' level of social reorganization and the embedded forms of motives.
2. The specific "objectified" forms of motives in these youngsters as they correspond to the "possibilities of information" given to them.

Finally she is able to plan a pedagogical intervention. This will be a conscious and systematically planned mediation of information in the form of "supply–information" (See Kaarle Nordenstreng (1979) and Maja Lisina (1989) for aspects of communication–theory on this subject). See fig. 9.

The pedagogue faces a *task of mediation of information*, which begins with communication with the youngsters about the backgrounds and reasons for

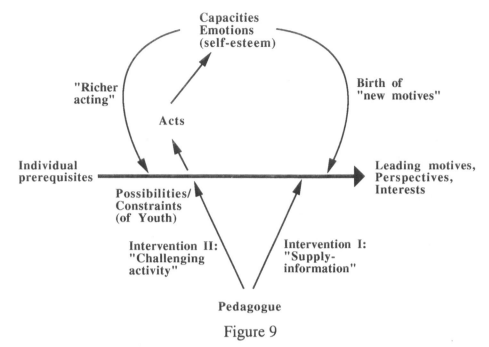

Figure 9

the concrete formation of their perspectives of life (see fig. 9). In this kind of communication it is of the utmost importance to adhere to the principle, *respect – not necessarily accept*. A too quick rejection of the youngsters' interests and perspectives will be experienced by them as a rejection of themselves as persons – this in view of the fact, that these leading motives form the "nucleus of the personality", the personal meaning of life.

The establishment of a mode of communication where "supply–information" is given, is aimed both at influencing the number and type of actual interests, as well as the oncoming change and the "birth" of new motives, which in turn must be conceptualized and put into words. The birth of new motives develops through the contradictions that arise when activities become more rich and grow out of the existing activity frameworks.

Intervention II

Making the activities more rich is the second area of intervention for the social worker in the youth club. Thus, the pure technical or didactic construction of a progressive increase in activities (e.g., curriculum) is not sufficient, as the youngster does not perceive all activities as relevant to himself. The relevance of an activity to the individual can only be seen in relation to the overall social reorganization and the individual's corresponding motives. When the social worker offers the youngster richer possibilities for acting (in the form of activities such as music, skateboarding and various workshops) it has to be on the basis of an analysis of the total situation of the youngster and his peer–group.

It is relevant to warn against a common tendency in various kinds of authoritarian pedagogical practice, a tendency we have met even inside a theory of activity framework. It is the authoritarian tendency to believe that the grown up "knows better" than the youngster does, what is meant by more rich acting. This ignores the fact that an activity is only relevant to a person if it helps him to carry out his motives. Even here it is not possible to find an absolutely societal, philosophical, psychological or technical reason for the "true" elaboration of the richness of activities.

On the other hand, there would be no purpose in pedagogical aim– and goal–setting, if the elaboration of the richness of activities was left to the youngsters themselves. The youngsters will – as was shown above with regard to the motives – carry out the acting– possibilities which are given them in the situation in an attempt to avoid the acting–*constraints* in their actual lives. These "possibilities" are both their own hitherto developed capacities (preconditions) and the outer given possibilities.

Thus new motives do not develop from nothing, but from two types of relations: The objective activity (that is the richness of available activities) and communication with others (which is limited by the available information, modes of expression, values, and so on, in the given (sub)culture). The "direction" and the "elaboration" of the future motives is in this way to a high degree dependent on the structure and content of the preceding activities.

Within the framework of our model this means that the development of the youngster will follow the direction of the resultant. The social worker must thus very carefully consider the implementation of activities which are directed towards making qualified self–determination the *leading motive* for the youngster in his future level of social reorganization.

Traditionally the pedagogical practice in the Danish youth clubs has been seen exclusively as a matter of offering and implementing activities (see Frost, 1989, and Agerschou et al., 1989). However, in this paper we have formed an alternative understanding of activities. That is, to look upon activities within the youngster's own sphere and perspective of development: 1) That the activities have to include "supply–information". 2) That the activities offered to the youngsters have to be relevant for their own motivated activity (the leading motives).

At the same time they have to be rich in such a way that they can plant the seed for the birth of new motives. These should be motives which promote a more optimum use of the possibilities in youth, the aim of which is qualified self–determination.

Instead of defining activities as just–free–to–take, we think – as mentioned above – that the form and content of activities have to be based on an analysis of the level of social reorganization of the group of youngsters, and its place in a "cell". The activity offered in this consciously well planned way to a group of youngsters is not in its outer form separable from usual club–activities (skateboarding, moto–cross, hiphop, music, wood– and metal workshops, theater, etc.), but in its inner form it is qualitatively different. We have suggested calling this kind of activity a "challenging activity".

Criteria for qualified intervention in the form of "challenging activity"

We have now moved away from an authoritarian pedagogical practice (in our view a pedagogy based on absolute criteria from individual psychology, technical sciences, etc.). We have also moved away from a laissez-faire pedagogical practice, founded on a sort of "canonization" of the youngsters' different kinds of "cultural" modes of expression (which in fact are no less absolute and dogmatic!). But with these two steps we face the problem that we lack relevant criteria for valuation (and evaluation) of the relevance of the established activities in terms of optimum development. In other words: How can we define an activity offered a certain group as a "challenging activity"?

We find it possible to establish relevant criteria for the valuation of the status of an activity as "challenging activity" based on the activity theory.

We find this basis in different works:

First in Holzkamp's categories "Subjektverhältnisse" and "Instrumentalverhältnisse" (Holzkamp, 1979, and 1983). Subject relations give developmental possibilities for optimum social and societal integration. They support the optimum interest of the development of the other and my self. In subject relations, the strategies for solving conflicts are directed towards the subject matter (and not person–directed). This makes for a true democratic atmosphere in this kind of relationship. In opposition to this, instrumental relations are restricted social and societal relations of integration. They retard a "true" personal interest in the other and they retard one's own development. Conflicts often end up in compromises and "exchanges" (just like selling secondhand cars). The result is low self–esteem, anxiety, diffuseness, etc. Subject relations arise in a group where there is a certain degree of merging, identity of interests in the common cause, and where this cause in itself is turned outwards – away from egoism and directed towards social and societal integration and responsibility for the other. An instrumental relation, on the other hand, expresses one person's egoistic exploitation of the other and shows disintegration and is turned inwards – narrowing itself around dysfunctional privacy.

The description of the subject relations can be used as "ideal" criteria for the analysis of whether an activity offered can achieve status of "challenging activity". This means that we have to decide:

1) Whether the activity offered to the group can be recognised by the group (and the individual in the group) as a common cause, which in itself might lead to social and societal integration.

2) Whether the conflict strategies in the implementation of the activity can be kept matter–oriented.

3) Whether it promotes a genuine mutual interest in the other's development.

4) Whether the individual in fact develops in the process of activity, (e.g., when higher self–esteem and anxiety–freedom are achieved).

Second: Petrovsky (1985) formulates similar criteria for evaluation of the group as a collective. He points out three criteria for valuation of the nucleus of the group (within the so–called stratometric model):

1) The level of societal integration (the success of participation in the social division of labour).

2) The degree of the group's correspondence to social and humanistic norms and values.

3) The degree of the group's ability to guarantee each member opportunities for complete and harmonious development.

To these criteria we would add that an activity should correspond to both the group's level of social reorganization and to the leading motives of its members. It is, for instance, of no use to offer a group aged 14–15 a pure technically oriented activity, if this activity does not at the same time satisfy the youngster's interest in human qualities and values and their interest in intimate communication.

Third: Haavind (1987) refers to similar criteria, which she has derived from Dreier (1977). She writes:

"A way of acting is relatively more developed than another when:

1) There is a relatively greater amount of *reciprocity* in the communication between the child and the other.

2) The child has a relatively *more expanded responsibility* for the consequences of his own acts.

3) The acts concerning the child are embedded in a more *extensive functional* coherence.

4) The acts rooted in the more extensive functional coherence open up a more *developed motivation* which give rise to new acts" (pp. 79–80).

Thus the criteria can be used not only to *plan* the activities offered and to *validate* the status of an activity as "challenging activity". They can already in the pre–planning stages be used as a tool to *evaluate* the level of development of a new group showing up in the club.

The criteria can also be used as the basis for evaluation of pedagogical processes, by setting up *criteria of success* for pedagogical processes (see fig. 3).

It is now possible to evaluate both the *quality* and the *content* of a certain pedagogical intervention, based on, for example, the three criteria of
Petrovsky and on the youngsters' own interests and modes of expression.

From here it will be possible to implement practical interventions that
satisfy the conditions of "supply–information" and "challenging–activities" with regard to specific problems or needs of youth groups.

References

Agerschou, T. et al. (1990): "Frontklubprojektet. Mellem 10–14", Copen-
    hagen.
Davydov, V.V. (1990): *Udviklende undervisning*, Copenhagen.
Dreier, O. (1977): *Familieværen og bevidsthed*, Copenhagen.
Döpping, J. (1991): Teoretisk forkortet, men praktisk anvendelig, *Udkast*,
    2, pp. 143–168.
Elkonin, D.B. (1982): "Problemet med periodiseringen af barns psykiske
    utveckling", In Hyden, L.–C. (ed.): *Sovjetisk barnpsy–kologi*,
    Stockholm.
Frost, S. (1989): "Virksomhedsteori og sociale klubber", In Hedegaard, M.
    et al. (eds.): *Et virksomt liv*, Aarhus.
Giddens, A. (1987): *Constitution of society*, Cambridge.
Haavind, H. (1987): *Liten og stor. Kvinners levekår og livsløp*, Oslo.
Holzkamp, K. (1979): "Zur kritisch–psychologischen Theorie der Sub-
    jektivität II: Das Verhältnis individueller Subjekte zu gesell-
    schaftlichen Subjekten und die frühkindliche Genese der Sub–jek-
    tivität", *Forum Kritische Psychologie* 5, pp. 7–47, Berlin.
Holzkamp, K. (1983): *Grundlegung der Psychologie*, Frankfurt.
Jensen, Torben B. (1992): Forklaringsantagelser og generering af viden.
    Udkast, 1, pp. 3–41.
Leontiev, A.N. (1983): *Virksomhed, Bevidsthed, Personlighed*, Copen-
    hagen.
Lisina, M. (1989): *Kommunikation og psykisk udvikling fra fødslen til
    skolealderen*, Copenhagen.
Ljungstrøm, C. (1984): "Differentiering og kvalificering", *Udkast*, 2, pp.
    133–170.
Mills, C.W. (1959): *The social imagination*, New York.
Mørch, S. (1985): *At forske i ungdom*, Copenhagen.
Mørch, S. (1990): Ungdomsteori og intervention, *Udkast*, 1, pp. 81–118.
Mørch, S. (1990): Youth reproduced and investigated, In Ehrnroot, J. &
    Siurala, L. (eds.): *Construction of Youth*, Helsinki.
Nordenstreng, K. (1979): *Kommunikationsteori*, Copenhagen.
Petrovsky, A.V. (1985): *Studies in Psychology. The Collective and the
    Individual*, Moscow.
Shotter, J. (1987): The social construction of an "us", In Burnet, S.P.,
    McGhee & D.Clarck (eds.): *Accounting for relationships*, London.